AF413121

WIN.

WIN.

THE CANDIDATE'S GUIDE TO WINNING BACK AMERICA

CHRISTOPHER PAUL GERGEN

BLKLYT Productions

Las Vegas, Nevada | United States of America

First Printing, 2023
Printed in the United States of America
ISBN-13: 979-8-218-20409-9 print edition
ISBN-13: 979-8-218-20410-5 ebook edition

BLKLYT Productions, LLC
1611 Spring Gate Lane | 371892
Las Vegas, Nevada 89134

"Victorious warriors win first and then go to war, while defeated warriors go to war first and then seek to win."

The Art of War | Sun Tzu

CONTENTS

WIN.

INTRODUCTION: PARABELLUM

Political campaigns are a bloodsport. Like ancient gladiators stepping into the arena, candidates enter the fray knowing that only one can emerge victorious. They must demonstrate strength, skill, and tenacity, for anything less will result in defeat. In this ever-changing world, conservative candidates must prepare for war if they wish to win back America and secure majorities in federal and non-federal legislative bodies. In the words of the great Latin adage, "*Si vis pacem, para bellum*" – "If you want peace, prepare for war." It is with this spirit that we embark on the journey laid out in this book, a journey that will arm you with the tools, tactics, and strategies necessary to triumph in the political arena. But be forewarned, for the path to victory is not an easy one, and it demands your unwavering commitment to excellence.

The success of your campaign will be determined by two vital factors: the quality of the candidate and the quality of the campaign. These are the pillars upon which victory is built, and their importance cannot be overstated. A candidate of exceptional character, knowledge, and conviction can inspire the masses and earn their trust, while a well-executed campaign can mobilize those supporters and transform their passion into tangible results.

Throughout this book, we will delve into the intricacies of both candidate and campaign development, examining the principles that underpin success and offering practical guidance to help you navigate the treacherous waters of political warfare. From pre-campaign analysis and setup to the final push for victory in the general election, each chapter is designed to provide you with a comprehensive understanding of the battlefield and the methods you must employ to emerge as the victor.

As with any great undertaking, the journey begins with understanding the rules of the game and recognizing the players on the field. In Chapter 1, we will lay the groundwork for your campaign, ensuring that you are well-versed in the language of politics and aware of the obstacles that lie ahead. Knowledge is power, and to enter the fray unprepared is to invite disaster.

In Chapters 2 through 7, we will explore the five phases of a successful campaign, from launch to the final push for undecided voters. At each stage, you will face unique challenges and opportunities, and it is imperative that you adapt your tactics accordingly. A skilled warrior knows when to advance and when to retreat, and the same holds true for political candidates.

Fundraising is the lifeblood of any campaign, and in Chapter 9, we will examine the art of building your war chest. Money may not guarantee victory, but it can provide the resources necessary to wage an effective battle. As you will discover, a well-funded campaign can amplify your message, allowing you to reach a wider audience and sway the hearts and minds of voters.

The power of storytelling cannot be overstated, and in Chapter 10, we will delve into the art of crafting a compelling narrative. Your story is your armor, and when wielded effectively, it can inspire loyalty and devotion among your supporters. By presenting your candidacy as a crusade for a better future, you can rally the troops and prepare them for the battles ahead.

Coalition-building is a critical aspect of any successful campaign, and in Chapter 11, we will explore the art of uniting forces. Allies are invaluable in the world of politics, and by forging strategic partnerships, you can strengthen your position and enhance your credibility. As the old saying goes, "United we stand, divided we fall." A well-crafted alliance can be the difference between victory and defeat.

In Chapter 12, we turn our attention to opposition research and the darker aspects of political warfare. While it may be distasteful to some, understanding your opponent's vulnerabilities and weaknesses is a crucial element of strategy. By anticipating their moves and capitalizing on their shortcomings, you can outmaneuver them and seize the advantage.

Finally, in Chapter 13, we will discuss the campaign calendar and the importance of having a master plan. The art of war is, at its core, a game of timing and coordination, and a well-structured calendar can guide your efforts and keep you on the path to victory. Like a skilled general surveying the battlefield, you must be able to adapt your plan as circumstances change, always staying one step ahead of your opponent.

As you embark on this journey, remember that the path to victory is paved with perseverance, determination, and a commitment to excellence. The road may be long, and the obstacles may be many, but with the right mindset and the proper tools at your disposal, you can overcome the odds and emerge victorious. The America First candidate who is willing to embrace the challenges and seize the opportunities presented in this book will stand tall in the face of adversity, proving once and for all that the spirit of America can never be defeated.

In the timeless words of the renowned Roman general Julius Caesar, "*Veni, vidi, vici*" – "I came, I saw, I conquered." This succinct yet powerful statement captures the essence of success, emphasizing the importance of seizing opportunities with determination and resolve. By preparing for war, you will be ready to seize the opportunities that arise during the course of your campaign, turning the tides of battle in your favor and leading your troops to victory. As you progress through these pages, let the spirit of "Parabellum" guide your actions and shape your destiny, for it is only through preparation and resolve that you can win back America and restore her rightful place as the shining city upon a hill.

It is my sincere hope that this book serves as a beacon of inspiration and a source of strength for all those who embark on the noble journey of political candidacy. For in the end, it is not merely the title of office that we should seek, but the opportunity to serve our great nation and to shape her future for generations to come. May the wisdom contained within these pages empower you to rise above the fray and claim victory, for the future of America rests in your capable hands. Now, dear warrior, the time has come to prepare for war. The battle for the soul of our nation begins with you. Steel your resolve, gather your resources, and step boldly into the arena, for it is only through courage and determination that we can win back America and secure a brighter future for all.

Christopher Paul Gergen
March 28, 2023

CHAPTER 1

THE RULES OF GAME AND THE PLAYERS ON THE FIELD

POLITICS IS SALES. It is nothing more and nothing less. In the grand scheme, campaigns serve as the avenue through which the sales process unfolds, and elections represent the moment when voters render their decisive verdict. Before we examine the specific strategies and tactics that pave the way to triumphant campaigns, to be discussed in subsequent chapters, it is paramount to discern and comprehend the rules that dictate the game, the players who tread the field, and the manner in which the game is conducted. Upon grasping the essence of what it means to win an election and the principles that steer the process, you will be better equipped to participate effectively. Merely submitting your name on the ballot and trusting in fortune will not secure victory. Relying on hope is not a strategy. It is imperative to understand the workings of the process, the identities of the players involved, and the underlying reasons for the process's structure.

POINT TO REMEMBER

At its core, an election is a formal process of decision-making that enables the public to choose one or more individuals to hold public office.

DIFFERENT RULES FOR DIFFERENT GAMES

The regulations that preside over international elections diverge across countries, with no universal system that nations employ to appoint their leaders. In autocratic regimes such as Venezuela, Bolivia, and Cuba which are led by dictators, elections amount to little more than a formality, as the outcomes are frequently predetermined by the ruling party. Consequently, the populace lacks a legitimate voice, irrespective of their capacity to cast a vote. In an array of European nations, a minimum turnout percentage must be realized for an election to be deemed binding, while other nations enforce mandatory voting laws that oblige citizens to partake. Nonetheless, the United States of America deviates from these models. Ours is a republican form of government, where the voice of the people is epitomized by the "one person, one vote" principle, and the duty to vote rests with the citizens.

While the United States employs a democratic election process to select our public servants and endorse state-level initiatives and referendums, this system is confined to elections and does not impinge on individual rights.

Citizens' rights, enshrined in the United States Constitution, cannot be revoked or modified by a mere majority vote. Our founding fathers deliberately crafted our system to shield the individual from the so-called "tyranny of the majority." The role of government is to safeguard the rights of the individual from being curtailed or abolished entirely. The government does not confer rights; our founders astutely maintained that an individual's rights are innate and divinely conferred upon each citizen of the United States of America. Disregard the daily clamor about preserving our democracy. What we must preserve is our republic.

In contemporary American politics, phrases such as "America First" or "Constitutional Conservative" are employed by candidates nationwide and at every level to signify their fundamental convictions. But what do these terms genuinely denote? If I champion one policy over another, does it imply that I am an America First or Constitutional Conservative candidate? If I repudiate one policy but endorse another, does that suggest I am not an America First or Constitutional Conservative? The situation can be quite befuddling.

The essence of Constitutional Conservatism (or America First, if you prefer) lies in electing public servants who shall act on behalf of the citizenry to manage the affairs of our communities, states, and nation, while simultaneously guaranteeing the protection of individual citizens' rights by restricting the functions and authority of government to those explicitly delineated in the United States Constitution and individual State Constitutions, in accordance with the framers' original intentions.

The United States Constitution and each State Constitution function as the operating manuals for government—in essence, these documents are the employee handbooks for our public servants. As a candidate, you must acknowledge this truth and revere its significance.

POINT TO REMEMBER

Upon being elected to public office, you assume the role of a public servant rather than a public leader. This is the essence of the United States' governmental system, and as a candidate, your foremost responsibility, should you be elected, is to enforce the restraint of governmental power and safeguard citizens' rights while proficiently managing the people's affairs within the capacity to which you are elected, in accordance with the limitations delineated in the United States Constitution and your State Constitution.

THE TWO BASIC TYPES OF ELECTIONS

In the United States, elections can be classified into two main categories: federal and non-federal (also known as state and local) elections.

Federal elections are divided into three main groups:

1. Congressional (House of Representatives)
2. Senatorial (United States Senate)
3. Presidential

Non-federal or state and local elections are broken down into many different offices, including but not limited to:

- Governor

- Lieutenant Governor

- Secretary of State

- Lower House (State House of Representatives)

- Upper House (State Senate)

- Countywide (Commissioners, Sheriffs, Auditors)

- Judicial (Judges)

- Municipal (Mayoral, City Council, School Board, etc.)

It is crucial to recognize that each state is distinct, and every state determines for itself, based on its State Constitution, the positions to be elected and those to be appointed. Non-federal elections exhibit considerable diversity. A mayoral race may greatly surpass a County Commission race in magnitude, contingent upon the anticipated number of participating voters. For instance, a mayoral race in Tampa, Florida (population 396,000) will be substantially larger and more intricate than a County Commission race in Liberty County, Florida (population 7,900).

Frequently, aspiring candidates are drawn to run for a federal seat (US House of Representatives or US Senate) due to the fame and allure associated with these positions. Nonetheless, elections should not be viewed in this light. They are not inherently hierarchical, and numerous federal races are considerably smaller than other state and local races. Moreover, all politics is local, signifying that the most pressing issues confronting citizens often stem from challenges encountered within their own communities. Public service ought to be regarded as an opportunity to serve one's fellow citizens in a capacity that enhances their daily lives and cultivates a flourishing community. The most immediate means of impacting your locality is by running for local or state office.

FEDERAL ELECTIONS

Federal election reporting and campaign rules are standardized across all 50 states. A candidate running for Congress in Florida adheres to the same federal campaign rules as one running for Congress in Nevada. The Federal Election Commission (FEC) oversees and enforces these standards, offering candidate manuals for individuals to familiarize themselves with election and reporting rules. At the time of writing, this information can be accessed at www.fec.gov. More detailed information will be discussed later in this book.

THE UNITED STATES HOUSE OF REPRESENTATIVES

Elections for the United States House of Representatives determine the individuals who will represent the people—not the state—within a specific Congressional District in a given state. In total, there are 435 Congressional Districts, predominantly apportioned equally among all states based on population. The average population size of a Congressional District is 710,000, with Montana's population at approximately 994,000 on the high end and Rhode Island's at approximately 528,000 on the low end. Consequently, less populous states like Wyoming have a single member of Congress, while larger states such as California have 52 seats in Congress.

Once consolidated, the political party representing the majority of seats in Congress is designated the majority party, while the party with fewer representatives is designated the minority party. The majority party then elects a member of their caucus as the House Majority Leader, while the minority party elects a member of their caucus as the House Minority Leader.

All 435 members of the House of Representatives nominate an individual to serve as the Speaker of the United States House of Representatives (commonly referred to as "The Speaker of the House"). Established by the United States Constitution in 1789 in Article I, Section 2, the Speaker of the House is not required to be a member of the United States Congress. Although every Speaker of the House in our nation's history has been a member of Congress, it is not a prerequisite.

Congressional elections occur every two years, and members may serve in the House of Representatives for as many terms as they can secure re-election. There are no term limits. According to Article 1, Section 2 of the United States Constitution, there are three basic qualifications to run for the House of Representatives:

1. The candidate must be 25 years old when elected.
2. The candidate must be a US citizen for the past seven years.
3. The candidate is not required to live in the Congressional District they wish to represent, but they must live in the state whose citizens they wish to represent.

Congressional elections are always held on even-numbered years on the first Tuesday after the first Monday in November.

THE UNITED STATES SENATE

Senatorial elections ascertain who will represent each state in the United States Senate. Comprising a total of 100 members, the United States Senate has two Senators elected from each state. The longest-serving Senator in a state assumes the role of the Senior Senator, while the shortest-serving Senator becomes the Junior Senator. Both Senators possess equal authority, with no distinction in their functions; however, Senior Senators enjoy preferential committee assignments, choice of offices, and other benefits associated with seniority.

Analogous to the House of Representatives, the majority party in the United States Senate selects a Senate Majority Leader, while the minority party chooses a Senate Minority Leader. Contrary to the United States House of Representatives, the United States Senate does not elect a "Speaker of the Senate." Instead, the Vice President of the United States serves as the President of the Senate, and the Senators in the United States Senate elect one Senator (typically the most senior Senator) as the *president pro tempore* of the United States Senate (commonly referred to as the *president pro tem*). The responsibility of the *president pro tem* is to act on behalf of the President of the Senate in their absence.

Before 1913, Senators were elected by the legislatures of individual states. Owing to the issue of vacancies in the Senate, the Seventeenth Amendment, enacted in 1913, altered the method of electing Senators, introducing popular votes by the people and thus terminating these types of vacancies (though vacancies still arise, usually due to death or resignation, special elections are held to elect a Senator to serve the remainder of the vacating Senator's term).

According to Article I, Section 3 of the United States Constitution, there are three basic qualifications to run for the United States Senate:

1. The candidate must be 30 years old when elected.
2. The candidate must be a US citizen for the past nine years.
3. The candidate must be a resident of the state they seek to represent.

United States Senators serve six-year terms and may serve as many terms as they can win re-election. Senatorial elections are staggered, so approximately one-third of the Senators are up for re-election every two years to coincide with elections in the House of Representatives. Like the House of Representatives, Senatorial elections are held on the first Tuesday after the first Monday of November in even-numbered years.

THE PRESIDENT OF THE UNITED STATES

Presidential elections are momentous events, and justifiably so. According to the Federal Election Commission (FEC), the 2020 Presidential candidates collectively raised and spent over $4 billion during the 24 months preceding the election cycle—with "billion" spelled with a "B." Presidential elections determine who will serve as the President and Vice President of the United States. The President assumes the role of Commander-in-Chief of the United States military forces, undertaking duties related to administration, legislative powers, foreign affairs, domestic policy, and agenda-setting, among other responsibilities.

While the general election process employed for Presidential candidates resemble those used by Congressional and Senatorial candidates, the selection process for becoming a party's nominee after the Primary Election differs. This procedure is referred to as the Presidential Preference Primary Election (or a variation of the term).

In Presidential elections, candidates accumulate delegates based on their performance in individual state primary elections. Certain states follow a "winner-take-all" approach, while others apportion delegates according to the candidate's performance. The two major parties—the Republican Party and the Democratic Party—each possess their own delegate point system. However, both parties award delegates in accordance with the party's rules in individual states. Once the delegates have been allocated, they pledge their support for a candidate at the party's national convention, typically held in July or August. The candidate with the majority of pledged delegates at the party convention emerges as the nominee who will vie for the presidency in the general election.

Each state maintains its distinct rules for the Presidential Preference Primary Election. Voters ought to contact their state's election governing body to acquaint themselves with their state's specific regulations.

According to the United States Constitution Article II, Section 1, Clause 5, there are three basic qualifications for holding office as President of the United States:

1. The candidate must be a natural-born citizen of the United States
2. The candidate must be at least 35 years of age
3. The candidate must be a resident of the United States for at least 14 years

However, even if a candidate meets the minimum criteria for holding the office of President of the United States, the Constitution has three disqualifying conditions:

1. Article I, Section 3, Clause 7 holds that any person having been impeached, convicted, and disqualified from holding further public office prior to running for President (or other federal offices) is not eligible.

2. According to the 14th Amendment, Section 3, no person who previously swore an oath to support and defend the Constitution of the United States and later recanted or rebelled against the United States is eligible to hold the office of President of the United States (or any public office).

3. According to the 22nd Amendment, no person may be elected President of the United States more than twice. This rule was added after the death of President Franklin D. Roosevelt who won four terms as President, serving three and dying in office shortly after winning his fourth term.

The President of the United States serves a single four-year term and may serve a maximum of two terms. These terms may be consecutive, as has been the case since the adoption of the 22nd Amendment, or staggered—potentially occurring for the first time since the 22nd Amendment's adoption if President Trump successfully runs for a second Presidential term in 2024. Like the House of Representatives and Senatorial elections, Presidential elections are held on the first Tuesday after the first Monday of November in even-numbered years.

NON-FEDERAL ELECTIONS

Due to the variety of state and local positions available, we will not cover specific offices at the non-federal level. State and local elections can occur at various times throughout the year. There might be state elections for positions such as Governors, Secretaries of State, County Commissioners, School Board Members, Water Board Members, State Legislators, or numerous other elected offices. Additionally, ballot initiatives and referendums can be presented for a vote as permitted by a state's specific election laws.

If you opt to run for a non-federal office at the state or local level, contact your state election governing body (such as the Department of Elections or Secretary of State). Moreover, you must research the specific rules, financial reporting requirements, prerequisites (like law enforcement certification, medical certification, bar association membership), marketing requirements (including disclosure requirements on campaign material, TV/Radio advertising, signs, etc.), contribution limits, and crucial deadlines for filings, declarations, ballot mailings, early voting dates, voter registration deadlines, and election dates.

No standardized approach governs how each state manages its campaigns and election requirements. Every state is unique. Before initiating any campaign effort for a non-federal public office, research all the election-related information and rules for your particular state, county, and municipality.

CAMPAIGN CYCLES

In the United States, campaign cycles are broken down into two distinct elections. One full cycle is comprised of two distinct elections:

1. Primary Elections
2. General Elections

PRIMARY ELECTIONS

Primary elections, or primaries, give voters the opportunity to choose their preferred candidate to represent their party in the general election. There are four types of primary elections used in the United States: closed, semi-closed, open, and top-two or "jungle" primaries.

Please check with your state's Secretary of State office for the most recent information regarding which primary system your state uses. Some states have multiple systems that may be different for local races, state level races, statewide races, and races at the federal level. The following information is correct as of this writing.

Closed Primaries

A closed primary is where registered voters in the major parties (Republican and Democratic) vote for candidates within their parties to determine who will appear on the general election ballot. Unaffiliated or non-partisan voters may not participate unless they register as Republicans or Democrats. Currently, 14 states and Washington, D.C., use the closed primary system.

These states are Connecticut, Delaware, Florida, Kentucky, Maine, Maryland, Nevada, New Mexico, New York, Oklahoma (only Republican and Libertarian Party), Oregon, Pennsylvania, South Dakota (only Republican,

Libertarian, and Constitution Party), Utah (only Republican Party), Washington DC.

Semi-Closed Primaries

In a semi-closed primary, unaffiliated or non-partisan voters have the option to choose to vote in either the Republican or Democratic primary without registering as a member of that party. Currently, 16 states use the semi-closed primary system.

These states are Arizona, Colorado, Idaho, Kansas, Massachusetts, Nebraska, New Hampshire, New Jersey, New York (only Reform Party), North Carolina, Oklahoma (only Democratic Party), Rhode Island, South Dakota (only Democratic Party), Utah (only Democratic Party), and West Virginia.

Open Primaries

An open primary allows registered voters in the major parties to vote on either partisan primary ballot, and unaffiliated or non-partisan voters may choose which ballot to cast. Currently, 21 states use the open primary system.

These states are Alabama, Arkansas, Georgia, Hawaii, Illinois, Indiana, Iowa, Michigan, Minnesota, Mississippi, Missouri, Montana, North Dakota, Ohio, South Carolina, Tennessee, Texas, Vermont, Virginia, Wisconsin, and Wyoming.

Top-Two or "Jungle" Primary

A top-two or jungle primary allows any registered voter to vote for any candidate on the ballot, and the top two vote-getters, regardless of party, move on to the general election. Currently, three states use the top-two or jungle primary system for state-level and federal elections (Nebraska uses the system only for non-partisan state legislative elections. The balance of their elections uses the semi-closed primary system). These states are Washington, California, and Alaska (which has a top-four variant).

GENERAL ELECTIONS

General elections are held on the first Tuesday after the first Monday in November, and they are similar to the championship game at the end of a tournament. There are no prizes for second place, so it is important to play to win.

THE DEFINITION OF WINNING

The objective of running for office is to win, but the definition of winning an election is not as simple as it may seem. Your ultimate goal is always to receive over 50% of the votes cast, thereby achieving a majority. However, this is not always necessary, especially in races with multiple candidates.

Primaries often have numerous candidates, and the winner is determined by which candidate secures the most votes, known as a "plurality." For instance, if five candidates are running for mayor in a primary election and candidate A receives 34% of the vote, candidate B gets 32%, candidate C earns 20%, candidate D obtains 10%, and candidate E garners 4%, the candidate with the most votes, in this case candidate A, will win and proceed to the general election. This is not always the case in "Jungle Primary" states, where the top two vote-getters, irrespective of party, advance to the general election.

In general elections, the winner is usually determined by a majority of votes cast, but in some states, minority and independent candidates are allowed on the general election ballot, and the winner is then determined by a plurality.

In Presidential general elections, the winner is determined by the electoral votes cast by each state's elector (electors are members of the "electoral college"), not by the popular vote. This is because the states, not the people, elect the President. The candidate who receives 270 or more of the 535 available electoral votes from the states emerges as the winner, regardless of the nationwide popular vote.

Before starting any race, it is essential to understand the rules of the game and how the winner is determined, both in the primary and general elections. Knowing the definition of winning will help you better prepare for the race. In the next section, we will focus on the team members involved in your campaign and their roles.

THE PLAYERS ON THE CAMPAIGN FIELD

Embarking on a triumphant political journey calls for more than the sole efforts of the candidate. A political endeavor is an intricate and arduous affair, demanding the unwavering commitment of a team of individuals, each driven to manifest the candidate's vision. Victory is elusive to the candidate who presumes to run their own campaign, for politics is an art of capturing the hearts of the multitude. To achieve this end, a candidate must assemble a team of proficient, coordinated volunteers and professionals, all working harmoniously to execute a strategic plan.

CAMPAIGN MANAGER: THE CENTRAL PLAYER

At the helm of this campaign vessel is the campaign manager, charged with the oversight of the entire operation, ensuring a seamless and effective course. This individual masterminds the campaign strategies, assembles the team, and makes critical strategic and tactical decisions throughout the journey. Among their essential responsibilities are:

- Developing the campaign strategy
- Making the campaign budget
- Recruiting staff
- Training and developing the staff
- Managing the fundraising effort
- Overseeing advertising
- Ensuring compliance with campaign finance laws
- Serving as the primary point of contact for the candidate
- Maintaining clear communication with all team members

The successful campaign manager is a mosaic of diverse skills and attributes. Possessing excellent communication skills, they delegate effectively and inspire their team. A disciplined, focused, and budget-conscious individual, the campaign manager is well-versed in election laws and regulations. Furthermore, they are strategic, creative, and adept at garnering valuable publicity.

It is crucial to remember that the campaign manager must always serve the candidate as the ultimate authority, never overshadowing their role in any capacity. The campaign manager's purpose is to bolster the candidate, breathe life into their vision, and guide them toward the realization of their aspirations.

Political Consultants: These individuals play an advisory role and specialize in certain aspects of campaign planning and execution. Campaigns may hire consultants when their current volunteers and staff lack the necessary expertise or time, or when it is more cost-effective to do so. For example, in a state-wide race, a campaign may seek the help of consultants in areas where the candidate, key supporters, and staff have few connections and little experience. Consultants can work independently or for consulting firms. There are consultants for every aspect of a campaign, but the most common are listed below.

- General Consultant (GC): When a campaign hires a general consultant, they typically help the candidate and campaign manager develop the overall strategy and plan for the campaign. They also assist in navigating significant issues and events, and may manage the narrative, messaging, and advertising. A general consultant may have extensive knowledge and experience as a former campaign manager and may work on multiple campaigns at the same time. My firm, Dark Horse Political, is an example of a general consultancy.

- Fundraising Consultant: A fundraising consultant's expertise lies in advising the campaign's finance director on how to raise funds effectively. They are usually familiar with the donor community and have experience introducing candidates to potential benefactors, event hosts, and bundlers. They may also be familiar with fundraising through event planning, telephone programs, mail, and the internet.

- Media Consultant: The media consultant manages the creation of advertisements and provides advice on messaging and strategy. Campaigns may hire consultants with expertise in specific forms of media, such as radio, television, digital/online, and direct mail. Campaigns may also retain individuals or companies that buy ads on television, cable, or digital platforms (these are known as media buyers or ad buyers).

Communications Director (Comms Director): The communications director oversees the entire campaign's interactions with media outlets and press members and leads the communications team. In a small campaign, the communications director takes care of the press, but in a larger campaign, the communications team typically consists of several aides. These aides share information with editors and journalists to generate press coverage for the campaign, and they also manage all web and social media activity to ensure that the campaign's message is spread across all platforms. The communications director reports directly to the campaign manager and/or the general consultant.

Field Director: The field director manages the grassroots organization of a campaign. At the start of a campaign, they create a plan outlining the tasks needed to achieve the campaign's objectives for voter identification, persuasion, and participation among target groups. The field plan includes efforts such as canvassing and Get Out the Vote (GOTV). The field director is accountable to the campaign manager and may oversee other field directors (often referred to as deputy field directors or assistant field directors) during the campaign. In larger campaigns that cover large geographic areas or areas with high population density (urban areas), it is not uncommon to have multiple field directors.

Field Organizer: The volunteers involved in the grassroots campaign to identify, persuade, and mobilize targeted voters are recruited, trained, and managed by a field organizer. They also recruit other volunteers, who are typically Precinct Committee Officers or Precinct Committee People (PCOs or PCPs). Field organizers are typically given smaller, specific geographical areas and report to the field director or deputy field director.

Finance (or Fundraising) Director: The finance director is also responsible for managing a portion of the candidate's time for personal fundraising appeals. It's important to note that the presence of a finance director does not relieve the candidate of their responsibility to raise money for the campaign. Typically, the candidate should dedicate four to six hours of their day to fundraising and interacting with donors and influencers. The role of the finance director is crucial in the success of a campaign, and therefore, campaigns place great emphasis on raising funds. The finance director works closely with the campaign manager and other staff members to ensure that the campaign has the necessary resources to achieve its goals. They must stay up-to-date with the latest fundraising techniques and best practices to help the campaign achieve its financial objectives.

Social Media Director: This person is responsible for organizing and implementing strategies for social media outreach to specific audiences. The social media function may be a part of the communication department on some campaigns or a senior function or consultant role that reports directly to the campaign manager.

Speech Writer: The speech writer is accountable to the communications director and writes speeches for the candidate and possibly other campaign representatives. They collaborate with the candidate, campaign manager, policy advisors, researchers, and staff members in charge of communications.

Pollster: The pollster is responsible for conducting focus groups and survey research for the campaign, evaluating the results, and determining how they will affect the messaging and strategy of the campaign. They typically report to the campaign manager and/or the general consultant.

Treasurer/Bookkeeper: The treasurer is required to sign the campaign finance reports to ensure their accuracy in accordance with campaign laws. In smaller campaigns, this role may be combined with the bookkeeper's responsibilities, which include paying bills, directing the deposit of contributions, managing the budget, and ensuring adherence to campaign finance laws, such as preparing campaign finance reports of donations and expenses. It is important to note that the candidate should **never** handle compliance reporting responsibilities.

Policy Advisor: This person analyzes information and devises and shapes the candidate's public policy agenda. They report to the campaign manager and may also collaborate with the speech writer or communications director to craft messages for the campaign.

Scheduler: The scheduler is responsible for scheduling and maintaining the candidate's calendar. They are in charge of prioritizing all requests for the candidate's time and collaborate closely with the campaign manager and the candidate.

FINAL THOUGHTS

In our final thoughts, let us reflect on the essential facets of the complex world of elections and political campaigns. There exist two principal categories of elections: Federal, encompassing the House of Representatives, the Senate, and the Presidency, and Non-Federal, which includes state and local-level elections. Every two years, the nation witnesses the election of the House of Representatives and one-third of the Senate, while the selection of the President occurs quadrennially.

Annual state and local elections follow the unique laws and regulations of their respective jurisdictions. The diverse election systems employed across the states to elect their public servants range from Closed Primaries and Semi-Closed Primaries to Open Primaries, Top-Two "Jungle" Primaries, and General Elections. In the case of Presidential Primary elections, each state abides by the rules of the major party, with the popular vote and state party regulations serving as the foundation.

As we delve into the intricacies of political campaigns, we recognize the indispensability of assembling a proficient team. At the core of a small campaign team are the campaign manager, treasurer, and field director, whose roles are crucial to the campaign's success. Expanding the team to accommodate a larger campaign may involve enlisting the expertise of a general consultant, finance director, communications director, social media director, field organizer, speech writer, policy advisor, pollster, and scheduler (to name a few).

Embarking on the arduous yet rewarding journey of running a political campaign is a task that demands unwavering dedication, strategic planning, and the wisdom to seek guidance when necessary. Should you require assistance in launching or fine-tuning your campaign, reach out to campaign@dhpolitical.com or visit www.dhpolitical.com/campaign. The opportunity to connect with you and contribute to your journey would be a privilege. Remember, the pursuit of success in the political arena is a testament to one's character, vision, and the burning desire to serve the greater good.

CHAPTER 2

PHASE 1:
PRE-CAMPAIGN ANALYSIS &
SETUP

IN THE PURSUIT OF VICTORY, it is vital to remember that champions are molded through diligent preparation and unwavering commitment, rather than in the heat of the battle itself. A candidate's success is often determined by their pre-campaign analysis and groundwork, rather than the events of election day. Indeed, many campaigns falter before they truly begin, as inadequate preparation or an ill-fated candidacy can doom a campaign from the outset.

In the realm of politics, only a select number of races are genuinely competitive, as gerrymandering and voter registration trends have led to the division of statewide and congressional districts into safe and contested territories. Consequently, there are fewer swing districts, intensifying the struggle for these decisive battlegrounds. A meticulous and comprehensive approach during the pre-campaign stage increases the likelihood of competing in a winnable race and positions you as a formidable candidate throughout the campaign.

WHY DO YOU WANT TO
RUN FOR ELECTED OFFICE?

Embarking on this journey begins with a moment of introspection to determine the driving force behind your decision to run for public office. This crucial first step cannot be overlooked, as campaigns are inevitably fraught with both triumphs and tribulations. The inevitable challenges and setbacks demand a powerful, unwavering "why" to sustain your resolve and motivation.

Contemplate the true motives behind your aspirations: Are they rooted in vanity, ego, financial or professional gain? Or do they stem from deeply held values, a sense of service, patriotism, or the belief that your unique skillset is indispensable for your community's betterment? Your "why" must be genuine, compelling, and reflect your most profound convictions. Anything less will leave you vulnerable when adversity strikes, as it invariably will. Once you have crafted a compelling "why" statement, distill it into one or two sentences and keep it close at hand as a beacon of inspiration during trying times.

SWOT ANALYSIS

Having ascertained your reasons for pursuing public office, the next vital step is to undertake a thorough SWOT analysis of yourself. This process, designed to furnish you with an honest appraisal of your strengths, weaknesses, opportunities, and threats, is instrumental in determining whether you ought to run for a specific public office. It is imperative that you remain brutally honest and objective in this exercise; self-deception or sugarcoating the answers serves no purpose. Engage in this exercise with intellectual and emotional honesty, and consider involving trusted advisors to offer unbiased feedback. If you cannot or will not complete this task for any reason, it is best not to run for public office.

SWOT analysis is a widely-used tool for gauging the strengths, weaknesses, opportunities, and threats faced by organizations and individuals in a given environment. Employed by Fortune 500 companies and the United States military, it is a valuable resource for decision-making. As you engage in this exercise, leave no stone unturned. Examine your resume, personal relationships, community involvement, hard and soft skills, emotional IQ, communication abilities, and sales experience or aptitude. Evaluate your opponents and their strengths, threats they pose, and how these factors match up against your weaknesses. By asking such questions, you gain invaluable insights into your potential as a candidate.

For a comprehensive approach, conduct a SWOT analysis on your known opponents as part of your opposition research. Understanding your opponents enables you to better anticipate their strategies and actions, facilitating success. It allows you to stay ahead of the game and navigate challenges with ease.

VOTER SEGMENT DEFINITIONS

In the realm of political campaigning, understanding the different voter segments is essential for developing an effective strategy. When examining the electorate, voters can be categorized based on their participation in the last four elections. This system of classification ranges from 4/4 (pronounced four-four) voters, who participated in all four recent elections, to 0/4 (pronounced zero-four) voters, who abstained from all four. It is imperative for candidates to understand these definitions for the purpose of voter identification (voter ID) and voter targeting.

Seven key voter segments should be carefully considered by candidates seeking to connect with their constituents. The first segment comprises the Hard Right Voters, typically registered Republicans, who participated in three or four of the last four elections (3/4 or 4/4 voters). Second, Soft Right Voters, also usually registered Republicans, are those who took part in one or two of the last four elections (1/4 or 2/4 voters).

The third segment encompasses Right-breaking Independents, voters who generally lean conservative but are not affiliated with the Republican Party, often due to a distaste for party politics. This segment can be further divided into Hard Right-breaking Independents, who participated in three or four of the last four elections (3/4 or 4/4 voters), and Soft Right-breaking Independents, who took part in one or two of the last four elections (1/4 or 2/4 voters).

Swing Voters form the fourth segment and are known for voting for both Republican and Democratic candidates across different elections. Hard Swing Voters, who participated in three or four of the last four elections (3/4 or 4/4 voters), and Soft Swing Voters, who took part in one or two of the last four elections (1/4 or 2/4 voters), constitute this segment's primary groups.

The fifth segment, Left-breaking Independents, includes voters who typically lean liberal but refrain from affiliating with the Democratic Party, often due to their aversion to party politics. This segment can be further subdivided into Hard Left-breaking Independents, who participated in three or four of the last four elections (3/4 or 4/4 voters), and Soft Left-breaking Independents, who took part in one or two of the last four elections (1/4 or 2/4 voters).

The sixth segment is composed of Soft Left Voters, typically registered Democrats, who participated in one or two of the last four elections (1/4 or 2/4 voters). Lastly, the seventh segment consists of Hard Left Voters, generally registered Democrats, who took part in three or four of the last four elections (3/4 or 4/4 voters).

In the pursuit of victory, it is crucial for conservative candidates to concentrate their efforts on engaging with the voter segments that are most likely to support their cause. The power of focused action is an essential element in transforming desire into reality, and this principle applies to political campaigns as well. A conservative candidate must first identify their most reliable supporters – the 3/4 and 4/4 voters who consistently vote for conservative candidates and are eligible to participate in the primary election. These voters embody the steadfast base that must be energized and mobilized to ensure victory in the primary election. Their unwavering loyalty to conservative principles makes them invaluable assets in the candidate's quest for electoral success.

In addition to rallying the core supporters, a wise candidate must also recognize the potential of those who can be persuaded to support their cause. These voters may not have a steadfast allegiance to conservative principles but may be swayed by the candidate's message, personality, or stance on specific issues. It is in these persuadable segments that a candidate can find the additional votes needed to secure victory, particularly in tight races.

However, it is equally important for a conservative candidate to avoid expending precious time, energy, and resources on voters who are unlikely to support them. Typically, these segments include the hard left, soft left, hard left-breaking independent, and soft left-breaking independent voters. In the context of commerce, a successful enterprise directs its efforts towards customers who are predisposed to purchase its products and those who can be persuaded to do so, while disregarding those who have no inclination to buy.

Just as a wise businessperson understands that they cannot appeal to everyone, a conservative candidate must acknowledge that certain voter segments may never support their cause. By focusing on those who are most likely to provide support – the 3/4 and 4/4 conservative voters – and those who can be persuaded to join their ranks, the candidate can optimize their campaign strategy for maximum impact.

In summary, one of the keys to a successful campaign lies in the art of focusing on the voter segments most likely to contribute to victory. By energizing and mobilizing the base of 3/4 and 4/4 conservative voters, while simultaneously appealing to persuadable segments, a candidate can create a formidable force for victory. At the same time, they must be prudent in conserving their resources and not squander them on attempting to convert those who will never align with their cause. By adhering to these principles, conservatives can confidently embark on the path to victory, fueled by the power of focused action.

RACE ANALYSIS

Data is the foundation of victory. Begin by analyzing voter registration, voter participation, and election results compared to the Cook PVI (Partisan Voter Index) Score of the congressional district. This information is vital to determine the winnability or competitiveness of a race. The Cook PVI gauges a district's partisanship in relation to the nation. For instance, a D+2 or R+5 rating implies that your district leans Democratic or Republican compared to the national average, respectively. An "Even" rating signifies that your district aligns with the national average.

Though the definition of a "Swing District" according to Cook PVI ranges between D+5 and R+5, realistically, it falls between D+3 and R+3. Flipping districts with margins beyond this range becomes increasingly difficult, though not impossible in wave election years. Another useful measure for analyzing districts is the Dark Horse VRP (Voter Registration Parity), which assesses registration parity between Democratic and Republican voters without considering past election results' partisan leanings.

For example, let's examine Iowa's 3rd Congressional District. As of 2020, this district had a Cook PVI of R+3. However, this Republican-leaning district was represented by a Democrat who won a narrow victory by 1.4% in the 2020 election cycle (this seat was targeted and flipped back to Republican control in 2022). The Cook PVI alone doesn't tell you why a Democrat won this Republican-leaning district, but the Dark Horse VRP reveals why.

The district had a total of 464,438 registered voters. Of those voters, 164,234 were Democratic active registered voters, and 160,778 were Republican active registered voters. The balance of active voters, 139,426 in total, were active voters registered as third party or no party (sometimes called NPA or independent).

With this information, we can calculate the Dark Horse Voter Registration Parity (VRP) using this simple equation[1]:

$$\frac{Total\ Registered\ Democrats}{Total\ Registered\ Republicans} = Dems\ per\ Reps\ (VRP)$$

If we insert the numbers from our example above, the equation looks like this:

$$\frac{164,234\ Democrats}{160,778\ Republicans} = 1.02\ VRP$$

In this district, the presence of 1.02 Democrats for each Republican indicates an almost perfect equilibrium in voter registration. If both parties were to achieve 100% turnout on election day, the Democrats would have a slight edge in voter numbers. Despite this, the Cook PVI reveals that this district has consistently favored Republicans by 3% more than the national average in the last two Presidential elections. The objective, therefore, becomes capturing the support of third-party and no-party voters — the crucial swing voters.

To accurately gauge the winnability of your race based on the district's VRP, comprehend that a VRP of 1.25 or higher renders the race exceedingly challenging for Republicans. With 100% turnout for both parties, 1,250 Democratic voters would emerge for every 1,000 Republican voters. Generally, there is no significant difference in partisan turnout rates between the two

---

[1] The Dark Horse Voter Registration Parity equation is a shortcut to understanding the math behind the required turnouts to achieve parity. For example, if average voter turnout for Democrats in IA-03 is 78%, we can expect 164,234 x 78% or approximately 128,103 Democrat voters will participate. To determine the Republican turnout percentage required to achieve the same number of voters divide 128,103 (the expected number of Democrat voters to turnout) by the number of registered Republicans.

Therefore, **128,103/160,778 =** *approximately* **80%.** The Dark Horse VRP represents and simplifies this process.

major parties, not enough to compensate for the shortfall once the VRP surpasses 1.25. For Republicans to triumph, they must secure third-party and no-party voters at an implausibly high rate.

On the other hand, a VRP of 0.75 or lower (signifying fewer Democrats than Republicans) makes the race equally demanding for Democrats. They too would need to win third-party and no-party voters at a near-impossible rate.

POINT TO REMEMBER:

Winnable races for either party typically fall between:

0.75 and 1.25 Dark Horse VRP

and

D+3 and R+3 Cook PVI

Anything outside that margin becomes extremely difficult to win—assuming historical turnouts remain consistent.

Regarding the race in Iowa, it appears that the Democrat won swing voters in urban areas in 2020 while performing well enough in rural areas to secure a narrow victory. This is evident when reviewing the actual election data. Iowa's 3rd Congressional District encompasses 16 counties, the largest of which is Polk County, home to Des Moines, the state capital. The Democrats won Polk

County and lost in the remaining 15 counties. This suggests that the Republican did not effectively win swing voters in the urban center (Des Moines) and did not outperform their historical averages in the rural counties they did win. These dynamics are manageable in future races.

Therefore, when analyzing Iowa's 3rd Congressional District, we find:

1.   Cook PVI: R+3
2.   Dark Horse VRP: 1.02
3.   2020 election results: D+1.4%

As a candidate or advisor in this district, considering the initial review, I would deem this race winnable for a Republican, given the district's partisan leaning, current voter registration, and historical performance.

In sum, during the race analysis process, it is vital to comprehend the factors behind the district's performance in the past two election cycles. Investigate news articles about the race, scrutinize financial statements, and assess the candidates to ascertain any elements that might have influenced the race's outcome. The Cook Political Report offers a downloadable Cook PVI Scorecard for every Congressional District in the US, easily discoverable through an internet search. Official results from previous elections can be obtained from county or state elections offices, typically accessible online at no cost. Upon completion, the race analysis process should yield a lucid comprehension of the factors behind the victory and defeat, substantiated by relevant data. This knowledge should significantly impact your decision to pursue the political office in question.

COST ANALYSIS

As disclosed by Open Secrets, in the 2020 Congressional races for the House of Representatives, victorious challengers who defeated incumbents raised and spent an average of $3,866,224. Losing incumbents, despite raising and spending more with an average of $5,094,005, were still defeated. Of the 435 House races, merely 15 challengers triumphed over incumbents, while 372 incumbents prevailed against challengers (the remainder were uncontested). Victorious incumbents in reelection campaigns raised and spent an average of $2,257,443, whereas defeated challengers raised and spent an average of $840,444. A successful federal campaign necessitates the readiness to amass considerable funds. Even at the local level, fundraising and appropriate campaign support are of utmost importance.

A seated incumbent enjoys a fundraising edge over a challenger, leveraging their influence to persuade donors and special interests to back their campaign, in addition to party support. Although uncommon, it is not impossible for a challenger to outraise a sitting member of Congress. Therefore, strive to match your opponent's fundraising dollar-for-dollar or achieve at least 75% to 80%. Anything less renders the task of funding vital campaign operations and keeping pace with your opponent increasingly arduous. Some campaigns have emerged victorious with limited funding; however, these instances are exceptions rather than the norm. Winning without being competitive in fundraising is improbable.

Establishing your average monthly fundraising target is essential for setting a performance benchmark. After determining your campaign's total monetary requirement, divide this figure by the months dedicated to fundraising and reporting to the Federal Elections Commission. The resulting number is your average monthly fundraising target. Although actual monthly figures may fluctuate, if you are near your overall target by the campaign's conclusion, your average should be close to this number, barring extraordinary circumstances.

BUDGETING

Your general consultant or campaign manager should collaborate with you to formulate a budget. Comprehend budgets on two levels: macro and micro. Macro budgeting encompasses all resources needed from the campaign's inception to certification, not merely election day. Budgeting solely until election day may leave you resourceless if your race necessitates a challenge or recount.

Micro budgets break down the entire campaign effort into specific timeframes, including:

1. Campaigns using a quarterly approach that corresponds to the FEC's reporting requirements
2. Campaigns using a monthly approach that is similar to most state-level contests
3. Campaigns dividing their budgets into phases

There is no single correct approach to structuring the budget, provided it adequately funds the campaign and clearly informs the candidate of the allocated percentages for specific campaign aspects. Campaigns resemble a sales and marketing endeavor undertaken for 6 to 18 months (or longer). Consequently, the majority of the funds should be designated for voter contact (marketing/advertising), typically 70% to 80%. Allocate 12% to 18% to fixed costs such as staff and recurring expenses (rent, utilities, internet, etc.), no more than 8% to 12% for general consulting retainers, and around 5% reserved for legal challenges. Bear in mind these are guidelines; your particular race may necessitate slight adjustments, but they should not diverge significantly.

Salary ranges for requisite staff will vary depending on the staff member's experience, role, race size (number of voters), location, and race level (congressional, statewide, legislative, or local). A congressional race Campaign Manager typically earns between $5,000 and $9,000+ per month. This range increases to between $7,500 and $12,000+ per month for statewide races, and decreases to between $2,500 and $6,000 per month for legislative and local races. The race size significantly impacts these figures; running a mayoral race in Los Angeles, CA, differs from one in Reno, NV. A statewide race in Montana is distinct from one in New York. Size is crucial, especially for determining salaries.

Finance directors should receive slightly less compensation than campaign managers, with 70% to 90% of the campaign manager's income being adequate. Field directors should earn 50% to 70% of the campaign manager's salary. Your general consultant (GC) or campaign manager will determine the appropriate pay scale to attract exceptional personnel for your team. Nevertheless, monitor their salaries to ensure competitiveness.

Media consultants, digital media consultants, direct mail consultants, fundraising consultants, and field operations consultants usually do not receive salaries. Their fees are commonly paid as commissions or flat fees for service. Some fundraising firms charge a retainer plus commission; however, these retainers should be reasonable and tied to specific outcomes. Avoid paying a retainer to a fundraising firm merely for their affiliation. They must deliver value in exchange for the retainer. Often, fundraising firms provide creative content, ads, email lists, or other valuable items. The particulars of fundraising will be addressed in a subsequent chapter.

MINIMUM TEAM REQUIREMENTS

Campaigns are built upon teamwork. No matter the position you seek, a dedicated team is crucial for a victorious race. It is nearly unattainable for a candidate to singlehandedly steer a successful campaign. When assembling your team, the foremost inquiry should be, "Who is essential to set this campaign in motion?" At the very least, a Campaign Manager and a Treasurer are necessary, even for the smallest races.

As explored in the preceding chapter, numerous roles exist, but not all must be immediately filled. In Phase 1, identify who is needed to adequately operate the campaign organization through Phases 1 and 2 and the capital required to hire these staff members. Envision this process as establishing a small business from scratch, asking who is needed to start, and determining the necessary digital and physical assets, marketing materials, and internal systems. Campaigns follow the same principles and logic.

For a successful congressional race, the minimum team you need to assemble in Phase 1 includes:

- General Consultant
- Campaign Manager (who also handles communications in this phase)
- Treasurer
- Fundraising Director and/or Fundraising Consultant

The team size may vary depending on your race's scope and available funds. Nonetheless, this foundation is ideal for launching a credible Congressional race in a winnable district with a formidable candidate. For a US Senate race or other statewide races (Governor, Lt. Governor, Secretary of State, etc.), your initial team will require additional members and a substantially larger initial capital.

GENERAL NARRATIVE CREATION

The quintessential aim of a campaign is to convey a story illustrating why you are the finest candidate for a specific public office. Every story possesses a "narrative arc," gradually revealing the storyline to the audience. This holds true for political campaigns as well. Many novice candidates unveil their campaign's entire story in the introduction, leaving voters pondering, "Now what?" A gripping tale requires suspense and tension to maintain interest. This is precisely what occurs when candidates disclose everything in their first public interaction or neglect to weave a coherent narrative.

REMEMBER:

Candidates with compelling narrative arcs are successful and win elections, while those without persuasive narrative arcs lose elections.

Though we will explore narrative arc development in a later chapter, it is vital during Phase 1 to comprehend your fundamental narrative. To achieve this, clarify the rationale and story prompting your run for public office by answering two questions: "What is the rationale for your candidacy, and what is the story behind your decision to run?"

To determine the viability of your campaign, you must also answer the following questions:

1. Am I at the appropriate experience level for this position?
2. Am I currently in a position personally, professionally, and politically to take advantage of this opportunity?

Addressing at least one of these questions positively enables an engaging campaign story. Write down the answers, and create a narrative centered around the problems and issues concerning voters. Once established, you will have a general narrative for your initial launch. We will discuss the complete process of crafting a fully developed narrative arc later. For now, let's examine an example.

John Hopeful is a 38-year-old technology consultant with 13 years of career experience in IT project management working with Fortune 500 clients on multi-million-dollar budgeted projects. The candidate has a bachelor's degree in Computer Science from the University of Southern California. After 8 years of marriage, the candidate has two small children, ages 5 and 7 years old. He has no political experience, but is very active in his local community through charity work and has an extensive professional and alumni network. Mr. Hopeful has $25,000 of his own money to contribute or loan to the campaign as start-up money. Recently, a spike in crime, increased cost of living, and a downward deterioration of education in his state has worried his family regarding their futures. After extensive conversations with his wife, close friends and business associates, and carefully considering the district and what it will take to unseat an incumbent, he's decided to run for Congress.

From this candidate profile we have enough information to answer the rationale and story questions posed above. Using this information, the rationale and story statement might look something like this:

John Hopeful is a well-qualified and experienced leader with the necessary skills and dedication to bring about positive change in his district. Just like you, John is deeply concerned about the increasing crime rate, the high cost of living, and the worsening state of education in his district. With his extensive experience in managing complex projects and his strong commitment to his community, John is ready to lead in Washington DC. By electing John Hopeful to Congress, our community can be confident that they have a competent and passionate representative who will advocate for their needs and uphold the conservative values that keep our communities safe and affordable. After careful consideration and discussions with his wife, close friends, and business associates, as well as a thoughtful evaluation of the district and what it will take to challenge an incumbent, John has officially decided to run for Congress.

This statement offers a concise overview to pique voter interest in the candidate and their campaign, inspiring them to learn more about the candidate and their platform. It serves as a foundation for building core support by directing voters into the commitment funnel on the candidate's website. From here, the candidate can elaborate on the problems facing voters and present their solutions. Recognize the distinction between problems and issues. Problems represent the challenges faced by voters, while issues are the solutions to these problems. Avoid confusing the two.

For example, if a community grapples with increased crime, a high cost of living, and insufficient education, the issues to address could include implementing stricter crime policies, fully funding law enforcement and enacting necessary police reforms, reducing taxes and regulations contributing to the rising cost of living, and empowering school districts to offer high-quality education while curtailing federal bureaucracy by defunding the Department of Education. Clearly delineating problems and issues is crucial for crafting a narrative that builds upon the campaign's core rationale and story message. Combining the rationale, story, problems, and issues forms the general narrative statement used in all initial communications during the campaign launch. This narrative will expand and develop into a more detailed pitch during Phase 3 and reach its climax in Phase 4.

SETTING UP FOR LAUNCH

OPTICS MATTER because *perception is reality*. Perception is paramount, as voters form their opinions of you and your campaign through the branding and imagery you present. It is vital to project a polished, professional image to leave a strong impression on the electorate. In the following sections, you will learn the steps to create a professional image for your campaign and the specific actions to take just before launch.

THE PHOTOSHOOT

Securing professional-quality photographs is essential for a polished, professional image. Investing in a professional photographer, typically costing between $1,000 and $2,000 for a photoshoot, is a worthy expenditure. Refrain from using low-quality images captured by friends or family members with mobile devices or featuring selfies on your website or printed materials.

YOUR WARDROBE

Selecting the appropriate wardrobe for your photo shoot is crucial, as your appearance in these images will be the first introduction to voters, shaping their perceptions of you and your campaign. Authenticity is key; present yourself genuinely through your attire. However, be mindful of voters' expectations for different offices. For instance, casual attire may suit a local race, while a formal business suit or dress is expected for a federal race. To avoid confusion, examine the attire of successful elected officials and business leaders for guidance. Investing in a professional tailor to ensure proper fit is also advised, signaling competence and determination to voters. Finally, consult a local clothier for advice on what to wear.

PHOTOSHOOT SITES

After selecting your wardrobe, scout locations for your photoshoot. Outdoor locations tend to offer better lighting, with morning hours before 11:30 am being more favorable than the afternoon. Capture images in recognizable locations within your district. For statewide office campaigns, consider photographing in various parts of the state, showcasing diverse geographies. For gubernatorial races, include images near the state capitol building and, if possible, in front of the United States Capitol Building for federal races. Local photographers can offer valuable insights on ideal shooting locations.

HEADSHOTS

Headshots are the most vital set of photos, as they will appear in media outlets, on your website, social media platforms, printed materials, and advertisements. When capturing headshots, opt for a horizontal orientation rather than vertical, as horizontal images can be adjusted to appear vertical, while the reverse is not always possible. Capture images with you positioned on the left, center, and right sides of the frame to accommodate your web developer and graphic designer's needs for adding text or logos.

Request your photographer to take head-on and three-quarter view shots, useful for marketing materials and social media posts. Avoid cropping your head or shoulders in any images, as your graphic designer will require complete head and shoulder shots. When posing in front of an outdoor background with depth, ensure the background is slightly blurred, emphasizing you in the foreground. This effect can be added during post-production, but it is more convenient for your graphics team if the original photograph is taken this way. Lastly, smile! While serious images have their place, smiling photos convey authenticity and approachability. Voters choose candidates they know, like, and trust.

FAMILY PICTURES

The decision to involve your family in your campaign biography is a personal one. Should you opt to include a family image, capture it in a warm setting or a natural environment, such as a park or near water. Experiment with different poses and wardrobes, featuring just your spouse, your spouse and children, or a posed family portrait. If you decide to include family pictures, ensure they present your family in a positive, unified light.

ACTION PICTURES

Action shots portray you engaged in an activity or task, appearing natural and genuine rather than staged. Steer clear of fabricated images, such as posing as a worker with rolled-up sleeves and a concerned expression. For authenticity, have a photographer document your workday, whether in the field or an office. Though this may require additional time and resources, the investment yields genuine, marketable images. Photos of you speaking at a rally or event or capturing powerful moments can also bolster your branding.

PHOTOGRAPHS WITH TARGETED VOTER SEGEMENTS

Capture images with individuals likely to support you, such as veterans, first responders, farmers, small business owners, parents, teachers, and minority groups. Include pictures with existing supporters to emphasize your genuine community involvement. By engaging with these individuals, you can create personal connections and obtain their consent to use the images in your marketing materials. This approach not only makes them feel valued but also reinforces the notion of inclusivity. **Note the importance of obtaining permission** and, in some cases, signed release forms from supporters before using their images in marketing materials.

PHOTOGRAPHS WITH HIGH-PROFILE INDIVIDUALS

Photographs featuring you with well-known, respected individuals who endorse your campaign can enhance your credibility and elevate your profile among voters. However, exercise caution when employing these images, ensuring your target voters hold the high-profile individual in high regard. Otherwise, using the photo may backfire, leading to a negative narrative leveraged against you by opponents or hostile media sources.

BRANDING, MARKETING AND ONLINE DEVELOPMENT

The significance of branding in politics and campaigns is paramount. Businesses allocate substantial resources to branding as it establishes an identity and conveys non-verbal cues about their values, offerings, and overall image. The same principle applies to politics. The Democratic Party and liberal organizations have excelled in branding, while Republicans and conservatives have lagged. In 2016, then-candidate Trump harnessed the strength of his well-known brand to triumph over adversaries and secure the election. His robust branding and skill in utilizing it to capture media and voter attention were instrumental to his success.

Even without the resources of a billion-dollar brand like President Trump, you can lay a solid branding foundation for your campaign. This is especially crucial in federal and statewide races, though it can also apply to down-ballot contests with the appropriate strategy.

Bear in mind that a logo and a brand are distinct entities. A brand encompasses the values and presentation that differentiate your campaign from competitors, while a logo serves as the visual embodiment of the brand. A logo lends credibility to your campaign, and when paired with robust branding, it becomes the face of your organization, conveying your values to voters.

LOGO DEVELOPMENT

Upon solidifying your brand values, the subsequent step involves crafting your logo. While your involvement in the process is necessary, it is advisable to entrust the actual design work to a professional graphic artist. Your general consultant should have connections to such experts who can generate multiple options based on your input and refine the design until you possess an iconic logo suitable for use in future elections.

Your campaign will need various versions of the logo for use in both digital and print materials. The basic files you will need include:

1. General Use 1: The primary logo on a white square background
2. General Use 2: The primary logo on a secondary color square background
3. Transparent 1: The primary logo on a transparent square background
4. Transparent 2: The primary logo in black and white on a transparent square background
5. Favicon: The primary logo formatted to 32x32 pixels or larger, saved in both SVG and PNG for use on your website tab.

Your general use and transparent logos should be saved in multiple file formats, including PSD, AI, PDF, JPG, and PNG, with a minimum resolution of 300 dpi. It's also important to have the logo saved in a vector format, which allows you to use it in large-scale images like billboards or buildings. Your graphic designer can provide additional file formats if needed.

DIGITAL DEVELOPMENT

In today's political campaigns, a robust website and digital presence are indispensable. Although a website or digital ingenuity alone will not secure an election, a poorly designed website or insufficient digital presence can certainly impair your chances. A common error committed by candidates is constructing their website solely for informational purposes or attempting to create their own website to save funds. This frequently results in protracted, unfocused websites that do more damage than good. It is crucial to engage a professional to build your website, as the data it generates and the conversion of visitors to voters are too vital to be managed by novices.

Your campaign website should fulfill five primary functions: capturing leads and integrating them into the commitment funnel, gathering contributions and incorporating them into the commitment funnel, enlisting volunteers and involving donors in the commitment funnel, conveying information about issues significant to voters and events they can attend, and offering contact information and press releases for media outlets. Moreover, your website ought to have a concise and easily memorable web address, an SSL certificate for security, optimization for tablet and mobile devices, SEO optimization, and, if appropriate, an online store for merchandise sales. Your website must serve as the bedrock of your online presence, with social media acting as a supplementary tool.

Employ social media as an instrument to achieve specific objectives for your campaign, such as delivering targeted messaging, reacting to current events, and reinforcing your campaign's narrative. Nonetheless, the instantaneous nature of social media may also give rise to impulsive messages and repercussions, making it crucial to exercise caution when posting. Your campaign should maintain a presence on the core social media platforms of

Twitter, Facebook, Instagram, and YouTube, ensuring consistent branding across all channels. For advertising purposes, it is essential to secure verification with Google and Facebook and to display identically branded headers and profile pictures on all accounts to prevent voter confusion.

PROMOTIONAL MATERIAL

As your campaign progresses to Phase 2, you will need promotional materials, including business cards and palm cards, to give to voters seeking more information about your campaign at live events. There are three essential promotional pieces that you should have ready from the start:

1. Business cards - Use a standard 2 x 3.5 inch business card that features your campaign's established branding.
2. Vertical palm cards - The most common size for palm cards is 4 x 9 inches. Vertical palm cards are usually used to introduce the candidate to the voter and briefly highlight the main issues of the campaign.
3. Horizontal palm cards - Create a second version of your palm card with a different layout but the same branding. This version should focus more on the issues of your campaign and your overall message.

GENERAL DIGITAL AD SET CREATION

During Phase 2, a lot of effort must be put in a short period of time, usually 30 to 45 days. To kickstart your campaign, a digital ad campaign should be launched on the day it is announced. This requires producing at least four to eight ad sets in Phase 1, so they are ready for use in Phase 2. There are four commonly used sizes in digital advertising:

1. 300px x 250px
2. 320px x 50px
3. 320px x 480px
4. 728px x 90px

Each ad set should have these four sizes included, resulting in a total of 16 to 32 (or more) separate graphics for your digital advertising push in Phase 2. The branding on these ads must be consistent with the overall branding of the campaign. Later, we will discuss what these ads should contain.

YARD SIGNS

Differing opinions exist regarding the efficacy of yard signs in today's digital era. Certain studies, such as one undertaken by Columbia University in 2015, propose that yard signs could account for a 1-2 percentage point difference in elections. Though this might not appear as a substantial impact, it could nonetheless be consequential in tight races. Conversely, some contend that weighing the cost-benefit analysis of employing yard signs against alternative marketing strategies makes it challenging to justify their use when more effective tools are accessible.

In my experience, yard signs tend to yield greater results in contested primaries as opposed to general elections. In general elections, voters are already acquainted with the candidates, whereas in primaries, especially those involving numerous contenders, voters may lack knowledge of the ballot. This holds particularly true for down-ballot races that do not attract as much media coverage as federal and statewide races. I have managed campaigns without utilizing yard signs and others where we deployed 20,000 signs across the state—both candidates emerged victorious in their respective races.

Should you opt for yard signs, it is crucial to maintain simplicity and clarity. Yard signs serve the purpose of identification rather than detailed issue discussions. They ought to incorporate your logo, website, campaign slogan (if applicable and available), and the requisite disclaimer. Three sizes of yard signs should be prepared for Phase 2: 18" x 24" for residential zones, 2' x 4' for high-visibility areas, and 4' x 8' for fields, buildings, and high-visibility locations. Your initial order need not be vast, but ensure you have some 18" x 24" signs available during the first 30-45 days of your campaign. If you distribute 80% of your signs, you can place a larger order, but exercise caution not to immobilize excessive capital in signs during your campaign's early stages.

INITIAL FUNDRAISING CALLS PRIOR TO THE LAUNCH

Two to three weeks before announcing your candidacy for public office, you should compile a Top 200 List. This list consists of the top 200 individuals in your network whom you believe will provide financial support to your campaign. If you have exhausted your list of potential financial supporters, proceed to those who may back you financially and then to those whose support remains uncertain.

WARNING:

Completing this exercise is not optional. **Do not skip this exercise, especially if you are a first-time candidate.**

REMEMBER, YOU SAID YOU'D DO THE WORK.

Upon initiating your campaign, your foremost priority should be establishing a Top 200 List of prospective supporters and contacts. This list serves as the foundation for your fundraising and email list, commonly known as your House File. These individuals should possess a familiarity with you, hold trust in you, and display a likelihood of offering financial support.

It is crucial to contact these individuals before officially filing your candidacy, adhering to regulations set by your state or the FEC (if running for a federal office). Once a commitment of financial support is secured, arrange to collect the check either in person or via mail. However, bear in mind that in most states, retaining these checks for over 5 to 7 days before officially announcing your candidacy is not permitted, making it vital to consult your local public disclosure office before acquiring any funds from donors.

The prospect of asking for money can be intimidating, particularly when reaching out to unfamiliar individuals. Most people experience unease or discomfort in making such requests, yet it is imperative to persevere and make these calls. Conquering the fear of soliciting funds is critical for your campaign's success. Refrain from allowing imposter syndrome or other factors to deter you from making these calls. While making donor calls may be challenging, remember that virtually every candidate who has run for public office has shared this sentiment. The intimidating act of calling and requesting money is crucial to undertake in order to confront and overcome this fear.

SET UP CANDIDATE COMMITTEE WITH FEC AND/OR STATE REGULATORY BODY

If you are running for a federal position, your treasurer will likely handle FEC registration, obtaining an EIN number from the IRS, bank setup, and donor portal setup, as the accuracy of the reporting is the treasurer's legal responsibility. Conversely, treasurers for state or local races may or may not provide these setup services. If you must arrange these elements yourself at the state level, the process typically involves the following order:

1. Registering your campaign with the relevant state authority. For details, visit your state's Secretary of State or Elections Department website.

2. Obtaining an EIN number from the Internal Revenue Service for your campaign committee (e.g., Dawson for Governor) instead of your personal name. After registering online at www.irs.gov, **make sure to print out the EIN document** so you have proof of registration and an IRS letter containing your EIN number when you secure a PO Box.

3. Securing a campaign PO Box at your local post office for mail and contributions.

4. Opening a bank account for your campaign.

5. Registering your campaign on donor portals such as www.anedot.com or www.winred.com to receive online contributions. These two solutions are known to be the best for conservative candidates and least hassle.

LAUNCH

Upon completing all tasks in Phase 1, you are ready to launch your campaign. Although the actual day of your official campaign launch may not be thrilling, careful planning is essential. Launching your campaign on a Monday is recommended, as the week's news cycle is just beginning and media outlets are more likely to take notice. Avoid Thursdays or Fridays, when the news cycle is concluding and media attention may wane. Ideally, distribute press releases at 4 a.m. on your launch day, particularly to unfamiliar media outlets. For media outlets with whom you have established relationships, notify them of an impending major announcement a few days prior and email them directly on your launch day.

Media coverage hinges on diligent follow-up. Strive to secure as many radio, TV, and print media appearances as possible on your launch day. Your Campaign Manager should actively schedule numerous media opportunities.

The scale of your race will dictate whether an event for your official announcement is warranted. If you are running for a statewide or federal office, it is advisable to organize a modest event with a strong supporter turnout. The manner in which this event is conducted will set the tone for your campaign and establish expectations. Further details on this subject will be addressed in the following chapter.

FINAL THOUGHTS

As we conclude our exploration of Phase 1: Pre-Campaign Analysis and Setup, let us reflect on the key insights and strategies discussed, which will form the bedrock of your successful campaign. Remember that the journey to public office requires a blend of astute planning, a strong foundation, and a deep understanding of your target audience.

Cost analysis is an essential aspect of laying the groundwork for your campaign. By diligently scrutinizing your campaign's financial requirements and developing a sustainable fundraising strategy, you will be able to allocate resources efficiently, ensuring that your message reaches and persuades the right voters. Race analysis plays a critical role in determining the winnability of the race you plan to enter. This entails researching the historical electoral trends and patterns, gauging the political landscape, and assessing your potential opponents. By selecting a winnable race, you increase the likelihood of success and make the most of your time and resources.

SWOT analysis, or the evaluation of your campaign's strengths, weaknesses, opportunities, and threats, provides a comprehensive understanding of the internal and external factors that will shape your campaign's trajectory. Armed with this knowledge, you can devise strategies to capitalize on your strengths and opportunities while addressing your weaknesses and mitigating potential threats.

Throughout this phase, it is essential to remember the importance of branding, including crafting a compelling logo and website to convey your values and message effectively. Additionally, establishing a robust digital presence will allow you to connect with supporters and amplify your campaign's impact.

Building your Top 200 List and mastering the art of asking for financial support will provide your campaign with the resources needed to thrive. Furthermore, understanding the various voter segments and focusing on those who are most likely to support your conservative candidacy will allow for a more efficient and targeted use of resources.

As you work through the tasks in this chapter, bear in mind the idea: How you do anything is how you do everything. The more excellently you execute these tasks, the more formidable your campaign will be. With thorough planning, unwavering determination, and a keen understanding of your audience, you will be well-equipped to conquer the challenges that lie ahead and ultimately secure a victory in your chosen race. In the forthcoming chapters, we will delve deeper into the strategies and tactics that will help you realize your goals and achieve success in the noble endeavor of public service.

CHAPTER 3

PHASE 2: LAUNCH – THE FIRST 30 TO 45 DAYS

THE LAUNCH PHASE of a political campaign is a crucial period that can determine its success or failure. The launch phase should last between 30 to 45 days, with a maximum of 60 days, and requires massive effort and hard work from the candidate and the campaign team. During this stage, the candidate should work long hours to create momentum and establish a dominant position in the race.

In this chapter, a clear and easy-to-follow Massive Action Plan (MAP) will be provided to guide the campaign through the launch phase and ensure its success. The MAP will help the candidate and the team to take action and achieve their goals, making it difficult for the opponent to match their efforts. By launching the campaign with great momentum, the candidate can set the pace for the rest of the race and solidify their position as a front-runner.

THE MEDIA

Before you embark on your MAP (Massive Action Plan), it is crucial to gain a clear understanding of the media. Dismissing the entire media as a mere extension of the Democratic Party is both intellectually lazy and, at times, inaccurate. Overlooking the media can hinder your ability to harness its power for your benefit, and to counter any unfair or damaging pieces that may be published about you. The media is a formidable force that warrants respect, not avoidance. However, be aware that some individuals within the media may attempt to undermine you if given the opportunity. This occurs because many in the media do not merely report the news; they report the narrative. Always remember, everyone has an angle they are attempting to pursue.

Therefore, to effectively engage with the media, you need to understand the six types of stories that they look for. Journalists look for stories that fit into one of these categories:

1. **Urgent/Timely** - News and information have a limited lifespan, and what was considered newsworthy for weeks 30 years ago may only be relevant for a few days today or not at all. When you pitch a story to the media, you must make a compelling case for why it matters to their readers right now.

2. **Locality** - People generally show more interest in news that affects them directly. Local media outlets focus on local news, regional media on regionally and nationally important news, and national media on news of national significance or if the regional news impacts the nation or a larger national narrative. Down-ballot races typically receive limited national attention, while top-of-the-ticket races tend to receive more media coverage. When you pitch information to the media, make

sure you target the right audience. Don't send a press release to the Associated Press about your local school board race unless it has a national impact. Instead, send it to your local news outlets.

3. **Gravity -** The media covers stories that matter to their readers in a meaningful way. If you are running for County Land Commissioner, the media will ask, "So what?" You must provide a compelling answer to this question, especially if you lack broad name recognition. Create a narrative that creates gravity and your campaign will receive coverage.

4. **Uniqueness -** Media outlets look for unique stories. They won't run a lead story about a dog chasing a squirrel, but they may run a story about a group of angry squirrels chasing a dog because it's unique and unexpected. Make your story unique and interesting to increase its chances of being covered.

5. **Conflict -** Conflict sells, and the media loves a good fight. If a story lacks an element of struggle or an us vs. them dynamic, it will likely be overlooked. Donald Trump is a prime example of this. He is the perfect villain/champion for media stories and they are addicted to all things Trump. Mr. Trump knows this and uses it to his advantage to gain earned media (media the candidate does not pay for). During the 2016 election, Donald Trump received a significant amount of earned media due to the nature of conflict that naturally surrounded his campaign. According to a New York Times analysis, he amassed close to $2 billion worth of media attention from television, print, and social media throughout his campaign. This amount was about twice the all-in price of the most expensive presidential campaigns in history.

6. **Human Interest -** People are naturally curious about other people, especially those with a level of celebrity. As a candidate, you are thrusting yourself into the public eye, and voters will be curious about your personal life. The media runs two types of human-interest narratives: the "get to know the candidate" narrative and the "uncover the personal faults of the candidate" narrative. Of the two, negative pieces are more interesting to the media because they create conflict, which sells newspapers or drives online clicks.

To create a compelling narrative that will make your campaign launch newsworthy, you should focus on the six types of stories that the media looks for. These include stories that are urgent, localized, have gravity, are unique, have conflict, and have human interest.

In addition to understanding these six categories, it's also important to understand the mindset of the media. Journalists will only cover a story if it passes the "so what" test and if it's relevant to their audience. As a candidate, you need to make a case for why your story is important to the media's audience and why they should cover it. By crafting a compelling narrative that fits into one or more of the six categories, you can increase the chances of your campaign launch being covered by the media. This is important because earned media, which is the media coverage you receive without paying for it, is typically worth four to five times more than the value of media you can purchase (unearned media).

YOUR MASSIVE ACTION PLAN (MAP)

THE DAY OF LAUNCH

Once your campaign is officially registered with the appropriate authorities (such as your state election commission or the Federal Election Commission), and you have set up your bank account, donor portal, website and email responder, and have all your collateral materials ready, it's time to announce your candidacy to the media.

To do this, send out your press releases via email between 8:00 AM and 2:00 PM local time on the Tuesday, Wednesday, or Thursday after the completion of Phase 1. Plan your official launch event for the Monday or Tuesday evening following the day you sent out the press release. Often these events are scheduled for 7:00 PM to 8:00 PM local time, so people have time to finish work and attend. If you believe you can gather a large crowd during the day, schedule the event for 10:00 AM to 11:00 AM local time; this will benefit the media who have afternoon deadlines

The same day you send out your press release, send an op-ed piece to your local newspapers to be published in their weekend edition. The op-ed should effectively outline the rationale and story leading to your candidacy along with your general narrative, and be well-written (free of grammar and spelling errors). Your campaign manager should also be on the phone with media outlets to schedule interviews. The goal is to book as many interviews with as many outlets as possible, including traditional print media, local TV affiliates, talk radio, podcasts, and social media shows. Your schedule for the week of your announcement should be filled with media appearances to discuss your candidacy and your general narrative.

Starting on day one, you need to begin collecting the financial pledges you have already set up and make donor calls for four to six hours a day. A strong fundraising total and positive attention to the campaign will help relieve stress and create buzz around your campaign. I have dedicated a whole chapter to fundraising and will provide all the information you need to be successful, including details on your 90-in-30 fundraising program.

LAUNCH YOUR
DIGITAL MARKETING CAMPAIGN

In addition to your other day of launch activities, a well-orchestrated digital strategy must be employed to deploy your digital and social media advertisements and capture the attention of conservative 3/4 and 4/4 voters within your district. Harnessing the power of digital platforms such as Google, Facebook, and Instagram will enable you to reach your target audience effectively and achieve four goals: Build name recognition, build your social media audience, drive traffic to your website, and build your email list.

For non-social media digital advertising, it is essential to optimize your campaigns with carefully crafted keywords and audience targeting. By selecting the right phrases and words that resonate with your target voters, your ads will appear when they search for relevant information. To maximize your reach, use location targeting and focus on your district, ensuring that your message is delivered to the right audience. Employing different ad sizes will allow you to adapt to the various display spaces available across the ad network, thereby increasing visibility and engagement.

Allocate your budget among the various digital channels and ad formats at your disposal, such as search engine marketing, display ads, video ads, and native advertising. Consider the priority of each target segment and the platform when deciding where to focus your spending. For instance, you might allocate a higher percentage of your budget to search engine marketing if you find that it's driving the most traffic to your website or to video ads if they're generating the most engagement.

In addition to setting appropriate budget levels, it's crucial to structure your spending efficiently. Utilize automated bidding strategies and cost-per-impression (CPM) or cost-per-click (CPC) pricing models to optimize your bids based on your campaign objectives, ensuring that you achieve the best possible outcomes within your budget constraints. As you progress, consistently analyze your ad performance and adjust your budget and spending structure accordingly.

Turning to Facebook and Instagram, these social media platforms provide an invaluable opportunity to connect with your target voters on a more personal level. Create engaging content that highlights your key messages and positions, ensuring that your ads resonate with your audience. Utilize the audience targeting features available on both platforms, narrowing your focus to your specific district and prioritizing conservative voters. This precision targeting will ensure your ads reach the right audience and maximize your return on investment.

To maximize your visibility on Facebook and Instagram, it's essential to allocate a budget that aligns with your goals while maintaining a balance between reach, frequency, and cost efficiency. The optimal budget level varies based on the competitive landscape of your region, the specific target audience, and the desired outcomes. Begin by establishing an initial daily or lifetime budget for your campaigns, keeping in mind that a higher budget will result in increased reach and visibility. It's wise to start with a modest budget and gradually increase it as you monitor the performance of your ads and gather data on the most effective strategies.

Distribute your budget between the various ad sets, taking into consideration the priority of each target segment and the platform. You may choose to allocate a higher percentage of your budget to Facebook if you find that your target audience is more active and engaged there, or you may decide to focus more on Instagram if it better resonates with your audience.

In addition to setting the appropriate budget levels, it's crucial to structure your spending efficiently. Employ Facebook and Instagram's automated bidding strategies to maximize your results while maintaining cost efficiency. These algorithms will help you optimize your bids based on your campaign objectives, ensuring that you achieve the best possible outcomes within your budget constraints. As you move forward, regularly analyze your ad performance and adjust your budget and spending structure accordingly. By diligently monitoring the metrics and making data-driven decisions, you will optimize your visibility and impact on these platforms.

THE ANNOUNCEMENT EVENT

Optics matter—**always**. This includes your official announcement event. On June 16, 2015, Donald Trump, along with his wife, descended the escalator at Trump Tower in New York City to a crowd of supporters, friends, family, and the media, to announce his candidacy for the presidency. The event was meticulously planned, from his entrance to the descent down the escalator to his actual announcement. A well-planned announcement can set the tone for a successful campaign. Research shows that leading presidential candidates have made powerful first impressions in their announcements in the past 30 years.

Planning a fantastic announcement event is a crucial step for any candidate in a political campaign. This event is often the first opportunity for the candidate to make an impression on potential voters, donors, and media representatives. A well-planned and executed event can create a positive perception of the candidate and their campaign, while a poorly planned event can have the opposite effect.

Creating a successful announcement event can increase the candidate's visibility and generate media coverage and social media buzz. This increased visibility can lead to increased donations, volunteer support, and word-of-mouth endorsements, all of which are crucial for a successful campaign. High-quality events also create a perception of legitimacy for the candidate, particularly for those who are new to politics or have never held office before. A well-organized and professional event demonstrates that the candidate is serious, competent, and worthy of consideration, which can lead to increased support and more positive coverage in the media.

Additionally, the announcement event is a great tool to kick-off fundraising efforts for the campaign. By impressing attendees with a professional and engaging event, candidates can increase the likelihood that attendees will donate to the campaign. This can provide crucial funding for the campaign and help establish momentum early on. Finally, the announcement event is an opportunity for candidates to clearly communicate their message and platform. By organizing a well-planned event with engaging speeches and a clear program, candidates can ensure that attendees understand their goals and priorities. This can help create a sense of enthusiasm and support among attendees and provide a solid foundation for the campaign moving forward.

THE STEPS TO PLANNING YOUR EVENT

1. **Choose a Venue:** The venue you choose should be large enough to accommodate the anticipated number of attendees and should be easily accessible. Consider venues such as community centers, hotels, or convention centers, as they often have large spaces with ample parking. When choosing a venue be sure to find a venue that will hold 75% to 80% of your expected turnout. The event should look full even if 25% of the invitees don't attend. Additionally, the venue should be in good condition on the outside and the inside. When choosing a venue, also consider the candidate's message and audience, as the venue should be in alignment with both.

2. **Develop a Theme:** The event's theme should be based on the candidate's general narrative and message. For example, if the candidate's message is centered around individual freedom, liberty, and limited government, the event theme could be "Empowering Communities, Building Freedom." This theme should be incorporated into all aspects of the event, including the decor, invitations, and speeches.

3. **Set the Tone:** It's important to set a professional and upbeat tone for the event, as this can create a sense of competence and legitimacy for the candidate. Consider hiring a professional emcee to keep the event flowing smoothly and to add an air of professionalism. This person can help introduce the candidate, moderate discussions, and provide entertainment as needed.

4. **Create Invitations:** The invitations should be high-quality and reflect the candidate's brand and the event theme. They should be sent out well in advance to allow attendees to plan accordingly. Physical

invitations should be sent to targeted high-dollar donors and followed up with a phone call from the candidate to personally invite the donor to the event and to spend some private time together in an exclusive green room area. Digital invitations can be a cost-effective option, and they can be used to increase response rates and facilitate easy RSVP tracking.

5. **Script the Program:** The program should be engaging and communicate the candidate's message clearly within a window of 60 to 90 minutes maximum. Consider including speeches by the candidate, guest speakers who are aligned with the candidate's views, and even a brief Q&A session to engage attendees. The program should be well-organized, with clear timing and musical transitions between speakers. This will ensure that attendees stay engaged throughout the event and leave with a clear understanding of the candidate's message.

YOUR 90 IN 30 PLAN

The 90 in 30 Plan is a very simple yet crucial aspect of a successful campaign. Its aim is to raise enough funds to cover the expenses for the first 90 days of the campaign within the first 30 days after launch. The campaign budget created in the first phase should provide the monthly spending rate of the campaign, known as the burn rate. For instance, if the budget requires $20,000 in expenses each month, the 90-day fundraising target should be a minimum of $60,000 ($20,000 x 3 months). The goal should be to raise $60,000 in the first 30 to 45 days of the campaign. The numbers may vary for local, state-level, senatorial, or statewide offices.

The 90-day target is then broken down into daily and hourly goals. Fundraising calls should be made six days a week, for a minimum of four to six hours a day. If there are 26 calling days in the first 30 days, the daily goal would be $2,307 ($60,000 divided by 26 days). To determine the hourly goal, divide the daily goal by the number of hours spent calling, which in this example is four hours, giving an hourly goal of $577.

Each hour, the campaign should aim to make between 40 and 50 calls, connecting with 3 to 6 potential donors. The conversation should last a minimum of 5 minutes to a maximum of 15 minutes, with a minimum donation request of $250. For federal races, it is best practice to establish benchmark amounts such as $6,600[1], $3,300, $1,000, $500, and $250 to ask for. Along with fundraising calls, the campaign should also deploy a digital and email fundraising strategy. Money raised through these efforts should be **in addition** to the funds raised through calls, *not subtracted* from the call time goal.

In Phase 2, the focus should be solely on fundraising and media. Raising money and increasing name recognition are the most important goals at this stage. If the campaign fails to raise sufficient funds and gain traction with its base, it may fall into what is referred to as "The Pit of Despair," which is difficult to recover from and the subject of the next chapter. Therefore, it's crucial for the campaign to achieve momentum within the first 30 to 60 days for long-term viability and success. The focus should also be on building name recognition and driving traffic to the campaign website, which serves as the centerpiece of the marketing effort. The priority goals of the marketing effort in the first two months should be to increase the email list, text alert list, and

---

[1] The current full cycle maximum for federal FEC regulated races in 2024.

social media community. This will pay dividends in the form of small dollar fundraising numbers in later phases.

FINAL THOUGHTS

As we conclude the chapter on Phase 2: The Launch, it is essential to reflect upon the principles that govern the initial steps of a successful campaign. As the adage goes, well begun is half done, and thus, the importance of a powerful launch cannot be overstated. Through unwavering determination and meticulous planning, a candidate can create a lasting impression and set the stage for a victorious race.

In navigating the complex world of media, the candidate must comprehend the characteristics of newsworthy stories and craft a compelling narrative that resonates with their target audience. By weaving tales that are urgent, localized, weighty, unique, contentious, and human-centric, the campaign can capture the interest of the media and amplify its message.

During the first 30 to 45 days of the campaign, the Massive Action Plan (MAP) serves as a guiding light, illuminating the path to success. It ensures that the candidate and their team take decisive, strategic actions that propel the campaign forward and make it difficult for competitors to keep up. By initiating the race with immense momentum, the candidate establishes themselves as a formidable front-runner.

On the day of the launch, a well-executed digital marketing campaign, coupled with a memorable announcement event, can make a lasting impact on potential supporters. These efforts, in conjunction with the 90 in 30 Plan, lay the foundation for a thriving campaign. By raising the necessary funds within the first 30 to 45 days, the candidate can confidently meet the challenges of the race, knowing they have the resources to fuel their activities.

CHAPTER 4

THE PIT OF DESPAIR

CAMPAIGNS THAT ARE UNABLE to gain momentum in the first 45 to 90 days of their efforts in contested primary elections often face defeat. This is because they reach a level of mediocrity that the candidate and the campaign leadership are unable to surpass. This dynamic is easily identifiable in federal and non-federal races at every level. Escaping this pit of despair is harder than maintaining momentum from the start, which is why many campaigns fail to do so.

CHARACTERISTICS OF A PLATEAUED CAMPAIGN

There are several signs that a campaign has fallen into the pit of despair, which can lead to eventual failure. One of the most critical signs is the inability to raise the funds necessary to cover the expenses of the first 90 days of the campaign within the first 30 to 45 days after launch. This lack of financial support can be a significant hindrance to the campaign's progress and may indicate that the message is not resonating with the intended audience. In addition to this, a plateaued campaign may also experience a lack of interest from volunteers and supporters, resulting in a shortage of manpower and resources. Furthermore, a campaign that is not gaining traction may also face difficulty in securing media attention and coverage, which is crucial for reaching a wider audience and spreading the message.

In order to overcome these challenges, the campaign needs to reassess its strategy and approach. This may involve revising the messaging, target audience, and outreach efforts. The team may also need to explore new fundraising methods and seek out new sources of support. It is crucial for the campaign to remain vigilant and proactive in its efforts to overcome these obstacles and regain momentum. With the right approach and persistence, a plateaued campaign can still achieve its goals and succeed in the race—possibly.

IGNORED BY THE MEDIA AND THE BASE

If a campaign does not garner sufficient attention from the media and the conservative base, raising the necessary funds to support the campaign can become exceedingly difficult. This issue is particularly acute for self-funded candidates, as being overlooked may result in major setbacks, potentially leading to the campaign's failure. Viability can be swiftly discerned by the amount of money raised from the constituency. For instance, a candidate who raises $10,000 from five donors will typically have less support than a candidate who raises the same amount from 50 donors.

Being ignored by the media and the base often occurs when the candidate failed to properly complete Phase 1, which involves identifying the rationale and story, researching the base, creating a commercially acceptable brand, and crafting a compelling general narrative. Campaigns that rush into Phase 2 without properly executing Phase 1 will almost always fail, as both the media and the voters can easily recognize a candidate who did not prepare adequately.

If the campaign has at least 180 days (120 days for smaller campaigns) left before the primary election, there may be a chance to overcome being passed over, but it will require a significant amount of effort and money. The first step is to go back to Phase 1 and complete it properly, which may require finding new leadership if the current general consultant and campaign manager were involved in the failure to execute Phase 1.

The campaign will then relaunch without an announcement event, instead focusing on a publicity effort through digital marketing, social media marketing, a media blitz, and targeting voters who were not exposed to the previous brand. A significant amount of rebranded content will need to be pushed out, and the voters who previously overlooked the candidate's brand will need to be retargeted later. The campaign will also need to increase fundraising efforts to cover the budgeted burn rate and catch up on funds that were not raised prior to the relaunch, which will require making at least six hours of calls per day to known donors and running targeted digital fundraising ads.

While the restart may save the campaign, there is no guarantee of success, as it depends on the quality of the restart and how much damage was done to the campaign's brand prior to the restart. This emphasizes the importance of a campaign-wide commitment to excellence, starting with the candidate and extending throughout the organization.

POOR FUNDRAISING

Lack of successful fundraising in Phase 2 can often be attributed to the candidate and the senior leadership of the campaign. The ultimate responsibility of raising the necessary funds to support the campaign lies with the candidate. If the campaign is struggling to raise money, it may be due to the candidate not making enough fundraising calls. On the other hand, if the candidate is making calls but still not receiving enough support, it is likely because the foundation of the campaign, established in Phase 1, was not strong enough. This could be due to a poorly developed rationale and story or a lack of compelling general narrative.

If the issue of poor fundraising is simply due to the candidate not making enough calls, the solution is straightforward - make more calls. However, it will be even more challenging as the campaign is already behind in funding its budgeted burn rate and must also make up for the funds that were not raised previously. The candidate must make a minimum of 6-hour call sessions to known high dollar contributors and implement a digital fundraising effort. Building and targeting the campaign's email list for low to medium dollar contributions is also essential.

If the issue is a lack of response from donors when the candidate makes calls, it is a clear sign that Phase 1 was not executed properly. The rationale and story of the campaign must be revisited and presented in a more compelling manner. However, this is a difficult task as the candidate is trying to re-establish credibility with voters who have already dismissed them as not viable. In such cases, it is unlikely that the campaign will be successful even after a restart of Phase 1. It is crucial to understand the importance of establishing a strong rationale and story in a successful campaign. These elements provide credibility to the candidate and without credibility, a campaign is unlikely to succeed.

RIGHT TARGET. WRONG MESSAGE.

Occasionally, a strong candidate may struggle with raising funds and connecting with the appropriate base voters because their general narrative is not resonating with the voters. This is because they may not be discussing issues that matter to the voters in a compelling manner. In such cases, it is important to adjust the general narrative to align with the priorities of the donors and the base. This means listening to the questions and concerns raised by the voters and addressing them in the general narrative. The candidates must understand that voters are interested in issues that impact their lives, rather than what the candidate finds important.

To resolve this issue, the campaign must revise its general narrative and the candidate must increase their call time to cover the expenses and make up for the previously missed contributions. The campaign must also update all its marketing materials, social media, and emails to align with the new general narrative. If the lack of resonance with the voters is the reason for the campaign's failure, realigning the general narrative should put the campaign back on track. However, this is not a common cause of campaigns falling into the pit of despair.

WRONG TARGET. RIGHT MESSAGE.

It is common for campaigns to be on track with their general narrative but to go wrong with their targeting. This occurs when the campaign targets too broad an audience, instead of focusing on the 3/4 and 4/4 voters who have a history of voting conservative. This dilutes the campaign's efforts and reaches people who are not politically engaged, have different political views, or have a history of not contributing to campaigns.

To avoid this problem, accurate data analysis and voter ID is crucial in Phase 1. If the leadership suspects this is a problem, they should reanalyze the voter data and adjust their targeting efforts. Winning campaigns don't target everyone, they focus on registered voters who have a history of being actively engaged in primary elections, contributing financially to campaigns, and are identified as conservatives. If the problem is caught in time, adjustments can be made, but if it is caught too late, it is likely that one of the candidate's opponents has already targeted the right voters and won their support.

BREAKING THROUGH AND AVOIDING THE PIT OF DESPAIR

Campaigns can avoid falling into the pit of despair by properly executing all steps in Phase 1 and taking decisive action in Phase 2. This involves accurately identifying and targeting the right voters with the right message, and making calls with maximum effort until the set goal is reached. In marketing, if the campaign has a goal to add a certain number of subscribers to the email list, they should take immediate action to reach that goal and even push harder if they surpass it.

The success of a campaign ultimately depends on the candidate's and the leadership's commitment to winning. The candidate sets the pace and determines the fate of the team. It is important to adopt a "breakthrough" mentality, where the focus is on making progress towards the goal, instead of making excuses for failure. The candidate is the leader of the campaign, and it is up to them to steer it towards success. As the candidate, you set the pace. You choose the fate of your team. **It's your ship. Lead it.**

FINAL THOUGHTS

In the twilight of a failed endeavor, one may find themselves standing at the precipice of the Pit of Despair. This abyss, however, is not an inevitability, but rather a warning, a signal to recognize the necessity of perseverance and determination in the pursuit of success. As you, the reader, reflect upon the lessons within these pages, let it be known that the power to overcome the Pit of Despair lies within you. The circumstances that led a campaign to this pit may vary, but the underlying principles remain the same. The mastery of these principles and the unwavering faith in your ability to succeed are what will propel you past the obstacles that may arise.

To triumph over adversity, one must have a clear vision of their goal, a burning desire to achieve it, and a firm understanding of the path that leads to it. It is of utmost importance that you engage with the right audience, conveying a message that resonates with their core beliefs and values. And, as you navigate the treacherous terrain of fundraising, let not the fear of failure hinder you, for it is through perseverance that success is ultimately achieved.

In moments of doubt and struggle, remind yourself that failure is but a stepping stone on the path to greatness. Embrace the wisdom gained from each misstep, for it is through adversity that our character is forged and our resilience is strengthened. In this journey, you will undoubtedly encounter obstacles, but remember, the power to overcome them lies within you.

CHAPTER 5

PHASE 3:
BUILDING YOUR BASE

THE FOCUS OF YOUR campaign in Phase 3 is to build a broad base of support through winning the early majority of engaged conservative voters during the run-up to the primary election[1]. In Phase 2, the campaign focus was laying a solid foundation of support from fully engaged conservative 3/4 and 4/4 voters. The efforts the campaign put into Phase 2 allowed the candidate to avoid the Pit of Despair and move into Phase 3. The campaign activity in this phase should expand your efforts to win the support of the early majority of conservative and conservative leaning voters you know are going to participate in the primary election. Phase 4 will shift the campaigns focus to winning the late majority of conservative and conservative leaning voters.

---

[1] This group of voters is determined by the type of voting system the candidate's state uses. For example, in partisan primary states, only Republicans can participate in Republican primary elections. Meanwhile, for example, in Washington State, there are no partisan races and any voter can vote for any candidate and the top two vote winners move onto the General Election. Be sure to clearly understand who can participate in your primary election.

WARNING:

There is a commonly held belief that campaigns should not waste their time and resources reaching out to 3/4 and 4/4 voters, as they are likely to participate in the election regardless of whether they receive outreach from the campaign. Instead, the focus should be on reaching 2/4 voters and encouraging them to cast their ballots.

This is entirely **INCORRECT** and will destroy your campaign.

In business, there are three types of buying behavior: those who *always purchase* your product, those who *may purchase* your product, and those who will *never purchase* your product (even if it's offered for free). Why would you market to individuals who may purchase your product and ignore those who you know will always purchase your product if given the opportunity? It doesn't make sense. Businesses always start with buyers, then target individuals who can be persuaded to become buyers, and ignore those who will never buy. The same principle applies in political campaigns.

The 3/4 and 4/4 voters are the most engaged and invested in the campaign, contributing the most money, volunteering the most often, acting as brand ambassadors, and providing the campaign with the best source of free word-of-mouth advertising. Additionally, they are typically more active on social media, professional associations, and community leadership. In a later chapter, we will discuss building a narrative arc. One of the key principles we will delve into is the idea that businesses sell what people are buying. If the market wants apples, don't sell them oranges. Sell them apples. In politics, this translates to discussing the issues most important to 3/4 and 4/4 voters, even if they are not important to the candidate.

To build and broaden support, the campaign's focus in Phase 3 should revolve around two main activities: selling buyers what they want within the context of a well-crafted narrative arc, and expanding fundraising efforts. In Phases 1 and 2, the majority of fundraising efforts were carried out by the candidate. In Phase 3, we add more fundraising elements and create multiple streams of income, in addition to the candidate's ongoing fundraising calls. Through continuous data analysis, the campaign will utilize targeted digital and social media advertising to drive traffic to the website and convert visitors into email subscribers. This email list will then be targeted with low-dollar fundraising appeals and campaign updates.

POLLING: THE PULSE OF THE CAMPAIGN

In the realm of political campaigns, it is the master strategist who understands the value of accurate information and utilizes it to create a roadmap to victory. Polling, when properly employed, serves as a vital instrument in the hands of such strategists, offering insights into the hearts and minds of the electorate. This knowledge empowers campaigns to refine their message, allocate resources judiciously, and devise strategies that resonate with the voters. Let us examine the multifaceted ways in which polling contributes to the art of political campaigning.

Should your campaign possess the resources to undertake polling, it is advisable to initiate this process during Phase 3, or even earlier if circumstances permit. In recent times, polling has faced criticism for producing results that deviate significantly from the actual outcomes. However, the astute strategist recognizes that internal polling still holds a vital place in contemporary campaigns. Among its many advantages, polling enables the candidate to pinpoint or corroborate key issues, evaluate the candidate's performance in their current contest, thoroughly analyze voter demographics, offer valuable data to direct resource allocation and strategic focus, and supply supplementary opposition research. These benefits, when leveraged effectively, can significantly enhance a campaign's chances of success.

The wise campaign comprehends that capturing the hearts of the voters is predicated upon first captivating their minds. To achieve this, one must understand the concerns that weigh heavily upon the electorate during a particular election cycle. Polling serves as the guiding light in this quest, revealing the issues that command the utmost importance for the voters. Armed with this knowledge, candidates can tailor their message to resonate with these concerns, demonstrating an unwavering commitment to discovering effective solutions. This approach not only fosters a connection with the voters but also conveys empathy and understanding, showing the candidate as a true champion of their cause.

As the campaign proceeds, it is crucial to maintain a vigilant eye on the evolving concerns of the electorate. Regular polling ensures that the candidate remains in tune with the shifting sentiments, adjusting their message accordingly to maintain its relevance and potency. By consistently aligning their message with the most pressing concerns of the voters, candidates can solidify their connection with the electorate, bolster their credibility, and substantially increase the likelihood of winning their support. In essence, the wise candidate understands that the key to electoral success lies in forging a genuine bond with the voters, built upon a foundation of shared values and priorities. Through the judicious use of polling, the campaign can continually fine-tune its message to ensure that it resonates deeply with the hearts and minds of the electorate, ultimately paving the way to victory.

As a campaign unfolds, it is essential to keep a watchful eye on the performance of the candidate. Properly executed polls (commonly referred to as "clean polls" as opposed to "push polls.") serve as a reliable barometer, allowing campaigns to evaluate the efficacy of their strategies, messaging, and events. In response to shifting voter sentiments, astute campaigns can fine-tune their approach, thereby maximizing their chances of success. A firm I use frequently with my clients and recommend is Spry Strategies, a public opinion research and data analysis firm that specializes in providing political, non-profit, and corporate clients with survey research, data analysis, and strategic consulting services. The firm is owned by my friend Ryan Burrell, a political veteran who has worked with numerous conservative candidates, organizations, and causes.

Their methodology often includes using various data sources, such as voter files, consumer data, and survey research to create a comprehensive understanding of public opinion and voter behavior. By combining these sources, Spry Strategies provides accurate and actionable insights to their clients, helping them make informed decisions in their political campaigns or organizational strategies.

In the realm of politics, knowledge indeed constitutes power, and gaining a comprehensive understanding of the demographics of one's supporters and potential voters can be the master key to achieving success. Polling data serves as a treasure trove of vital information, encompassing aspects such as age, gender, income, education, and political affiliation (this information is often referred to as "crosstab data"). This wealth of knowledge equips campaigns with the necessary insights to meticulously target their efforts, forging connections with key voting blocs that may ultimately determine the outcome of the election.

By delving into the nuances of the electorate's composition, campaigns can devise tailored strategies that cater to the unique preferences and concerns of different demographic groups. This targeted approach not only amplifies the campaign's message but also creates a sense of inclusivity, demonstrating to the voters that their individual needs and aspirations are recognized and valued. Moreover, the astute campaign strategist knows that the dynamics of the electorate can shift over time, influenced by factors such as socioeconomic changes, evolving social attitudes, and fluctuating political landscapes. Regular polling empowers the campaign to stay attuned to these changes, ensuring that their strategies and messaging remain relevant and impactful in the face of an ever-changing demographic landscape.

The art of political campaigning is a delicate dance, necessitating not just an inspiring vision, but also the prudent management of resources. In this intricate balancing act, polling data emerges as a crucial compass, guiding campaigns toward the geographic regions and voter demographics where their endeavors will yield the most abundant fruit. By judiciously allocating time, money, and energy, campaigns can optimize their impact, amplifying their message and significantly enhancing their prospects of success on Election Day. Polling data not only identifies the areas where a candidate's message resonates most powerfully but also highlights regions where additional effort may sway undecided voters. This invaluable information enables campaigns to formulate targeted strategies, directing resources toward the mobilization of supporters, persuasion of undecided voters, and the fostering of enthusiasm among the base.

In addition, the allocation of resources is an ongoing process, requiring continual evaluation and adjustment in response to evolving circumstances. As the campaign unfolds, polling data can reveal fluctuations in voter sentiment, enabling the campaign to respond with agility, reallocating resources as needed to maintain momentum and seize emerging opportunities. Furthermore, the strategic management of resources extends beyond financial investments and time commitments. It also encompasses the efficient utilization of human capital – volunteers, staff, and the candidate themselves. By harnessing polling data to guide the allocation of these valuable assets, campaigns can ensure that their message is conveyed effectively, bolstering support and fostering a sense of unity and shared purpose.

A keen awareness of not only one's strengths but also the vulnerabilities of one's opponents is paramount to success. Polls serve as a valuable source of insight in this regard, illuminating areas where the opposing candidate may be susceptible to critique or challenges. To truly master the art of exploiting an opponent's weaknesses, a campaign must first engage in thorough research and analysis (a subject we will discuss later in the book). Polling data provides a foundation upon which to build, revealing key indicators such as the opponent's unfavorable ratings, areas of policy vulnerability, and potential controversies. By carefully examining this information, a campaign can identify the most effective lines of attack, crafting messages that resonate with the electorate and cast doubt upon the opponent's qualifications or credibility.

Beyond merely identifying weaknesses, the astute strategist recognizes the importance of timing and execution in the deployment of these attacks. By monitoring polling data and gauging voter sentiment, a campaign can determine the optimal moment to strike, maximizing the impact of their message and catching their opponent off guard. In addition, the method of attack must be carefully considered, with the campaign weighing the risks and benefits of direct confrontations, subtle insinuations, or third-party involvement. Moreover, in the pursuit of exploiting an opponent's vulnerabilities, the wise campaign remains ever vigilant of their own weaknesses. By conducting self-assessments and evaluating their own vulnerabilities, campaigns can anticipate potential counterattacks and prepare their defenses accordingly. This proactive approach not only ensures the campaign remains on the offensive but also prevents an opponent from gaining the upper hand.

Polling is a vital tool in the arsenal of the modern political campaign, offering invaluable insights into the ever-changing landscape of voter sentiment and behavior. By skillfully harnessing the power of polling data, campaigns can chart a course to victory, navigating the treacherous waters of politics with confidence and determination. In the end, it is the master strategist who seizes opportunity and turns the tide of battle, securing triumph where others falter.

THE GENERAL BRAND AWARENESS: DIGITAL/SOCIAL MEDIA CAMPAIGN

The ads created in Phase 1 and launched in Phase 2 were centered around a general narrative. In Phase 3, these ads will be refined and focused on the first hot-button issues the campaign identified as important to voters, forming the opening act of the narrative arc. While they are still more general than specific, they will target the key issues. After the first wave of ads is launched, the second wave will focus on another important issue, and this sequence will continue until the entire narrative has been presented.

The primary goal of the ad push is to increase brand awareness, but the ultimate aim is to drive people to a landing page or website and capture their contact information. From there, they will be contacted and given opportunities to contribute financially, purchase merchandise, order signs, become volunteers, join social media ambassador groups, or help organize events, among other things.

At the same time, a social media marketing campaign should be initiated, including a combination of organic content posting and targeted paid ads. Viral marketing is no longer free, as social media companies now monetize most viral marketing. Be prepared to pay for social media exposure, as it is a marketing platform with an associated cost.

WARNING:

There is **<u>NO</u>** correlation between the size of a campaign's social media following and election outcomes. Any assertion that a correlation exists is myth.

While there are numerous social media platforms and online forums, campaigns typically use Facebook, Instagram, YouTube, and Twitter as their main outlets. Despite the criticism of censorship and bias, these platforms still offer the largest reach of voters among social media platforms.

In 2022, Facebook had 240 million users in the United States, accounting for about 71% of US citizens. The majority of the voters the campaign needs to reach can probably be found and targeted on Facebook. Instagram, which is owned by Facebook, has 160 million users in the US, or approximately 47% of US citizens. By utilizing these two platforms, the campaign can likely reach the majority of the voters it needs to build support. Ignoring these two platforms will limit the campaign's ability to reach voters where they spend most of their time: on their phones.

YouTube is a unique platform, as it is not technically a social media platform (it is the second-largest search engine after Google), but it has elements of discussion (comments) and a broad reach, along with the ability to micro-target specific audiences with video content and advertising. In the US, around 247 million people watch YouTube, with 70% of them watching it on their mobile devices. Additionally, videos on YouTube are typically shareable on other social media platforms.

The usefulness of Twitter for conservative campaigns changed significantly after Elon Musk purchased the platform in October 2022. At the time of writing, Twitter has 57 million users in the US and is expected to grow its user base in 2023 and beyond. Twitter cannot be used for political advertising, but it is useful for interacting with the media and informing the public about policy positions, campaign narrative, and overall brand exposure. Additionally, the media typically follows the Twitter profiles of credible candidates.

THE KEY TO DIGITAL MARKETING IS AD QUALTY, VOTER TARGETING, AND FREQUENCY OF SERVICE

As previously noted, perception is reality, and brand perception is built on the quality of advertising delivered. Poorly crafted advertisements can have a devastating impact on a campaign. Voter targeting and frequency of service are important, but the visual creative the campaign broadcasts through their digital marketing efforts will determine how the ads are received by the target market. The narrative is important, but not as important as the visual aspects. Campaign marketing should always be crafted by professional graphic designers.

Studies conducted in Europe show that only 9% of ads are viewed for longer than one second, and a mere 4% are viewed for longer than two seconds. Nearly 44% of ads were viewed for less than one second, and 35% of ads weren't viewed at all. This highlights the fact that most advertisers don't understand marketing and graphic design, and this includes many political advertisements.

To avoid these mistakes, campaigns should aim for simplicity and visual appeal in digital advertising. The image must grab the viewer's attention for longer than two seconds so that the ad copy can deliver the message. The next step is to create a compelling headline. The goal of any digital advertisement is to get the viewer to click on it. The first "hook" is how it looks, the second is the message, and the third is the call to action (CTA). Two emotions drive action: fear and greed (or hope). The ad must connect with these emotions and invite the viewer to take action.

The rule that guides powerful ad copy is the idea that you're not trying to talk to everyone, you're trying to talk to *someone specific*. This is why voter profiling and data research are so important in Phase 1. The campaign must know exactly who to reach with their compelling narrative arc. The CTA must be clear and specific, as a confused mind always says no. An example of a compelling CTA is "Learn how you can cut your taxes with my one policy change." This CTA, targeted to an over-taxed voter segment, will likely drive traffic to the campaign's website.

In the realm of political campaigns, a timeless principle holds sway over those who endeavor to inspire and win the hearts and minds of the electorate. This guiding tenet, the "Rule of 7," harkens back to the annals of history, yet its wisdom resonates just as profoundly in the modern age of political persuasion. The origins of this political marketing doctrine can be traced to the depths of advertising antiquity in the late 1800s. Its essence has been adapted from the world of commerce, offering invaluable insights for those who seek to forge a connection between a political candidate and the discerning voters.

The 1930s' movie industry, where the Rule of 7 truly took form, sowed the seeds of a notion that would later blossom in the fertile ground of political campaigns. Those orchestrating the art of persuasion recognized that a message must be delivered a minimum of seven times before it could truly captivate the audience and spur them to act. Over time, this tenet has evolved and expanded, with some proponents arguing that even seven exposures may be inadequate to sway the hearts of the electorate. It is crucial to note, however, that no definitive scientific evidence exists to substantiate the precise number of exposures required for a political advertisement to make a lasting impact.

The road to winning the hearts and minds of the electorate is paved with myriad factors that can influence the effectiveness of a political advertisement. The complexity of the message, the context in which it is presented, and an individual's preexisting knowledge and sentiments towards the candidate or issue all contribute to the campaign's success. In the sphere of politics, campaigns must tailor their approach to the ever-shifting landscape. For issues of lesser consequence, a limited number of exposures may suffice to spark the interest of the voters. However, for matters of great import, such as economic policies or social reforms, a more substantial number of exposures is necessary to permeate the consciousness of the electorate.

Political campaigns must also be mindful that beyond a certain threshold, the impact of their message may begin to diminish. A delicate balance must be struck to ensure that the message is not lost amidst the cacophony of competing voices and ideas. And so, the lesson to be gleaned from the Rule of 7 for political campaigns is that while repetition can be a formidable weapon in the arsenal of the political strategist, there is no one-size-fits-all solution to the enigma of frequency. When plotting the course to victory, campaign leaders must consider the unique dynamics of their target audience, the message they endeavor to convey, and the ever-changing context in which their advertisements will be encountered. The campaign's general consultant or digital media director should be able to create, buy, and place advertising, or they should know someone who can.

THE KEY TO SOCIAL MEDIA IS CONTENT

Social media content and the frequency of posting it is crucial to building exposure, especially when it comes to video content. Platforms like Facebook, Instagram, YouTube, and Twitter all have short-form video content capabilities. Facebook and Instagram have a platform called "Reels" with a 60-second video length for Facebook and 90 seconds for Instagram. YouTube has a platform called "Shorts" for videos 60 seconds or less, and Twitter has the capability to upload videos up to 140 seconds. Additionally, YouTube offers traditional long-form video content.

The optimal length for political video content is 30 to 60 seconds, which can be uploaded to all of these platforms. Short videos should be recorded as MP4s and in a 9:16 aspect ratio, making them easily shareable. Long-form YouTube videos for the campaign channel should be recorded as MP4s in a 16:9 aspect ratio and easily shared via a link.

Pictures are the second-best option for content, and they should be formatted in a 1:1 aspect ratio at 1200 pixels. Images are also easily shareable, although not as much as videos, unless they are memes. Every campaign event should have a team member taking pictures, and attendees who take pictures with the candidate should be encouraged to post the image on social media using the campaign's hashtag (e.g., #smith4congress, #sally4schools).

Text-only posts should be used sparingly, except for Twitter, which is text-based. With society becoming increasingly auditory and visual, most people do not read for comprehension, which explains the rise in popularity of audio books and video-based training and entertainment. It is recommended to limit text-only content to Twitter, as the other platforms either don't have the option for text-only content or limit its distribution, in the case of Facebook.

During Phase 3, content frequency should be at 100% of the recommended posting frequency. According to Hootsuite, a leading social media management company, social media content managers should post on Facebook 1 to 2 times per day, Instagram 3 to 7 times per week, and Twitter 1 to 5 times per day. BBTV (Broadband TV Corp.) suggests posting to YouTube Shorts at least 3 times per week. The same schedule should be used for Facebook and Instagram Reels to maintain content continuity. Keep in mind that these are minimums and the frequency of content can and should be increased, depending on the race. Typically, the higher the race on the ballot, the more content is required to build the brand.

The success of the campaign's social media content strategy depends entirely on two things: consistency and the quality of the narrative. Content must be posted regularly, and every campaign should have a social media content calendar integrated into their master campaign calendar (a topic we will discuss in a later chapter). Additionally, the content must support the overall narrative of the campaign, with voters hearing the same message from the candidate as they do on social media.

EMAIL AND TEXT MESSAGING

The most powerful tools a campaign has for staying in touch with supporters and potential supporters are a robust email and text messaging program that are integrated into a single marketing effort. Email serves as the main driver of communication, with text being used as a support piece to deliver important information immediately. Most people check their emails once or twice a day and political emails, specifically, have an average open rate of around 23% and an unsubscribe rate of 0.21%. According to recent data from Hubspot, SMS texting has an open rate close to 99%, with 97% of texts being read within 15 minutes of receipt.

Sending 500,000 emails per month, which is just 20 emails to a list of 25,000, can cost anywhere from $5 to $500, depending on the bulk mail provider. In comparison, sending the same number of SMS texts using opted-in (i.e., the target gave permission for the campaign to text them) bulk texting will likely cost over $2,500 at the very low end. For non-opted-in (i.e., the target did not give permission to receive texts) peer-to-peer texting, the cost would be more than $40,000. Additionally, SMS texting has a character limit, while email has no character limit.

Campaigns must use the correct tool to achieve a specific outcome. Email, by far, is the most cost-effective way for campaigns at every level to maintain communication with supporters and raise money. I believe email should be limited to a maximum of three to four times per week. If the campaign can send more than 20 emails a month without upsetting supporters, having high unsubscribe percentages, and not getting blacklisted as a spammer by the email exchanges, then go for it. However, I wouldn't risk it, as the risk-reward ratio doesn't support this type of behavior.

In Phase 3, the campaign should ensure their email sending frequency is 60% to 70% of the maximum frequency of emails they plan to send in the final 8 to 12 weeks (Phase 4) before the primary election. If the plan calls for a maximum of 20 emails per month in Phase 4, they should plan to send 12 to 14 emails per month in Phase 3, allowing the campaign to adjust the frequency based on supporter feedback.

Text messages should be used to advertise special events, fundraising events, breaking news, or other important communications. With the exception of Get Out The Vote (GOTV) efforts near Election Day, campaigns should not blindly text voters who haven't opted-in to receive messages, as this can backfire and cause the candidate to lose support. Because the open rate of text messaging is so high, people tend to feel violated if their phone is invaded by unrequested contact from a political campaign. We will discuss text messaging in depth in the next chapter.

THE MEDIA

Phase 3 requires the candidate to be in the media frequently, appearing for interviews or giving comments at least three to five times per week on average. This not only keeps the candidate at the forefront of voters' minds, but also undermines their opponents. A constant media presence reduces the opponent's relevance, as voters rarely see or hear about them in the press. Moreover, a busy media schedule provides material for the social media team, content for emails, and narratives for fundraising. A candidate can never be in the media too often, unless it's for negative reasons.

Every time the candidate appears in the media, they should promote the campaign website or social media. When used effectively, media can be one of the largest drivers of fundraising. For example, if the candidate has a media appearance that results in a great 30-60 second video clip, it can be repackaged into various pieces of content and sent to supporters as a fundraising request. Furthermore, viewers or listeners are likely to visit the campaign's website or social media and enter the commitment funnel, where they can make a financial contribution to the campaign.

Even better, if the opponent makes a mistake or takes a controversial stance in the media, the campaign should immediately make the candidate available for a reaction piece. This reaction can then be used as a fundraising appeal. There is no limit to the uses of candidate media appearances in a campaign. If the candidate is not in the media, this tool is lost and considered a missed opportunity. Once the campaign officially launches, media appearances should be a weekly staple in the campaign's activities.

For smaller races, aim to stay in the media at least once a week. Down-ballot candidates may find it more challenging to secure media hits, but that shouldn't stop the campaign from making the effort each week. Remember, you miss 100% of the shots you don't take, so shoot often and early.

FUNDRAISING

Lastly, in Phase 3, fundraising requires the candidate to continue making donor calls for 3 to 4 hours per day. Candidate fundraising calls are a regular weekly activity throughout the entire campaign. However, in Phase 3, the fundraising effort is expanded and includes multiple sources of income, in addition to the candidate's phone efforts. As mentioned earlier, email will play a significant role in the campaign's fundraising and voter outreach efforts. Every email should give voters the opportunity to contribute to the campaign, but the efforts should be divided into two distinct asks: a hard ask and a soft ask. A hard ask is a direct request for the reader to financially support the campaign, while a soft ask presents the appeal for a contribution as an addition to the message.

Example Email Fundraising Scripts

Here is an example of a hard ask a candidate might send to supporters as a direct appeal:

Sam,

We wish we had better news. We fell short of our fundraising goal for August by $7,971.

With less than 70 days to go until Election Day, we cannot afford to fall behind and let our nation fall into the grasp of radical leftists that want to turn it into another woke dumpster fire like California.

Can you pitch in now to help us make up for missed our goal?

<Donation Link>DONATE $15

<Donation Link>DONATE $20.23

<Donation Link>DONATE $50

We cannot let the radical progressive Joe Blow pull ahead of us during this crucial month. Our state and its future are at stake. Will you step up?

<Donation Link>RUSH IN A DONATION NOW

Thank you in advance for stepping up.

In freedom,

Team John Q. Candidate

The hard ask is concise, focused, and written with a sense of urgency that motivates the reader to take action. It's important to note that the call-to-action (CTA) should be specific, clear, and straightforward. Furthermore, each option for giving should be a low-dollar ask. Candidates who are apprehensive about this approach and worry about offending voters are also the ones who don't raise enough funds for their campaigns and end up losing. As they say on the street, "Scared money, don't make money." Therefore, it's essential to send the emails.

Here's an example of a soft ask from the America First Policy Institute in response to a piece of legislation they disagree with:

John,

The Big Government Socialism Bill, inappropriately named the "Inflation Reduction Act," has just passed in the House. With President Biden's signature the Leftist wish-list, poorly veiled as an economic recovery measure, is law. In reality, this bill is expected to worsen inflation and supercharge the Internal Revenue Service (IRS)!

The America First Policy Institute knows this bill for what it is—the wrong approach to fixing inflation and the weaponization of the IRS. Will you help us defeat the radical reckless spending spree and promote America First economic policies?

<Fundraising Link> Support American Prosperity

Make no mistake, the Big Government Socialism Bill is a revival of the Green New Deal with a new title. It attacks the heart of American small businesses to finance Congress' reckless spending spree. It will use 87,000 new IRS agents to conduct more than 1.2 million audits. The White House claims these audits will "make the rich pay their fair share" and that no additional audits will be conducted on Americans making less than $400,000 dollars a year.

The numbers say otherwise. Currently, 75% of IRS mail audits are conducted on citizens making less than $200,000—54% of those audits are conducted on individuals making less than $25,000.

The Big Government Socialism Bill weaponizes the IRS in an effort to attack small businesses and middle-class Americans. These efforts will raise taxes and cut jobs during a recession when Americans are already hurting.

The America First Policy Institute and our Center for American Prosperity called this legislation what it was from the beginning—and Americans are taking notice. Since our first statement on this legislation, an additional 138 leading economists have also condemned the bill as wrong for America. So far, 369 economists, along with thousands of Americans, agree the Big Government Socialism Bill will do nothing but increase inflation for hardworking Americans and grant boundless power to the IRS.

The Center for American Prosperity is doing something about it. We are informing the public of the deceitful tactics of the radical Left and promoting America First alternatives—including making the Trump Administration's tax cuts permanent. If you believe in our mission and want to support policies that promote American prosperity, please make a tax-deductible donation. We can't perform these critical actions without you.

<Fundraising Link> Support American Prosperity

The radical Left will stop at nothing to finance its socialist wish-list with your taxpayer dollars—making our mission more vital than ever. We will continue to strive for policies that benefit hardworking Americans, not a radical agenda.

America First, Always.

The Center for American Prosperity

The soft ask is notably more extensive, incorporating a wealth of information, with the goal of securing the reader's financial backing. The approach is straightforward: (1) present the current situation, (2) explain the actions being taken in response, and (3) suggest ways the reader can contribute.

This method proves beneficial for candidates across the board, irrespective of their position on the ballot. Soft ask emails seek to cultivate a sense of community and inclusion, conveying the notion that "you are an integral part of this movement."

It is crucial to recognize that soft ask emails generally generate less revenue than hard ask emails, though they do foster a feeling of camaraderie and teamwork. In contrast, hard ask emails do not contribute to community building; rather, they tend to have the opposite effect. To utilize these emails effectively, particularly for down-ballot contenders, several informative soft ask emails should precede the hard ask—typically on a 3 to 1 basis. The optimal ratio of soft to hard ask emails will vary depending on the specific race, and some experimentation may be necessary to strike the perfect balance.

End-of-quarter (EOQ) emails are a powerful tool for raising money for the campaign. At the end of each quarter, most local and state campaigns must file an itemized expense and contribution report, while all federal candidates must do so as well. In the week leading up to the end of the quarter, several hard ask emails should be sent to voters, emphasizing the impact of their support on the overall viability of the campaign.

OTHER FUNDRAISING AVENUES

Another source of revenue for the campaign is through the sale of campaign merchandise, such as hats, shirts, jackets, flags, signs, and mugs. Some campaigns have raised hundreds of thousands of dollars from merchandise sales. For example, a campaign I ran raised almost $250,000 just from selling yard and field signs in exchange for a contribution of $20 to $100. This turned a sunk cost into a source of profit for the campaign.

In Phase 3, the campaign begins to gain credibility with outside interests, such as political action committees (PACs) and large-dollar donors. Reaching out to these organizations for contributions is crucial, as a contribution from a PAC often comes with an endorsement that can be used to target supporters of the PAC. We will discuss this later in this book.

Meet-and-greet events are another tool that candidates can use throughout the entire campaign. These events can take the form of a simple meeting where the candidate gives their stump speech, followed by a question-and-answer session, and an appeal for financial support at the end. Merchandise is usually available for supporters to purchase at these events. Townhall events are a variation of meet-and-greet events, where a moderator discusses pre-scripted issues with the candidate and the candidate fields questions from the audience.

Dedicated fundraising events, such as breakfasts, lunches, dinners, auctions, or any other format the campaign can imagine, are held in various locations and hosted by various individuals or organizations. Attendees pay to attend the event, and an appeal is made near the end to raise additional money. The key to making these events successful is to advertise the event to drive attendance, provide value (an enjoyable event), and offer access to the candidate on a one-on-one basis at some point during the meeting.

For statewide and federal candidates, fundraising companies can also be useful, but they should not be the centerpiece of a fundraising plan. Typically, these companies charge a retainer (though candidates should be wary of high retainers) and a share of the money raised. Companies that don't charge a retainer typically take a larger portion of the fundraising haul.

It is important to note that fundraising companies should be used as a supplementary source of revenue, not as the main source. The campaign should have a solid plan in place and utilize other methods, such as email fundraising, merchandise sales, and events, before considering hiring a fundraising company. When working with a fundraising company, it is crucial to thoroughly research and vet the company before making a decision and that their fees and terms are reasonable and fair.

QUALIFYING FOR THE BALLOT

The distinction between announcing one's candidacy by registering with the Federal Election Commission and the state electoral body, often the Secretary of State's Office, and securing a place on the ballot is crucial. Generally, there exists a specific time frame in which candidates must file to appear on their state's ballot for the office they seek. Each state has its unique set of qualifying rules.

Commonly, candidates can qualify to appear on the primary ballot in one of three ways: submitting signatures and paying a fee, providing signatures or paying a fee, or merely paying a fee. These rules differ based on the office, the state, and whether the race is federal or non-federal. It is essential that you acquire a comprehensive understanding of the qualifications you must fulfill before the qualification window commences. Instances have arisen where candidates, unaware of ballot qualification requirements, were unable to satisfy these qualifications in time to secure a place on the ballot.

As the window for ballot qualification typically aligns with Phase 3, it is imperative that your team commences work on the ballot qualification process as the campaign transitions into this phase. The importance of adhering to this deadline cannot be overstated: **do not let it slip by unattended.**

FINAL THOUGHTS

As we reach the conclusion of this chapter on "Phase 3: Building Your Base," it is essential to revisit the key lessons we have discussed, ensuring that they are firmly etched in the mind of the candidate. First and foremost, we delved into the critical task of identifying which voters to focus on and who to ignore. By strategically directing your efforts towards the segments of the electorate that are most receptive to your message, you can efficiently allocate your resources and increase the likelihood of winning their support.

Polling emerged as a vital tool in this endeavor, providing invaluable insights into voter sentiment, demographics, and concerns. By harnessing the power of this data, you can continually fine-tune your message and strategy, ensuring that they resonate with the hearts and minds of the electorate. We also explored the crucial role of digital and social media in raising general brand awareness. The key to success in digital marketing lies in the triad of ad quality, voter targeting, and frequency of service. By mastering these elements, you can amplify your message and connect with a broader audience, fostering a sense of unity and shared purpose.

In the realm of social media, content reigns supreme. Engaging, authentic, and informative content can capture the imagination of your audience, spurring them to share your message far and wide. This organic growth can significantly bolster your campaign's visibility, credibility, and appeal. Furthermore, we examined the use of email and text messaging as effective means of communication with supporters and potential voters. By leveraging these platforms, you can provide timely updates, solicit donations, and maintain an ongoing dialogue with your base, strengthening their commitment to your cause. Media appearances were also highlighted as a potent tool in building your base. By engaging with the press, participating in interviews, and appearing on television and radio, you can increase your visibility, convey your message, and establish yourself as a credible and authoritative voice in the political arena.

In Phase 3, fundraising remains a critical aspect of your campaign. It is imperative to devise innovative and compelling strategies to engage donors, ensuring a steady flow of resources to fuel your campaign's ongoing efforts. Lastly, we provided example email scripts, offering a practical resource to guide your communications with potential supporters and donors. These templates can be adapted and refined to suit your campaign's unique needs and objectives.

Lastly, it is essential that your campaign team ascertain the precise dates for the opening and closing of the ballot qualification window, and work diligently to fulfill the requirements for ballot qualification. Should the window close and you have not met the qualifications, paid the necessary fee, or attempted to file late, your campaign will come to an abrupt end. The impossibility of having your name appear on the primary ballot will render all your hard work and dedication fruitless.

CHAPTER 6

PHASE 4:
ESTABLISH YOUR BASE

THE FOCUS OF YOUR campaign in Phase 4 should be to win over the late majority of undecided voters and right-leaning independent voters (if independent voters are eligible to participate in the primary election, as rules vary by state). Phase 4 is crucial for winning a contested primary election, as the candidate who wins the majority of undecided voters will likely win the election and advance to the general election. Any major missteps or challenges during this phase could result in a loss.

Phases 3 and 4 are similar in terms of marketing efforts (such as digital, social, email, and text), fundraising (including digital ads, email, events, merchandise, and candidate calls), coalition building, and media strategy. The main difference is the volume of activity. In Phase 3, the campaign should have been operating at 60% to 70% of the maximum effort required by the campaign strategy. In Phase 4, efforts should be increased to 100% for the duration of the primary campaign. This increased activity will come in the form of ground efforts, referred to as the "Ground War," and broadcast efforts, known as the

"Air War." The Ground War will include door-to-door canvassing, phone banking, texting, and direct mail, while the Air War will encompass broadcast, cable, OTT, CTV, digital radio, and terrestrial radio. If it makes sense to run billboards or other print advertising, these should be placed during Phase 4.

THE GROUND WAR

The Ground War encompasses door-to-door canvassing (including leaving literature at doors without speaking to anyone, known as "lit drops"), phone banking, texting, and direct mail. Of these four activities, door-knocking is a low-cost, high-return effort when carried out by volunteers. If canvassing teams are hired (which is common in larger races), the costs associated with door-knocking and lit drops will increase. Hiring canvassing teams will be more expensive in major cities like Los Angeles, Seattle, Miami, and New York, compared to smaller cities like Omaha, Jackson, or Spokane. Recruiting enough volunteers to carry out your targeted canvassing program can help save money that can be allocated to other advertising media.

Phone banking is also an effective way to reach voters. It should be noted that phone banking is not the same as robocalls, which I do not recommend. Phone banking involves volunteers calling voters, encouraging their support, and seeking a commitment. The cost of phone banking will depend on the size of your call list, the dialer system used, and whether the callers are paid.

Texting has gained significant popularity among campaigns at all levels in recent cycles, with typical open rates of over 95%. Texting almost guarantees that voters will receive and read the message. It is also versatile and can be used to raise funds, invite voters to events, share breaking news, organize volunteers, and more. The possibilities of texting are limited only by your imagination and budget.

Direct mail is a popular tool for political campaigns because it works. Although it may seem counterintuitive, studies have shown that direct mail is an effective way to target specific voter segments with specific messaging. The cost of direct mail varies, with a typical mailing (including postage) costing anywhere from $0.39 to over $1.00 per piece, including postage, for a standard mail piece. It's important to note that the per-piece cost may not include design costs or processing fees.

DOOR KNOCKING

Canvassing is the process of visiting voters at their homes or in their communities to talk to them about your campaign. Canvassers can gather information about voters and their opinions, deliver campaign materials, and encourage voters to take action, such as by supporting the campaign and voting early (or on Election Day).

Winning campaigns knock on doors. Period. Canvassing is a highly effective way to reach voters, especially those who are less likely to engage with campaigns through other channels like social media, television, radio, or direct mail. By knocking on doors and talking face-to-face with voters, canvassers can build personal connections and gain a better understanding of the issues that matter most to voters in a given community. This is important because it gives your campaign insight into what issues they need to discuss. Additionally, it allows you to know what issues are important to specific voters, to segment those voters by issue, and then micro-target them with messaging they will find useful.

There are many different strategies that campaigns can use when canvassing, such as targeting certain neighborhoods or voter groups, using data to inform which voters to visit, or using canvassing to mobilize voters who have already expressed support for the campaign. You may choose to use one or all of these approaches. Regardless of the approach, canvassing is a valuable tool for building support and getting out the vote on Election Day.

As mentioned above, canvassing is typically done by volunteers or paid campaign workers who are trained to engage with voters and deliver a consistent message about the campaign. Here is a general overview of how canvassing is typically conducted:

1. **Identify the Target Audience:** The campaign manager will use voter data to identify areas or neighborhoods with a high concentration of likely voters or supporters and then create walk lists. Often, datasets will have "likely support" scores that indicate the likelihood of whether the voter will support your campaign. These scores can be useful but are often not entirely accurate-they're a best guess. Take them with a grain of salt. In the old days when I started in campaigns, this was done by hand with binders full of voter data and we had to use paper maps to navigate the neighborhoods. Now, campaigns have cutting edge apps (there are many to choose from but some are better than others) that do all of this work virtually and guide canvassing groups via GPS. Later in the book, I will share specific app solutions I recommend.

2. **Prepare Materials:** Your Campaign should already have palm cards used for events and other campaign functions. You can use these palm cards as literature to leave with voters or you can create new literature specifically for canvassing and lit drops. For example, if your

campaign is targeting a specific voter segment you can create literature addressing the issues important to this segment. Whether you use a general use literature piece or a targeted literature piece always leave something in the hand (or at the door) of voters.

3. **Train Canvassers:** Before sending canvassers to knock doors, it is important to train them on the campaign's message, the issues that are important to voters, and how to engage with voters in a respectful and effective manner. Do NOT send canvassers out without training! This can hurt your campaign if canvassers do not know what to say or how to conduct a voter contact event. Canvassers must know how the canvassing technology (often referred to as a "walking app") works, what information to gather from voters, what to say to voters or how to conduct a survey, and how to handle questions and objections.

4. **Timing the Launch of the Canvassing Activity:** Some campaigns will launch canvassing efforts in the early phases of an election cycle to build momentum and encourage early support. This is specifically true of candidates with little or no name ID. Other campaigns will conduct canvassing later in the election cycle to drive a specific call to action (to support your campaign and/or vote early or on election day). The timing of the canvassing activity depends entirely on the specific conditions of your race. If the race is highly competitive, you have several credible opponents, and/or you have a large number of voters to reach, it's better to start canvassing in Phase 3 to reach early majority voters in your base. If your Phase 3 marketing has been effective at building early majority support, the race isn't competitive, and/or you don't have very many credible opponents, you can start canvassing in Phase 4. A word of caution: make sure to leave your team enough

time to actually knock on all the doors in the target groups. If you start too late, you may miss voters you should have contacted.

5. **Execute the Canvassing Activity:** Often campaigns will hold a "Super Saturday" campaign event where multiple voter contact events are launched simultaneously. For example, teams of door knockers may be deployed, phone bankers may start calls, text messages may be deployed, and a direct mail piece may hit mailboxes all on the same day. Other campaigns will launch each of their ground war efforts at different times. Regardless, the launch timing needs to make sense for the conditions of your specific race. As a best practice, it is effective to conduct all voter contact activity (door knocking, phone banking, and texting) between the hours of 9 am or 10 am to no later than 7 pm or 8 pm.

GATHER DATA

Canvassers will typically be equipped with a cell phone or tablet to record information about voters, such as their opinions on the campaign and the issues that matter to them. This information is **HIGHLY VALUABLE** and will be used in your direct mail, TV, radio, and digital marketing efforts. Additionally, it will inform your comms team about what messaging works with specific voter segments. **DO NOT** conduct canvassing activity without making an effort to collect information about voters and voter opinion.

---

6. **Follow-up:** Your campaign needs to follow up with voters after the canvassing efforts to reinforce the message and keep them engaged in the campaign. This can be done by creating a call list for the phone banking team and reaching out to voters (if there is no phone contact, send an email if an address is on file). These calls can serve to answer questions, follow up on volunteer commitments, and support fundraising efforts.

Canvassing can be time-consuming and labor-intensive, but it is highly effective in reaching voters and building support for your campaign. By using targeted and strategic canvassing, your campaign can engage with voters in a personal and meaningful way and build momentum towards Election Day. Campaigns that knock on the right doors win elections.

Example Door Knocking Scripts

Here is a sample script that a canvasser could use during your campaign:

Canvasser: Hello, I'm [Name], and I'm here today to talk to you about [Campaign Name]. May I have a few minutes of your time?

Voter: Sure, what's this about?

Canvasser: [Campaign Name] is working to [insert campaign message or platform]. We believe that [insert specific issue or problem that the campaign is addressing], and we're asking voters like you to support our efforts by [insert specific ask, such as voting for the candidate on election day or a commitment to vote early].

Voter: Hmm, that sounds interesting. Can you tell me more about the campaign?

Canvasser: Of course! [Insert more information about the campaign and the issues it is addressing]. We believe that [insert specific issue or problem that the campaign is addressing], and we need your support to [insert specific ask, such as passing a piece of legislation or electing the candidate].

Voter: OK, that makes sense. What can I do to help?

Canvasser: There are a few ways you can get involved. You can [insert specific actions the voter can take, such as voting, volunteering, or donating]. Every little bit helps, and your support is critical to our success.

Voter: OK, I'm interested. Can I sign up to volunteer or make a donation right now?

Canvasser: Absolutely! I have a form right here that you can fill out, or you can visit our website to learn more and get involved. Thank you so much for your time and your support!

This is just one example of a script that a canvasser could use during a door knocking session. The specific language and message will vary depending on the campaign and the audience, but the goal is always to engage voters, deliver the campaign message, and encourage them to take action. Before we move on, let us pause for a moment of reflection and acknowledge a fundamental truth: voter engagements are almost never as clean as the examples given here. Nevertheless, this example serves to illustrate the process of voter engagement.

Here is a sample script that a canvasser could use when conducting a survey during a door knocking session:

Canvasser: Hello, I'm [Name], and I'm here today to ask you a few questions about [Campaign Name]. Would you be willing to take a short survey?

Voter: Sure, I guess so. What do you want to know?

Canvasser: Great, thank you! We're just trying to get a better understanding of the issues that are important to voters like you. First, can I ask if you're registered to vote?

Voter: I'm registered as [insert party affiliation].

Canvasser: OK, thank you. And on a scale of 1 to 10, where 1 is not important at all and 10 is extremely important, how would you rate the following issues?

[Insert issue 1].

[Insert issue 2].

[Insert issue 3].

Voter: OK, let's see... [Insert answers].

Canvasser: Great, thank you! And finally, are you familiar with [Campaign Name] and our efforts to [insert campaign message or platform]?

Voter: Yes, I've heard of it.

Canvasser: OK, that's great. And would you be willing to support [Campaign Name] by [insert specific ask, such as voting for the candidate]?

Voter: Hmm, I'll have to think about it. Can I take a brochure or visit your website to learn more?

Canvasser: Of course! Here's a brochure with more information, and you can also visit [insert website] to learn more and get involved. Thank you so much for your time and your support!

The key to successful voter contacts on the doorstep is to **ALWAYS** be respectful. Canvassers should be well-groomed, smile, have a positive attitude, and not react negatively if a voter becomes hostile or angry. Remember, the purposes of canvassing are to build awareness and support, gather data, and increase voter turnout; not to win arguments.

PHONE BANKING

Phone banking is a method of voter contact that involves making phone calls to voters to communicate campaign messages and encourage them to take action. Phone banking can be used to reach large numbers of voters quickly and cost-effectively.

Here is a basic overview of how phone banking is typically conducted:

1. **Prepare a List of Voters to Call and Secure an Auto-Dialer System:** Ideally, this list can be obtained from your voter data file. The list should be targeted to the voters who are most likely to be supportive of your campaign. Additionally, the list should be segmented by voter behavior; specifically, 4/4, 3/4, 2/4, and then 1/4 voters, in that order. You want callers to connect with people you are certain will participate. Once the list is prepared, you will upload it into an auto-dialer system. There are many providers your campaign can use to facilitate the call banking. The costs vary between providers, as do the features. Some have the ability to leave a prerecorded voicemail (ideally, a prerecorded message from the candidate) while others do not. Some have the ability to take live surveys and enter notes while others do not. Make certain the provider you choose

offers the features your campaign requires to make the calls as effective and efficient as possible.

2. **Create a Script**: A script should be created that outlines what the callers will say to voters. The script should be concise and clearly convey the campaign's message, as well as any specific actions that the caller is asking the voter to take (such as voting, attending an event, or donating money). I have included two examples of what your call script could say later in this chapter. Ultimately, your script should be tailored to your specific race.

3. **Train the Callers:** Before the phone banking begins, the callers should be trained on the script, as well as any other important information about the campaign or issue. This training should help the callers feel comfortable and confident when making calls. Most auto-dialing systems now are virtual; meaning callers will log into the auto-dialing system from a laptop, enter their personal cell phone number, and then the auto-dialer will call the phone banker's cell phone and connect them to the system. Once the connection is made, the phone banker tells the system to begin calling by a click of a button. This allows volunteers to make calls from the comfort of their home if they are unable to come into a campaign office.

4. **Make the Calls:** Once the callers are trained, they can begin making calls. Callers should use the script to guide their conversation with voters (which is preloaded into the auto-dialer and will appear on their computer screen along with the voter information). They should also take notes on the responses they receive, so that they can follow up with voters later, if necessary.

5. **Track and Analyze the Results:** After the phone banking is complete, the campaign manager should track and analyze the results. Once the analysis is complete, the results should be shared with the appropriate staff to make adjustments revealed through the calling. This can help the campaign better understand what worked well, what areas need improvement, and what needs to change.

Phone banking is a powerful tool for engaging voters and building support for a campaign. However, it is important to conduct phone banking carefully and professionally, in order to ensure that voters have a positive experience and are more likely to take the desired action. Under no circumstances can callers be rude with voters even if voters respond rudely to their call. When conducting a phone banking campaign, it's important to consider the following best practices:

1. **Personalize the Call:** Whenever possible, callers should try to personalize their conversation with voters. This can involve mentioning the voter's name, as well as any other relevant information that the campaign has collected. Personalization can help establish a connection with the voter and make them more likely to listen to the message being delivered.

2. **Be Professional and Polite:** Callers should always be professional and polite when speaking with voters. They should avoid being confrontational or pushy, and instead aim to have a friendly, conversational tone. This will help the voter feel more comfortable and willing to listen to the message. People can feel smiles through the telephone.

3. **Keep the Call Concise:** Phone banking calls should be concise and to the point. Callers should aim to deliver the message and ask for any desired actions within a few minutes, so as not to take up too much of the voter's time. The goal of making calls is connection and volume. Be polite and build rapport but get to the point.

4. **Make Follow-Up Calls:** If a voter is unable to answer the phone during a call, the caller should make follow-up calls until they are able to reach the voter. This can help increase the chances of the voter taking the desired action. If your auto-dialer system has the ability to leave a voicemail, do so.

5. **Test the Campaign:** Before launching a large-scale phone banking campaign, it can be useful to test the script and the call process with a small group of volunteers. This can help identify any issues or areas that need improvement before the phone banking campaign is fully rolled out.

Phone banking can be a time-intensive process, but it is also very effective for reaching voters and building support for a campaign. By following these best practices, your campaign can help ensure that the phone banking efforts are successful and make a positive impact on election day.

Example Phone Banking Script

Here's an example of a phone banking script that incorporates a survey:

Intro

Hello, my name is [Your Name] and I'm a volunteer with [Campaign Name]. May I speak with [Voter's Name]?

Personalization

Hi [Voter's Name], I'm calling from [Campaign Name] to get your opinions on some important issues facing our community. We value your input and want to make sure that [Candidate's Name] is addressing the issues that matter most to you.

Survey Questions

On a scale of 1 to 10, how concerned are you about [Issue 1]?

How important do you think it is for [Candidate's Name] to address [Issue 2]?

What are your thoughts on [Issue 3] and its impact on our community?

[Candidate's Name] has a plan to [Issue 4]. How supportive are you of this plan?

Message

One last thing. [Candidate's Name] is running for [Office] because [Reason for Running]. [Candidate's Name] is committed to [Key Issues] and has a strong record of [Key Achievements]. We believe that [Candidate's Name] is the best choice for [Office] and will make a real difference for [Constituency].

Call to Action

Based on your responses to our survey, do you have any other questions or concerns about [Candidate's Name] or the campaign? And would you be willing to support [Candidate's Name] by [Action Requested]?

Closing

Thank you so much for your time, [Voter's Name]. Your feedback is important to us and we'll be sure to share it with [Candidate's Name]. Have a great day!

This is just one example of a phone banking script that incorporates a survey, and the exact questions and format will depend on the specifics of the campaign and the target audience. Remember, the goal is to gather valuable data while delivering a clear message, establishing a personal connection with the voter, and asking for a specific action. By combining these elements, your campaign will increase the chances of success with the phone banking efforts.

TEXT MESSAGING

SMS (Short Message Service) and MMS (Multimedia Message Service) and P2P (peer-to-peer) texting are increasingly popular channels for political campaigns to reach voters and supporters. These channels allow for the sending of targeted, personalized messages on a large scale, making them valuable tools for increasing voter engagement, mobilizing voters, and fundraising. SMS and MMS texting and P2P texting are the two different forms of text messaging used in political campaigns.

Texting is a widely used form of communication among most voters and is supported by almost all mobile devices. The open rate of political text messages varies and is influenced by several factors, such as the target audience, message content, timing of the message, and overall campaign strategy. On average, text messaging has an open rate of approximately 98%, meaning that nearly all messages sent are opened by the recipient. However, this does not guarantee that all recipients will take action based on the message, such as responding, donating, or voting. P2P text messaging, which is more personalized and targeted, has a higher engagement rate (the action the voter takes after opening the text message) compared to traditional SMS and MMS text messaging. The engagement rate for P2P text messaging can range from 50-90% depending on the target audience and message content.

It's important to keep in mind that the open rate of political text messages is just one metric to consider when evaluating the success of a text messaging campaign. Other factors, such as the response rate and donation rate should also be tracked and analyzed to fully understand the impact of the text messaging campaign.

SMS/MMS Texting

SMS/MMS text messaging is a type of text messaging that allows individuals to send and receive texts through a cellular network. In the context of political campaigns, it is frequently used as a mass communication tool to reach a large group of voters. Campaigns can use SMS/MMS text messaging to promote a candidate, provide information about an upcoming election, conduct surveys, or encourage a specific action. This method of communication is particularly effective for sending time-sensitive information and alerts, such as reminders to vote, updates on polling locations, or details about campaign events.

However, it is crucial for campaigns to consider the limitations of SMS/MMS text messaging. SMS messages are limited to 160 characters (although MMS messages may allow more), and there is no guarantee that all recipients will receive or read them. Additionally, SMS/MMS text messaging is subject to regulations and laws that govern telemarketing and political advertising, so campaigns must ensure that their use of this communication method complies with these regulations at the state and federal levels.

P2P Texting

P2P text messaging is a form of text messaging that utilizes an internet connection instead of a cellular network to send messages directly from one person's device to another. Unlike traditional SMS/MMS text messaging, P2P text messaging is not subject to regulations and laws governing telemarketing and political advertising. In political campaigns, P2P text messaging is often used for personalized and targeted communication with voters.

Campaigns can use voter data to target specific segments of their audience and send personalized messages directly to these segments. This allows for direct and personal conversations with voters, leading to increased engagement and a stronger sense of community. P2P text messaging also allows for large-scale messaging, as well as small-dollar fundraising efforts.

One popular P2P text messaging platform is Rumble Up, which allows campaigns and organizations to send targeted and personalized messages to their audience. The platform enables users to create segments of their audience based on demographic, geographic, and behavioral data, and then send targeted messages directly to these segments through individualized text message conversations. The platform also provides real-time metrics and analytics, allowing for data-driven decisions.

However, campaigns must still be mindful of the challenges of using SMS/MMS and P2P texting, such as ensuring message delivery and read rate, protecting data privacy, and avoiding message fatigue among voters. It is important to use best practices and platforms that are compliant with all applicable laws and regulations to ensure the success of text messaging efforts.

The Benefits of Using SMS/MMS and P2P Texting

SMS/MMS and P2P texting are becoming increasingly important for political campaigns that aim to reach and engage voters. With the advancements in digital communication, campaigns must utilize the latest technology to connect with their target audience. The advantages of using SMS/MMS and P2P texting in political campaigns are numerous and can have a significant impact on election results.

One of the key advantages is increased voter engagement. SMS/MMS and P2P texting allow political campaigns to have direct and personal conversations with voters, resulting in increased engagement and a stronger connection between the campaign and the community. Messages can be sent directly to voters' phones, providing them with quick access to information about the candidate, campaign events, and election news. This direct communication helps to build a stronger relationship between the campaign and the voters, leading to increased engagement and support.

Another advantage is personalized and targeted messaging. Campaigns can use voter data to send messages to specific segments of their audience, making the communication more effective and improving results. For instance, campaigns can target messages to specific age groups, geographic locations, or coalition members to ensure that the messages are relevant and personalized to the recipient. This targeted approach leads to more effective communication and reaches the right audience at the right time.

Reaching voters at scale is another benefit of using SMS/MMS and P2P texting in political campaigns. These tools allow campaigns to reach a large number of voters quickly and efficiently. In just a few seconds, campaigns can send a message to thousands of voters, ensuring that their message is seen by a large audience. This enables campaigns to reach a wider range of voters and provides the opportunity to connect with those who may have been difficult to reach through other channels.

Finally, improved fundraising efforts is another advantage of using SMS and P2P texting in political campaigns. These tools can also be used to solicit small-dollar donations from supporters, helping to build a more diverse and sustainable funding base. SMS/MMS and P2P texting enable campaigns to reach a large number of supporters quickly and easily, making it easier to solicit donations and build a more sustainable funding base. Additionally, campaigns can track donations and respond to supporters in real-time, improving the efficiency of their fundraising efforts.

Best Practices for Using SMS/MMS and P2P Texting

For your campaign to be successful, it must adopt a data-driven and strategic approach to text messaging. Segmentation of the audience using voter data is a crucial step in this process as it enables campaigns to send targeted messages that are relevant to each segment. The message itself should be brief, clear, and concise to ensure its effectiveness. Platforms such as Rumble Up can automate and streamline messaging, enabling campaigns to reach a large number of voters quickly and efficiently. However, it is equally important for campaigns to regularly test and refine their messaging strategy to ensure that they are using the most effective messages and approaches.

Example Text Messaging Scripts

For example, donation text messages could be:

"Help us reach our fundraising goal! Donate now to support [candidate's name] and bring change to [district/state/country]. Reply YES to give $10, or visit [campaign website link] to donate more."

"Only a few hours left in our fundraising drive! Your support can make a difference. Donate now to help [candidate's name] win. Reply YES to give $25, or visit [campaign website link] to give more."

And examples of GOTV text messages could be:

"Election Day is tomorrow! Have you made a plan to vote for [candidate's name]? Reply with YES to let us know you support [Candidate Name]!"

"It's time to make your voice heard. Help [candidate's name] win by voting today. Need a ride to the polls? Reply with your address and we'll arrange one for you."

These are just examples, and you will want to customize your messages based on your campaign's goals and audience. It's important to keep your messages brief, clear, and to the point to ensure that they are effective.

DIRECT MAIL

The use of direct mail in political campaigns has a long history, dating back to the early 20th century. Candidates and political parties recognized the value of reaching voters directly in their homes and began sending letters, flyers, and other forms of direct mail. One of the earliest notable uses of direct mail in political campaigns was by the Progressive Party in the 1910s, using it to reach voters and fundraise for their campaigns. Over the next few decades, the use of direct mail in campaigns continued to grow, and by the mid-20th century, it had become an indispensable part of elections.

During the 1950s and 1960s, direct mail became more sophisticated, with the use of new technologies and data analysis allowing campaigns to target specific groups of voters more accurately. In the following decades, direct mail continued to evolve with the advent of new technologies, such as personalized and digital printing, making it easier and more affordable to reach voters.

Putting Together a Direct Mail Effort

A successful direct mail campaign requires careful planning and execution. Here are the key steps to putting together a direct mail effort:

1. **Identifying the Target Audience:** The first step in any direct mail campaign is to identify the target audience. This may be based on factors such as demographics, political affiliation, voting history, and past behavior. The target audience will determine the content and design of the mail piece, as well as the lists used for mailing.

2. **Writing the Copy and Designing the Piece:** Once the target audience is identified, it's time to write the copy and design the direct

mail piece. The copy should be compelling, clear, and concise, and should include a call to action. The design should be eye-catching and consistent with the campaign's overall messaging and branding.

3. **Printing and Mailing Services:** Printing and mailing services are an essential part of any direct mail campaign-without it, there is no direct mail campaign. Direct mail is such an important aspect of my client's campaigns that I opened a marketing firm called Parabellum Strategic Group (www.parabellumstrategic.co) to standardize this process and deliver the highest quality direct mail and printing services at the best rates while streamlining the internal management of the process.

4. **Lists and Voter ID:** Lists and Voter ID are critical to the success of a direct mail campaign. By using smart voter targeting techniques, you can focus on the specific group of voters whose interests align with your message. Conversely, you can align your messaging with the specific group of voters.

Costs Involved in a Direct Mail Campaign

The cost of a direct mail campaign can vary widely, depending on several factors, including the size of the campaign, the size of the mail piece, the cost of printing, processing, and postage (I call this the 3 P's), the cost of lists, and creative and messaging costs.

1. **Printing and Processing Costs:** Printing costs will depend on the size of the campaign and the complexity of the design. Smaller campaigns may be able to get by with less expensive printing options, while larger campaigns may require higher-quality printing. A word of

caution: do not opt for low quality printing in an effort to save a few dollars. Voter perception of your mail piece will have a profound effect on how they view you as a candidate and your campaign. A low-quality mail piece comes from a low-quality candidate. A high-quality mail piece comes from a high-quality candidate. This is the lens through which voters will view your direct mail piece. Proceed accordingly.

Additionally, there are typically processing cost of getting your printed materials from the printer to the mail shop handling the actual process of applying postage and delivering the finished pieces to the post office. Some venders line item these costs on their proposals, while others roll the cost into the overall project. Either way, it is a cost you will pay. At my firm, Parabellum Strategic Group, we roll these prices into the overall project.

2. **Postal Expenses:** Postal expenses are a fixed cost set by the United States Postal Service and will depend on several factors including the size of the campaign, the size of the mail piece, and the actual cost of postage. Direct mail campaigns can be expensive, especially for large campaigns, but there are often discounts available for bulk mailing. That said, there are certain best practices you can use to limit cost overruns; specifically, keeping your mail pieces to a standard size of 6" x 11" or smaller unless your budget allows for the increased cost of larger pieces. Ultimately, the messaging and creative quality of the piece is more important than the size. Spend your money where it creates the biggest impact on voters. The more customized and non-standard the piece, the higher the printing, processing, and postage

costs will be. My recommendation is to keep it simple and focus on the quality of the visual and copywriting aspects of the piece.

3. **List Acquisition Costs:** List acquisition costs will depend on the size of the list and the quality of the data. High-quality lists are more expensive, but they will also be more effective in reaching the right people. That being said, your voter data file should have the most up-to-date voter information (which should always include mailing addresses) available. If your campaign does not have a voter data file by Phase 4, you need to acquire one immediately. If you executed Phase 1 properly, your campaign should already have this file and should be actively using it in all of your marketing efforts.

4. **Creative Costs:** Creative and messaging costs will depend on the complexity of the design and the size of the campaign. Typically, a high-quality mail piece will cost a minimum of $150 upwards to $750 to produce. This should include all of the design, graphic art, and messaging. A word of caution: unless you are a graphic designer and a skilled copywriter DO NOT attempt to do this yourself. As mentioned above, the quality of your mail piece will directly affect how you and your campaign are perceived by voters. If you think hiring a professional is expensive, wait until you hire an amateur. Once a direct mail piece is created and mailed to voters there is no way to rework it. The damage is done.

Direct mail is a powerful tool for political campaigns, but it can also be expensive-as mentioned above, typical final costs can run between $0.39 per piece including postage upwards to $1.00 per piece including postage or more. Careful planning and budgeting are essential to ensure the success of a direct mail campaign. Whether your campaign is a local race or a large national or statewide race, it's important to consider the benefits and costs of direct mail and to plan your campaign accordingly. Additionally, the importance of determining exactly how your direct mail campaign fits into the overall campaign strategy cannot be overstated. Sending mail just to send mail is a waste of time and donor resources. Determine the specific reasons and messaging behind the effort prior to beginning any type of direct mail effort.

THE AIR WAR

Smaller campaigns typically do not have the resources to launch a comprehensive air war campaign, as it involves multiple media platforms. However, for medium to large campaigns, it is crucial to utilize the available technology and reach their target audience through broadcast TV, cable TV, Over-the-top (OTT) platforms, Connected TV (CTV), digital radio, streaming radio, and terrestrial radio. In today's fast-paced media world, a well-executed and well-funded air war campaign can be the difference between winning and losing a close race.

DEFINING THE PLATFORMS AND THEIR USES

Broadcast TV is a traditional form of television that is transmitted over the airwaves, usually via an antenna or cable, to a large audience. It offers a broad reach and can be used to reach a large, diverse audience, making it well-suited for reaching older audiences and delivering campaign messages meant to educate and inform. On the other hand, cable TV is delivered through cable service providers like Comcast or Time Warner Cable, offering a more targeted reach by allowing campaigns to focus on specific geographic locations and demographic groups, making it ideal for reaching suburban and urban audiences.

Over-the-top (OTT) platforms, such as Netflix, Amazon Prime Video, and Hulu, deliver content over the internet without the need for cable or satellite service providers. These platforms offer highly targeted reach and are effective for reaching younger audiences and delivering highly targeted messages. Connected TV (CTV) combines the reach of traditional television with the targeting capabilities of OTT platforms, making it suitable for reaching a broad, diverse audience actively engaged with streaming content.

Digital radio uses digital signals instead of traditional analog signals, offering campaigns the ability to target specific geographic locations and demographic groups, as well as deliver more interactive and engaging content to listeners, making it well-suited for younger and more tech-savvy audiences. Streaming radio platforms, like Pandora and Spotify, deliver content over the internet and offer highly targeted reach for younger audiences actively engaged with streaming content. Lastly, terrestrial radio, which includes traditional AM and FM radio stations, provides broad reach for reaching a diverse audience, particularly in rural areas where other forms of media may not be available, making it well-suited for educating and informing a broad audience that may not have access to other forms of media.

Costs and Budgeting

The cost of each platform in a campaign's air war will vary depending on several factors, including the target audience's size, location, and duration of the campaign. For instance, broadcast TV and cable TV may be more expensive compared to OTT platforms and digital radio, while terrestrial radio could be a more cost-effective option. The cost of purchasing media is typically paid in the form of a commission, which ranges from 10% to 15% of the total cost, plus the cost of production. For instance, the cost of producing a 30-second TV commercial could be $8,500, and the budget to air the ad on cable TV could be $10,000, which would result in a commission of $1,000 to $1,500 to the media consultant, and the remaining $8,500 to $9,000 would be used to purchase spots on the platform. The total cost of the first run of the ad would be $8,500 for production cost plus $10,000 for the ad buy for a total first run cost of $18,500.

When planning a campaign's budget, it is crucial to consider the cost of each platform, its reach, and its strengths and capabilities, along with the target audience's demographics and the time slots available. There is no one-size-fits-all formula for dividing the ad budget among platforms, as the strategy will depend on several factors, such as the dynamics of the race, the location, the target demographics, the messaging, and the budget.

THE PHASE 4 BIG PICTURE

The marketing process of a campaign can become overwhelming, especially with the elevation of the ground war and air war in Phase 4, and the need to manage and track each aspect. However, it's important to maintain a broad perspective and not get lost in the details. Later in the book, we will cover the organization of this information into a manageable master calendar. A strong marketing strategy is crucial for a successful campaign, and a well-rounded approach is necessary to achieve broad name recognition and engage voters. This includes a combination of digital advertising, social media marketing, email marketing, in-person events, and candidate fundraising calls, which also serve as a form of advertising through word-of-mouth.

As you enter Phase 4, your campaign should focus more heavily on increasing digital advertising, targeting specific voters for the primary election. This advertising should be continuously monitored and optimized for best results. As always, all advertising should have a clear call to action, directing people to your website or a landing page for more information about your campaign and events, capturing their contact information, asking for support, and offering campaign merchandise. Digital advertising, not social media advertising, should be the foundation of your advertising strategy, as everyone in your target audience is likely online, but not necessarily on social media.

REMEMBER:

Digital advertising **first.** Then, social media advertising.

In addition to your daily baseline digital advertising effort, the campaign should continue running ongoing social media advertising. Your social media advertising efforts should be targeted and utilize video and graphics crafted to include your campaign's brand language. Your calls-to-action in your social media advertising should drive voters to the same landing pages as your digital advertising, and the messaging should be consistent with your digital advertising for message discipline. Additionally, the campaign should run fundraising advertising on social media, using a short 10 to 15 second video of the candidate making a quick appeal for financial support, as well as static images. The ads should feature a link that drives the voter to a donation landing page specifically set up for the ad.

The campaign should connect with voters on a weekly basis through well-crafted and visually appealing emails to keep supporters up-to-date on the campaign, important issues, upcoming events, and fundraising appeals. The email audience should receive an email from the campaign at least three or four times a week, and more frequently around fundraising at the end of the month and end of quarter reporting deadlines.

In-person (including virtual) events should be scheduled on a weekly basis. No amount of advertising, such as digital, social media, email, TV, radio, canvassing, or phone calls, can replace the candidate directly speaking to voters. The regularly scheduled in-person events that were established in Phase 2 and Phase 3 should continue in Phase 4, and even increase, if possible, especially for medium and large campaigns. This not only allows the candidate to interact with voters but also provides the opportunity to leverage earned media.

All of the activities outlined above should be part of the campaign's daily advertising activity and form the baseline. In addition to this established activity, there are the activities outlined in the ground war and air war campaigns, adding two more layers of voter contact and building momentum to a crescendo that should peak three to four weeks prior to primary ballots being mailed to vote-by-mail voters.

FINAL THOUGHTS

As you embark on Phase 4 of your campaign journey, let us acknowledge the significance of this moment. It is here, in the penultimate phase, that your campaign efforts gather momentum, propelled by your determination and creativity. The late majority of undecided voters and right-leaning independent voters hold the key to unlocking the door to success. Welcome them with open arms, for their support will bring you closer to the general election. Be vigilant, as even the smallest misstep could jeopardize your hard-earned progress. In this crucial stage, your unwavering conviction must guide you during difficult times.

Navigating the realms of marketing, fundraising, coalition building, and media strategy, your campaign's activity will amplify to its highest capacity. In this surge of effort, do not falter, but instead, find strength in the knowledge that your dedication shall be rewarded.

The Ground War and the Air War, vital components of your campaign's efforts, will harmoniously work together to reach the hearts and minds of the electorate. Every door-to-door canvass, phone call, text, and direct mail piece should stand as a testament to your unwavering commitment to the people. As you fill the airwaves with your message, remember that your voice has the power to inspire and galvanize the masses.

Phase 4 is the prelude to your final triumph for the primary election in Phase 5: Imposing Your Dominance. Embrace the challenge with courage, resilience, and an indomitable spirit. For it is in these moments that champions are forged and real progress in made.

CHAPTER 7

PHASE 5:
IMPOSING YOUR DOMINANCE

THE FOCUS OF YOUR campaign in Phase 5 should be winning over undecided voters in the final four to eight weeks leading up to the primary election. This phase is critical to securing close races and demonstrating your strength in contested races. Your campaign should have monitored voter engagement and response through canvassing and phone banking during Phases 3 and 4, which will serve as a rough indicator of your overall level of support. This information will also allow you to directly target undecided voters. Internal polling provided by your pollster can also be used to determine support levels. This poll, if positive, can be packaged into fundraising appeals, advertising creative, media opportunities, and social media content.

In Phase 5, your campaign will maximize get-out-the-vote (GOTV) efforts and adjust messaging to focus specifically on this goal. Phase 5 encompasses the "14-Day Plan." The 14-Day Plan usually starts one or two days after absentee or mail-in ballots are sent to voters. Note that this timing may not exactly align with 14 days prior to election day, as it used to in the past. These plans also involve conducting a "ballot chase," or reaching out to voters who haven't yet voted or returned their ballots during early voting or mail-in voting periods. Campaigns that implement a ballot chase are more likely to be successful in close races, especially if the overall campaign process has been executed correctly. This section will focus on these two plans, explain their purpose, and provide guidance on how to execute them effectively.

It is important to note that all Phase 4 activities should continue at the highest levels of effort that your manpower and budget can support. Maintaining this high level of output for more than four to eight weeks can quickly drain resources and exhaust your campaign team, so timing peak output levels to begin four weeks before Election Day will help ensure that your team doesn't burn out or run out of funds. Both will be necessary for the general election.

YOUR 14 DAY PLAN

The 14 days leading up to primary election day (or thereabout) are considered crucial in a campaign because they represent a critical period of time in which the campaign can still influence the outcome of the primary election. During this time, your campaign must focus on a variety of important tasks in order to maximize their chances of winning. Maximizing voter outreach and turnout is one of the primary goals during the 14-day period leading up to election day. This involves reaching out to as many voters as possible through phone banking, door-to-door canvassing, and other forms of voter outreach. Campaigns must identify the most supportive voter groups and target their outreach efforts towards those groups.

Promoting the candidate's message to undecided voters is another key objective during this time. Campaigns can do this by hosting rallies and speeches, creating targeted digital advertisements, and responding to negative news or attacks from the opposing campaign. By promoting the candidate's message and energizing supporters, campaigns can build momentum, increase voter engagement, and persuade the remaining undecided voters.

DAY 1-7 (14-7 DAYS BEFORE ELECTION DAY)
Voter Outreach Plan

Voter outreach is a crucial aspect of your campaign and plays a vital role in the 14-day plan leading up to Election Day. The goal of the voter outreach plan is to reach as many voters as possible and encourage them to cast their vote for the candidate. To create a comprehensive and effective voter outreach plan, campaigns must evaluate various strategies and tactics, including phone banking, door-to-door canvassing, and other forms of outreach. Phone banking involves making calls to voters to persuade them to vote for the candidate, while door-to-door canvassing involves visiting undecided voters in person to discuss the candidate and their platform.

To maximize the impact of voter outreach, campaigns must determine the most supportive voter groups and focus their efforts on reaching them. For instance, a campaign may concentrate on older voters who tend to have a higher voter turnout rate, or identified voters who are more likely to support a particular candidate.

For voter outreach to be successful, campaigns must also create a script for phone bankers and canvassers. The script should provide a clear and concise message about the candidate and their platform, tailored to the target audience. The campaign should also prepare materials and provide training for volunteers and staff who will be conducting voter outreach, to ensure they have the necessary information and tools to succeed.

Negative Media Coverage and Attacks

During the final stage of a political campaign, it is important to be proactive in anticipating and responding to negative news or attacks that may come from opposing campaigns or media sources. Negative information has the potential to harm the candidate's reputation and decrease voter support, so having a solid plan in place is essential.

To keep track of negative news or attacks, the campaign should monitor various news outlets and social media platforms. This task can be assigned to a team of staff members or volunteers, who may include the campaign's communications team. This team should be diligent in their monitoring efforts and should have a clear understanding of the campaign's goals and messaging.

In the event that negative news or attacks are detected, the campaign must have a well-prepared rapid response plan in place. This plan should outline the steps the campaign will take to address the negativity, including assigning responsibility for the response, deciding what information will be shared, and determining how the response will be communicated to the public. For optimal results, it is important that the rapid response plan be created well in advance of any potential negative news or attacks, and that the plan be rehearsed so that the campaign can respond quickly and effectively if and when such an event occurs. The response should be tailored to each specific situation and should aim to minimize the harm caused by the negativity, while still effectively communicating the campaign's message and goals.

Candidate Rallies and Speeches

Hosting rallies and speeches is a crucial aspect of a campaign's efforts to spread the candidate's message and energize supporters. During the final 14 days leading up to the election day, the focus should be on hosting a series of events in key communities to reach as many voters as possible.

To host effective rallies and speeches, it is important to first identify the key communities and organize events in those areas. The events should be held in locations that are easily accessible to voters and are likely to attract a large number of supporters. In addition to identifying the key communities, it is essential to prepare well-crafted remarks for the candidate and other speakers. The remarks should clearly communicate the candidate's message and platform. The candidate should be well-prepared and capable of effectively communicating their message to the audience. Finally, the events should be promoted through various channels, such as social media, digital advertising, email invitations to supporters, and local newspapers and media outlets. This will help reach a larger number of voters and increase attendance at the events.

Election Day Preparation

Election day is the climax of your primary election campaign, and it is imperative to be fully prepared for this crucial moment. Everything your team has worked on throughout the preceding months all culminates on this one day. Preparing for election day encompasses a range of tasks, including training election day workers, setting up legal teams, and keeping a close watch on polling stations for any potential problems.

To get ready for election day, first assemble and train your election day workers. This involves recruiting and training volunteers and staff who will be stationed at polling stations on election day. These workers must be familiar with the procedures and protocols involved in conducting an election, and should be equipped with the necessary tools and resources to carry out their duties efficiently.

Along with training election day workers, it is also important to establish legal teams (for large races) and keep an eye on polling stations for any issues that may arise. This includes having a team of lawyers ready to address any legal challenges that may come up on election day, and monitoring polling stations for any situations that could compromise the integrity of the election.

Finally, create a plan to deal with any issues or disputes that may arise on election day. This plan should outline the steps that the campaign will take in the event of any difficulties, including the individuals responsible for handling the situation, the information to be shared, and the method of communicating the response to the public.

The Ballot Chase

A campaign's goal is to ensure that every eligible and legal vote is counted in the election. One way to achieve this is through a process called a "ballot chase." This involves tracking the status of absentee and early ballots, reaching out to voters to remind them to return their ballots, and providing resources and support to help voters have their votes counted.

The campaign starts by monitoring the status of absentee and early ballots. They utilize data from the election department, which is usually updated daily, to identify which ballots have not yet been returned or have been rejected. This information is essential for the campaign as it provides them with an understanding of their position in the election and what actions they need to take to support their voters in having their votes counted. The ballot chase effort should continue until the polls close on election night. It cannot be emphasized enough how important it is to chase every single ballot, as one vote can make the difference between winning and losing.

Next, the campaign reaches out to voters who have requested absentee or early ballots but have not yet returned them. This is done through a dedicated team in the campaign's phone bank. The team reminds these voters of the importance of returning their ballots. This outreach can help ensure that every vote is counted, as it provides voters who may have forgotten or need help returning their ballots with the support they need.

A WORD OF CAUTION

Typically, where legal, ballot harvesting--collecting ballots from voters and submitting them on their behalf--is **NOT** legal for campaigns, but is legal for authorized organizations and official party organizations. However, each state has different rules, so be sure to check with your state's elections department for the specific rules.

In addition to reaching out to voters, the campaign also provides resources and information to ensure that every vote is counted. This may include information on how to fix a rejected ballot or where to drop off an absentee or mail-in ballot. By providing these resources, the campaign helps their voters have their votes counted, regardless of any challenges they may face.

DAY 8-14 (7-1 DAY BEFORE ELECTION DAY)
Intensified Voter Outreach Efforts

The campaign should aim to reach more voters and engage with them more effectively through phone banking and canvassing efforts. This can be done by increasing the number of callers and canvassers, as well as refining the scripts used for these outreach efforts. Additionally, campaigns may consider targeting specific voter groups that are more likely to support their candidate and adjusting their outreach efforts to best reach these groups. It is also important to make sure that the phone bankers and canvassers are well-trained and equipped with the information and resources they need to be successful. This may include providing them with updated voter data, detailed scripts, and effective communication tools.

Canvassing and Meet-and-Greets

Hosting a series of smaller events, such as canvassing and meet-and-greets, is an essential part of spreading the candidate's message and energize supporters in the last days before the election day. To host these events, the campaign must first identify crucial communities and organize canvassing and meet-and-greets in those areas. The events should take place in communities that have a high concentration of supporters and are easily accessible to voters.

Final Appeal to Donors

Sending a final appeal to past donors is a critical aspect of your campaign's fundraising strategy in the final days leading up to the election. This appeal serves as a final reminder to past donors of the importance of supporting the campaign and can help to generate additional funds that can be used to support voter outreach and other critical campaign activities.

To send a successful final appeal to past donors, campaigns must first carefully craft an email or direct mail appeal that is personalized to each donor. This may include addressing each donor by name, referencing their donation history, and highlighting the impact that their support has had on the campaign so far. Including specific examples of how their donations have been used can be particularly effective in inspiring further contributions.

It is also important to remember that a final appeal is not only about raising funds, but also about building relationships with donors and supporters. A well-crafted appeal can help to demonstrate the campaign's appreciation for past support and encourage further engagement with the campaign, even after the election is over.

Early Voting Trends

In addition to monitoring early voting trends and adjusting strategies, campaigns must also closely analyze their own voter data and compare it to the early voting data to determine their own level of support among early voters. This includes tracking the number of voters who have been contacted by the campaign and the response rate from these voters, as well as tracking the number of volunteers who have been engaged in voter outreach efforts. At Dark Horse Political, we use a new cutting-edge technology call Kingmaker to organize and analyze voter data. If you're interested in learning more about how this exclusive technology, Kingmaker, can benefit your political campaign, don't hesitate to reach out to the team at Dark Horse Political. This cutting-edge technology, developed by my good friend and brilliant political strategist, Matthew Woolbright, offers unparalleled capabilities in organizing and analyzing voter data compared to other campaign management software.

Campaigns can then use this information to refine their outreach strategies and target their efforts more effectively. For example, if the campaign is seeing lower support among a particular demographic of early voters, they may adjust their outreach efforts to target that demographic more heavily, or adjust their messaging to better resonate with that demographic.

In addition to tracking early voting trends and adjusting strategies, campaigns must also monitor the voting process itself, including any issues or concerns that may arise at the polling places. This may include monitoring for any instances of voter suppression or intimidation, and working with local election officials to resolve any issues that may arise. Often these efforts are led by or coordinated with County or State Republican Parties. If party involvement is not an option for your campaign (for whatever reason), the campaign should muster poll watchers.

PRIMARY ELECTION NIGHT EVENT

The moment all your campaign efforts have been leading up to has finally arrived: election night. This is the time to celebrate your hard work and gather with supporters to watch the results come in. While down-ballot candidates may attend election watch parties with state and county party leaders and volunteers, federal and top-of-the-ballot candidates typically host their own events to monitor the election returns. This is an opportunity to pivot into the general election with energy and enthusiasm from your base. A successful primary election night event is essential for setting the tone for the rest of the campaign.

The planning process for this event should commence when Phase 5 begins—or approximately six to eight weeks prior to election night. The following information will help guide your efforts to host a memorable election night celebration.

1. **Choose a Great Location:** The location for the event should be easily accessible and able to accommodate the number of supporters and media that will attend. It should have a large venue and appropriate audio and visual equipment to broadcast the candidate's message. Consider factors such as parking, public transportation, and proximity to campaign headquarters. As with other events, use the 75% to 80% Rule when determining the size of the venue. Specifically, secure a location that can hold 75% to 80% of the expected attendance. This will ensure the venue is full even if 20% to 25% of your expected attendees do not attend the event due to weather or some other reason.

2. **Get the Word Out:** Once you've chosen the location, promote the event through social media, email lists, and other marketing channels. Personal invitations should be sent to top donors, campaign volunteers, and other key supporters. Make sure to promote the event well in advance (begin advertising this event on day one of Phase 5) so supporters can plan accordingly.

3. **Invite The Media:** Inviting the media can help reach a wider audience and generate valuable media coverage. Reach out to local and national

media outlets and invite them to cover the event. This can increase the exposure of the candidate and lead to greater public support.

4. **Plan an Engaging Program but Stay on Message:** The program should engage and excite supporters. Provide audience appropriate live music, prepare canned music for interludes that do not have live music, the candidate should deliver a powerful victory speech, and other speakers should precede the candidate to share their support for the candidate and platform. The candidate's speech during the event should be inspiring and their platform should be presented in a clear and concise manner. It is important for the candidate and the campaign to maintain message discipline. This principle was highlighted in the case of Howard Dean's Iowa Caucus victory speech, which ironically resulted in the downfall of his campaign.

Howard Dean's presidential campaign in 2004 is perhaps best remembered for a particular moment during his victory speech after the Iowa caucuses, which was seen as a turning point that ultimately led to his defeat in the Democratic primary.

On the night of January 19, 2004, following the Iowa caucuses, Howard Dean gave a rousing speech to his supporters in Des Moines, Iowa, in which he proclaimed, "We're going to South Carolina, and Oklahoma, and Arizona, and North Dakota, and New Mexico, and we're going to California, and Texas, and New York...And then we're going to Washington, D.C. to take back the White House!" As he spoke, he became increasingly animated, shouting and waving his arms, and the crowd cheered in response.

However, as the speech continued, Dean's excitement seemed to get the better of him. He let out a loud, primal scream that came across as more angry than enthusiastic. The scream, which was played repeatedly on news broadcasts and late-night talk shows, quickly became a symbol of Dean's campaign and was widely ridiculed and parodied.

The media coverage of the scream, combined with criticism from other Democratic candidates and negative ads from outside groups, created a perception that Dean was too volatile and un-presidential to be a serious contender. His poll numbers plummeted, and he was unable to recover, ultimately losing the Democratic nomination to John Kerry. While the "Dean Scream" was not the only factor in his campaign's downfall, it certainly played a significant role in shaping public opinion of him and contributing to his defeat.

5. **Create a Production, Not Just an Event:** In the digital age, technology has become an essential tool for political campaigns. Utilizing technology at a primary election night event can generate buzz and reach a wider audience. Live streaming the event to broadcast it to a larger audience is a great way to get more supporters involved, and using social media to engage with supporters who can't attend the event is imperative. Encouraging attendees to share pictures and videos on social media using campaign hashtags can help to amplify the candidate's message and reach new audiences.

    Additionally, the event should incorporate lighting and other visual effects to create a stunning audio/visual production. This helps to engage supporters and creates a festive atmosphere. Humans love to be entertained, so a well-produced event can be an effective tool for creating excitement and building momentum for the campaign. The supporters should leave the event with a stronger conviction that the candidate is the right person for the job and that the campaign has the necessary resources and momentum to win.

6. **Thank Supporters:** An event like this is only possible with the help of volunteers and supporters, so be sure to thank them for their time

and effort. Consider offering campaign swag or other tokens of appreciation to show gratitude. This will help motivate supporters to continue their support.

7. **Look Forward:** During the event, it's important to highlight the key issues that the candidate will focus on during the general election campaign. This provides an opportunity to engage supporters and ensure they are fully aware of the candidate's platform and the key issues that they will be addressing throughout the campaign.

   The primary election night event is a great opportunity to set the tone for the upcoming general election campaign and get supporters excited about what's to come. By highlighting the key issues and policies of the campaign, the event can help to create a shared sense of purpose and build momentum for the candidate as the campaign heads into the general election.

   It's important to keep in mind that the primary election is just the first step in a full campaign cycle. A successful primary election night event can create a strong foundation for the campaign to build upon as it transitions into the general election. By setting the tone and outlining the key issues and policies of the campaign, voters can better understand what the candidate will achieve once elected and can stay engaged and informed throughout the coming months.

8. **Follow Up:** After the event, follow up with attendees. Send a thank-you email and encourage them to get involved in the campaign leading up to the general election. Keep supporters engaged and updated on the latest campaign developments.

THE PRIMARY "OCTOBER SURPRISE"

An "October Surprise" is a term used to describe unexpected political developments or revelations that occur during the final weeks of an election, which can refer to both primary and general elections. The timing of such events is critical, as they often occur too late in the campaign for the affected candidate to respond effectively or for the media to thoroughly investigate the matter. The occurrence of an October Surprise has the potential to significantly influence the outcome of an election. These developments can take many different forms, including a major scandal, a diplomatic breakthrough, a terrorist attack, a major economic development, or a significant health issue affecting one of the candidates. The surprise may be engineered by one of the candidates or their supporters, or it may be an entirely unexpected event that nobody could have predicted.

As mentioned above, an October Surprise-type event can also have an impact on a primary election, particularly in cases where the event occurs late in the primary season, after many voters have already cast their ballots. In some cases, an October Surprise that occurs during the primary season can be significant enough to swing the race in favor of one candidate or another, even if they were not previously seen as the frontrunner.

For example, in the 2008 Democratic primary election, then-Senator Barack Obama faced a significant challenge from Senator Hillary Clinton. As the primary season progressed, the race became increasingly contentious, with both candidates launching attacks on each other. However, in the days leading up to the key Pennsylvania primary, Obama made a controversial comment at a private fundraiser about working-class voters "clinging to guns and religion." This comment was leaked to the media and quickly became a major story, dominating the news cycle in the final days before the election. Some political analysts believe that this controversy may have contributed to Obama's narrow loss in Pennsylvania, which was a crucial primary state.

In the 2020 Democratic primary, the COVID-19 pandemic emerged as an unexpected and significant event that impacted the race. As the virus began to spread rapidly across the United States in March of 2020, many states were forced to delay or reschedule their primary elections. This led to confusion and uncertainty for both campaigns and voters, and many states eventually switched to mail-in voting in order to "reduce the risk of spreading the virus." The pandemic also highlighted the importance of healthcare and economic issues, which became key campaign themes for the remaining primary candidates.

NAVIGATING AN OCTOBER SURPRISE EVENT

An October Surprise can be a challenging event for a political candidate to navigate, as it often occurs too late in the campaign for an effective response. However, there are a few steps that a candidate can take to prepare for and respond to such an event:

1. **Anticipate Potential Surprises:** Anticipating potential surprises is a crucial aspect of preparing for an October Surprise event. While these occurrences are, by definition, unexpected, candidates can still take measures to identify vulnerabilities and risks that could affect their campaign. This process involves conducting thorough opposition research and inoculation research, analyzing their opponent's history, policy positions, public statements, and voting records to pinpoint areas of weakness or potential scandals. In addition, campaign teams may examine past election cycles to recognize events or revelations that significantly impacted previous campaigns.

Inoculation research serves as a defensive asset, enabling the candidate to proactively address potential vulnerabilities before they are exploited by their opponent. By using opposition research to counterpunch, the campaign can turn the tables on their opponent, placing them on the defensive and minimizing the impact of the surprise attack.

Once potential surprises have been identified, the candidate and their team can devise strategies to mitigate their influence. This may encompass developing messaging to tackle potential vulnerabilities, creating contingency plans for responding to adverse developments, or identifying supporters who can be mobilized in the event of a crisis.

Anticipating potential surprises is an ongoing process throughout the campaign, as new information and events can surface at any moment. It's vital for candidates to remain vigilant and be receptive to feedback and advice from their team and other advisors. With meticulous preparation and a strategic approach, candidates can be better equipped to navigate unforeseen events and minimize their impact on the campaign. By leveraging both opposition and inoculation research, candidates can turn potential setbacks into opportunities for growth and success.

2. **Have a Crisis Communication Plan in Place:** Having a crisis communication plan in place is an essential component of any campaign strategy, not only for preparing for an October Surprise but for any unforeseen event that could negatively impact the campaign. A crisis communication plan should include clear protocols for communicating with the media and the public in the event of a crisis. It should also outline a strategy for addressing any negative fallout that may arise as a result of the unexpected event.

The crisis communication plan should be tailored to the specific needs and circumstances of the campaign. It should identify potential sources of negative media attention and develop messaging to counteract these narratives. The plan should also identify key spokespersons who will be responsible for communicating with the media and the public, as well as a clear chain of command for decision-making in the event of a crisis.

The plan should also include strategies for maintaining the trust and support of the candidate's base of supporters, as well as for reaching out to potential swing voters who may be influenced by the unexpected event. This may involve deploying additional campaign resources to target key demographics, such as running additional ads, increasing voter outreach efforts, or holding additional campaign events.

Ultimately, a well-crafted crisis communication plan can help candidates to respond quickly and effectively to unexpected events, maintain public confidence, and minimize the impact of an October Surprise or any other unforeseen event. It can also help to ensure that the campaign remains on message and focused on the issues that matter to voters, even in the face of unexpected challenges.

3. **Be Ready to Punch, Pivot, and Communicate (PPC):** Being ready to counterattack and adapt is a crucial skill for any political candidate, especially when faced with unexpected events during a campaign. When an October Surprise or any other unforeseen event occurs, a candidate must be able to rapidly respond and adjust their messaging, media strategy, and campaign tactics accordingly.

Counterpunching in political messaging involves responding to an attack or negative message from the opponent by either highlighting the candidate's own strengths or attacking the opponent's weaknesses. Successful counterpunches can help shift the narrative of a campaign and maintain voter support. The form of a counterpunch can vary, depending on the nature of the attack and the message the candidate wants to convey.

During the 2004 US presidential election, a group of Vietnam War veterans called the "Swift Boat Veterans for Truth" launched a series of attacks against Democratic candidate John Kerry, claiming that he falsified his military service record. In response, Kerry's campaign launched a counterpunch, releasing ads that showcased his military service and criticized the Swift Boat Veterans for spreading what he claimed were lies. The truthfulness of the ads continues to be debated to this day.

Democratic candidate Hillary Clinton referred to some of Donald Trump's supporters as a "basket of deplorables" during the 2016 US presidential election. The comment was widely criticized as condescending and out of touch with voters by the mainstream media. In response, the Trump campaign launched a counterpunch, using the comment to rally his supporters (many of whom adopted the phrase and referred to themselves as "the deplorables") and paint Clinton as an elitist who was disconnected from the concerns of ordinary Americans.

Throughout the same 2016 US presidential election, Donald Trump and his supporters often called for Hillary Clinton to be "locked up" due to her criminal use of a private email server and the illegal deletion of 33,000 government emails while serving as Secretary of State. In response, the Clinton campaign launched a counterpunch, highlighting Trump's own ethical and legal problems, including his refusal to release his tax returns and the now-debunked investigation into his alleged campaign's ties to Russia.

Adapting requires a degree of flexibility and agility from the campaign team. In response to an unexpected event, the candidate and their team must first assess the situation and its potential impact on the campaign. They must then quickly determine how to modify their campaign messaging and tactics to address the new reality (the pivot) and reframe the conversation back to the campaign's core messaging (communicate).

This may involve adjusting campaign ads, creating new talking points, or redirecting the focus of campaign events to address the new issue. It may also involve reallocating campaign resources to areas that will be most affected by the unexpected event. The ability to respond to an unexpected event requires the campaign team to be nimble and responsive. They must be willing to adjust their strategy in real-time and experiment with new approaches. Additionally, they must communicate any changes to their supporters, donors, and staff in a clear manner.

Ultimately, the ability to effectively adapt in response to an unexpected event can make the difference between success and failure in a political campaign. Candidates who can quickly and effectively adjust their strategy can help minimize the impact of an October Surprise or any other unforeseen event and maintain their voter support.

FINAL THOUGHTS

As you stand on the cusp of Phase 5: Imposing Your Dominance, remember that this decisive moment in your campaign journey is a testament to your unwavering commitment and determination. In the final four to eight weeks leading up to the primary election, your focus must be to win over undecided voters and secure victory in close races.

Your campaign's tireless efforts in Phases 3 and 4 have provided you with valuable insights into voter engagement and response. Utilize this information to target undecided voters directly and strategically. Embrace the guidance of your internal polling to fine-tune your messaging and amplify your reach. In this critical phase, concentrate on maximizing your get-out-the-vote (GOTV) efforts and refining your messaging to achieve this objective. The 14-Day Plan and the ballot chase, crucial components of your campaign's endgame, will play a pivotal role in your success. Be diligent in executing these plans effectively, ensuring that every uncast vote is pursued with unwavering dedication.

As you continue to exert the highest levels of effort in Phase 4 activities, be mindful of your campaign team's well-being and the resources at your disposal. Timing peak output levels to begin four to six weeks before Election Day will help prevent burnout and resource depletion, preserving the vitality of your team for the challenges ahead in the general election.

In these final moments, remain steadfast in your pursuit of victory. Let your passion and conviction inspire those around you. Rise to the occasion and impose your dominance, for it is through your unwavering determination that your campaign shall leave an indelible mark on the hearts and minds of the voters and carry your mission into the general election.

CHAPTER 8

THE GENERAL ELECTION: WINNING THE WAR

YOUR PARAMOUNT OBJECTIVE throughout the march towards the culmination of the general election must be to retain the allegiance of voters who cast their ballots in the primary election, capture the support of those who participated in the primary but favored a conservative rival, and broaden your appeal to registered voters who abstained or were unable to vote during the primary election. This encompasses independent voters, conservative voters who sat out the primary election, and voters who backed one of your competitors in the primary contest. Furthermore, amplifying your fundraising efforts should be a top priority.

It is crucial to recognize that primary election dates vary, and as a result, the blueprint for a successful general election campaign will differ accordingly. The primary election may transpire as early as March or as late as September, with the general election taking place in November. However, primary election dates may shift annually, and some states might not have congressional or other primary elections in specific years. To stay well-informed, it is prudent to consult your state's election office.

Regions with primary elections in the earlier months (March to June) must brace for an extended general election campaign, posing challenges such as maintaining voter enthusiasm. Conversely, regions with primary elections in the later months (July to September) must strategize for a more condensed general election campaign, which presents hurdles like expeditious fundraising, efficacious publicity, and crafting a compelling narrative arc. In this chapter, we shall outline the vital goals and steps indispensable for prevailing in the general election. The timing of these endeavors will differ from one region to another, barring the 14-Day Plan, which should commence two days after ballots are dispatched and will be scrutinized in depth later.

THE GENERAL ELECTION: DAY ONE

You have emerged victorious in the primary election. What comes next? It is vital to remember that the general election lies on the horizon, and your tireless efforts must persist. While the allure of respite or leisure may be strong, succumbing to it could result in a costly misstep. I recall a previous candidate who forfeited the general election (spanning a 90-day cycle) by a scant 150 votes after embarking on a two-week Hawaiian vacation following their primary triumph. That time could have been more wisely allocated to campaigning, engaging the media, and soliciting donors. On the first day of your general election crusade, prioritize media engagements and calls to donors who deferred their contributions until the primary's conclusion.

The general election campaign's progression bears striking resemblance to that of the primary election. On the inaugural day, your team should commence by resuming various primary election Phase 1 activities. Upon completion of these tasks, your campaign should inaugurate a gentle launch of the general election with a Massive Action Plan (MAP), encompassing a torrent of fundraising, media, and air war activities (and ground war activities, should your general election commence post-July), akin to the primary election Phase 2. Subsequently, the campaign should advance to Phase 3 by amplifying fundraising endeavors, forging alliances, pinpointing conservative and right-leaning independent voters, engaging conservative voters who did not support you in the primary, and targeting undecided swing voters. Once these activities are in motion, the campaign should expand its efforts into Phase 4 by presenting a robust case for your candidacy, optimizing voter exposure to your narrative arc through vigorous ground and air war campaigns. Lastly, in Phase 5, the campaign should direct its attention towards the remaining undecided voters with your closing argument and mobilize your supporters to cast their votes (GOTV).

If your general election campaign commences in July or later, numerous activities within each phase will need to be undertaken simultaneously. Conversely, if the general election campaign initiates in June or earlier, the phases will generally be executed sequentially (though not entirely). If time is on your side, this permits a more deliberate approach to each activity. Nevertheless, some states possess exceedingly brief general election cycles of 90 days or less, with mail-in ballots distributed to voters a mere 60 days after the general election's onset. In these states, the incumbent enjoys a tactical advantage, as the challenger is compelled to amass substantial funds in a limited timeframe while simultaneously bolstering their name recognition and overall support within the district. Your comprehensive campaign strategy in states with truncated general election cycles must address these distinct challenges before your campaign's official launch.

LENGTHY GENERAL ELECTION CYCLES (PRIMARIES IN JUNE OR PRIOR)

Extended general election cycles can span from 5 to 8 months (or more), which may feel like a political eternity. Understandably, the intensity of campaigns in states with a prolonged general election cycle will diminish following the primary election. The dilemma in an extended general election cycle is preserving an appropriate level of activity throughout the campaign and escalating intensity evenly until it reaches its zenith just before election day (or upon mail-in ballots' arrival in voter mailboxes). Such campaigns demand stamina to endure the long haul. Often, otherwise well-executed campaigns wane late in the cycle due to insufficient activity maintenance during the general election, ultimately succumbing to inferior candidates who peak flawlessly near election day. This occurs because the campaign strategy or execution (or both) was inadequately structured, and the campaign exhausted its momentum too early in the cycle. Be vigilant of the challenges posed by a protracted campaign and ensure this misfortune does not befall you.

Following the primary election, it is imperative for your campaign team to meticulously analyze data, pinpointing areas of strength and vulnerability among the voters essential for victory in the general election. For instance, if your primary campaign flourished among suburban females with children but faltered with voters aged 65 and above, your team should construct "look-alike" cohorts, targeting voters akin to the suburban females who ardently supported you in the primary. Ascertain the messaging that resonated with this demographic, devise narratives that will engage this group, and, if feasible, transform them from mere supporters to dedicated volunteers. Simultaneously, your team should determine the reasons for the campaign's lackluster primary performance with the 65+ age group, the narratives that failed to connect, refine your messaging to this demographic, and convert them from opposition or undecided voters into supporters and donors. The objective of data analysis is to fully comprehend what succeeded, what did not, and why, allowing you to replicate the process or implement remedial measures.

For each targeted voter segment, your team should diligently analyze the data, reconfigure your communications plan, and update your marketing strategy and collateral. Once this is accomplished, the campaign can unveil the new advertising endeavor, which constitutes your general election Phase 2 launch. The emphasis of the general election Phase 2 effort should be on fundraising and maximizing exposure through media and advertising. The candidate must devote as much time as necessary on the phone with high-dollar donors to achieve the campaign's fundraising objectives. This process mirrors the efforts delineated in the primary election. The campaign should conduct another 90 in 30 fundraising push to amass as much capital as possible within the first 30 to 45 days of the general election.

Subsequent to the initial general election fundraising and marketing efforts, the campaign will have either gained momentum or lost it entirely, possibly culminating in a detrimental stagnation. If momentum is sustained and the 90 in 30 goals are realized, the campaign can transition to Phase 3, centering on targeting conservative voters who did not support the candidate in the primary, independent and swing voters who abstained from the primary, and any probable voters who were not contacted during the primary. The campaign should also maintain consistent communication with known supporters and gradually intensify it.

The activities from Phase 3 of the primary election should be replicated in Phase 3 of the general election, concentrating on targeting voters who consistently back conservative candidates but have not participated in the current cycle, or those who can be swayed to endorse a conservative candidate. The campaign should refrain from squandering time and resources on voters who will never rally behind the candidate or are unlikely to partake in the election.

Upon solidifying Phase 3, the campaign can progress into Phase 4, encompassing the repetition of activities conducted in Phase 4 of the primary election, albeit with distinct targeting. The campaign should thoroughly deploy their narrative arc and disseminate it to their targeted voter groups during this phase. Fundraising efforts ought to escalate to their zenith, as campaigns with vigorous support tend to amass significant capital in the later stages of the campaign. If fundraising starts to decelerate, it may signify a decline in overall support, voter enthusiasm, or interest in the election. Fundraising activities and performance in Phase 4 are crucial to the entire endeavor, as campaigns that exhaust their funds early typically succumb to defeat. Capital is essential to properly finance the marketing and Get Out The Vote efforts in Phase 4 and Phase 5. Without funding, the campaign will be unable to cover the burn rate, run advertisements, or mobilize the canvassing initiative.

Phase 5 represents the campaign's final stage, wherein the campaign should operate at its maximum capacity to secure commitment from voters. The candidate should implement another 14 Day Plan, akin to Phase 5 of the primary election, but with alternative targeting. The focus should be on targeting voters that the campaign needs to turn out on Election Day or for mail-in ballots. All efforts during this phase, including media interviews and campaign events, should be directed towards these voters.

General election Phase 5 is the concluding stage of the campaign. By this point, the campaign should possess a lucid understanding of whether the candidate has a substantial lead, is engaged in a close race, or is trailing. Irrespective of the circumstances, the solution remains the same: heightened activity. Politics is sales, and Phase 5 represents the final opportunity to persuade buyers (voters). The campaign should function at its full potential. During this phase, you will execute another 14 Day Plan, just as you did during the primary election. The sole distinction lies in targeting; the activity remains consistent. Chasing ballots is chasing ballots. Media interviews are media interviews. Campaign events are campaign events. The crux of the general election is to guarantee that all these efforts are aimed at the voters you need to turn out on Election Day (or cast their mail-in ballot).

SHORT GENERAL ELECTION CYCLES (PRIMARIES IN JULY OR LATER)

Prior to exploring the execution of a short general election, it is necessary to address what should have been achieved during the protracted primary election. Specifically, the fundraising effort should have considered a portion of the general election's financial requirements (this will be examined in detail in a subsequent chapter). For example, if your budget determines that your total primary and general election budget necessitates $600,000 to achieve victory, of which $200,000 is required to secure the primary and $400,000 is needed for the general election, you do not want to raise and expend $200,000 during the primary election and subsequently be forced to raise $400,000 within 60 to 90 days during the general election.

Short general election cycles necessitate campaigns to raise general election funds during the primary election, ensuring the campaign can continue functioning at its peak once the primary election is concluded. In this simplified example, if your campaign's timeframe spans 12 months for both primary and general elections combined, your average monthly fundraising target amounts to $50,000. If the primary election occupies 9 months, and the general election 3 months, the total primary election fundraising target should equate to 9 months multiplied by $50,000, yielding $450,000. You will expend $200,000 during the primary, leaving $250,000 for the general election on day one. This enables you to concentrate on raising the $150,000 of required contributions during your general election 90 in 30 efforts. Raising $150,000 in 30 to 45 days is considerably more manageable than attempting to raise $400,000 in 60 days.

Time is a scarce resource in short general election cycles, and it cannot be replenished. This compels your campaign to maximize time usage with high output from individual team members, executing virtually all campaign activities concurrently instead of sequentially. On day one of the general election, your team should analyze the data and obtain actionable information within a few days. Without this information, your campaign will struggle to accurately target the right voters, realign and update narrative, messaging, and advertising collateral, and devise a plan for your ground and air war efforts.

Simultaneously, the communications team should revamp your branding components to reflect the realities of the general election and a clearly defined opponent. Moreover, new narrative, editorials, videos, digital ad pieces, social media ad pieces, palm cards, and website updates should be in progress. Once the data is properly analyzed and appropriate targeting determined, the communications team will create new narrative and copy for each new design. This is particularly challenging for large campaigns; however, such campaigns typically possess larger teams of professionals and volunteers to handle the frenetic pace required to accomplish the launch of your general election campaign. Regardless of campaign size, this process is demanding and must be expertly managed to ensure success.

Upon completing general election Phase 1 efforts, Phases 2 and 3 commence simultaneously. The 90 in 30 Plan during Phase 2 should not exceed 30 to 45 days (though your fundraising efforts should persist until you cannot legally raise more money). Your Phase 3 efforts should begin concurrently with Phase 2 and last no more than 14 to 21 days, followed by Phase 4 efforts lasting 14 to 21 days. By October 1st at the latest, your campaign should have optimized the use of all human resources on the ground and advertising outlets. Throughout October, the campaign should be fundraising, making calls to voters, knocking on doors, sending direct mail, sending text messages, sending emails, attending rallies, meet and greet events and other voter contact meetings, participating in scheduled debates, sitting for media interviews, running TV advertising, running radio advertising, digital advertising, social media advertising, and placing any other advertising the campaign deems advantageous toward winning the election.

Typically, absentee ballots and vote-by-mail states distribute ballots two to three weeks prior to Election Day. This marks your transition into Phase 5 of the campaign, focusing nearly exclusively on undecided voters and turning out identified supporters. Your 14 Day Plan initiates, and all efforts are maximized based on the remaining financial resources at your disposal. The campaign team, candidate, and consultants will be fatigued. Everyone on the team has labored for 90 days at a breakneck pace—some working 12 or more hours a day without a day off. However, successful campaigns appear to possess an energy that propels people forward and maintains full engagement. Losing campaigns, on the other hand, lack this energy and often limp across the finish line.

In the final days leading up to the election, your campaign must maintain its momentum, enthusiasm, and drive. Even as everyone on the team experiences fatigue, it is crucial to remember the importance of the race and the impact the candidate could have in office. Harnessing the collective energy of the campaign, supporters, and volunteers will be vital in pushing past the exhaustion and continuing the hard work needed to secure victory.

As the final ballots are cast and the campaign comes to a close, the team should take pride in their efforts, regardless of the outcome. The experience, knowledge, and skills gained during the campaign will serve as valuable lessons for future endeavors. Moreover, the relationships formed throughout the campaign often prove long-lasting, forging connections that will benefit both the candidate and the team members in their respective careers.

Executing a successful campaign during a short general election cycle requires strategic planning, effective fundraising, efficient use of time, and unrelenting determination. By following the principles and tactics outlined in this chapter, your campaign will be well-positioned to achieve its goals and potentially secure victory on Election Day. Remember, the key to triumph lies in the unwavering commitment of the candidate, the campaign team, and the supporters who believe in the cause and work tirelessly to bring it to fruition.

ELECTION NIGHT

For victorious candidates, the election night celebration serves as a springboard into their new role, a time to reaffirm their commitment to the principles they campaigned on and to initiate the process of realizing their vision. It is crucial for the candidate to maintain the momentum and enthusiasm from the campaign and carry it forward into their term in office. To ensure a fitting celebration, the campaign should extend invitations to the media, the general public, supporters, volunteers, donors, and staff.

When organizing the celebratory event, it is essential to create an atmosphere of jubilation and triumph. To accomplish this, the campaign should draw upon the successful model used for the launch event at the beginning of the campaign. By replicating the energy and excitement of that initial gathering, the election night celebration will not only serve as a fitting culmination of the campaign's efforts but also as a powerful launching pad for the candidate's journey in public office.

For those who did not prevail, the election night gathering provides an opportunity to express gratitude to the dedicated individuals who supported the campaign and to encourage them to remain active in the political process.

A loss can be disheartening, but it is essential to view it as a stepping stone towards future successes. Candidates should take the lessons learned from the campaign and use them to refine their strategies, enhance their skills, and ultimately, better serve the people they sought to represent.

The election night event, whether a victory celebration or a gathering for reflection, serves as a pivotal moment in the campaign's journey. It is an opportunity to show appreciation, recommit to one's principles, and set the stage for the next chapter in the candidate's political career. Embracing the lessons learned and using them to grow and evolve will ensure that the candidate remains a force to be reckoned with in the ever-changing world of politics.

CANDIDATE DEBATES

When top-of-the-ticket political debates are televised, they frequently play a pivotal role in election campaigns, serving as a platform for candidates to persuasively articulate their ideas and sway voters. However, participating in these debates can be an anxiety-inducing experience, even for seasoned candidates, particularly if they are inadequately prepared. The significance of delivering a strong debate performance cannot be emphasized enough. A disastrous debate can—and has—derailed entire campaigns. This section provides insights on how to surmount the challenges of political debates and deliver a compelling performance.

IDENTIFY THE DEBATE STRUCTURE

To ensure a robust debate performance, it is crucial to begin by thoroughly familiarizing oneself with the event's rules and structure. The candidate must pay meticulous attention to time constraints for each debate segment, including opening statements, rebuttals, and closing statements. Grasping these time limits aids in crafting clear and concise arguments that fit within the allotted time frame. It is also vital to recognize appropriate moments for posing questions or responding to an opponent's assertions. Comprehending these dynamics can help prevent confusion or awkward situations during the debate and empower the candidate to effectively convey their message.

By preparing diligently in advance and acquiring a comprehensive understanding of the debate's rules and format, a candidate can approach the event with confidence and focus on presenting their arguments persuasively. In the end, proficiency in the regulations and structure of the debate is a critical first step toward success and can significantly influence the debate's outcome.

RESEARCH

Investigating the opponent's background, voting history, and policy positions is the second step. This tactic enables one to anticipate an opponent's arguments and develop rebuttals accordingly. Furthermore, it is essential to identify potential weaknesses or inconsistencies in their record that can be leveraged. This approach grants an edge during the debate, making the candidate appear well-prepared and knowledgeable, thereby increasing their likelihood of swaying undecided voters. Candidates should also possess a solid understanding of policy issues, stakeholders, dynamics, and the particulars of debate topics. This familiarity will instill a sense of ease, allowing the candidate to concentrate on what needs to be conveyed and how to articulate it, rather than frantically searching through notes for the correct response. Insufficient research or understanding can expose the candidate to committing a gaffe that could—and likely will—prove detrimental later.

During the October 6, 1976 presidential debate at the Palace of Fine Arts Theatre in San Francisco, California, President Gerald Ford made a statement that became widely recognized as a gaffe. Responding to a question, Ford asserted, "There is no Soviet domination of Eastern Europe." This claim was factually inaccurate, exposing his lack of understanding of the region's complex geopolitical realities. Democratic nominee Jimmy Carter capitalized on this opportunity to demonstrate his superior knowledge and experience in foreign policy matters. Carter utilized the incident to emphasize the importance of a president who could grasp the intricacies of the global landscape. This episode quickly became a major talking point throughout the campaign and was viewed as a pivotal moment in favor of Carter.

Ultimately, Carter won the election by a slim margin, with numerous political analysts attributing his victory, in part, to Ford's debate gaffe. The incident illuminated the potential consequences of a single mistake or misstatement during high-stakes political debates and underscored the necessity of thorough preparation and message discipline for candidates in such situations.

During the 2012 Republican primary debate on November 9, 2011, in Rochester, Michigan, Texas Governor Rick Perry experienced difficulty distinguishing himself amidst a crowded field that included frontrunners like Mitt Romney and Newt Gingrich. Perry, who initially entered the race as a formidable contender with a strong record as Governor of Texas, faltered during the debate when asked to identify the third government agency he would eliminate if elected president. Drawing a blank, Perry stumbled over his words and struggled to remember the agency's name (the Department of Energy). Perry's gaffe became a central topic of conversation in the media and on social media, with numerous voters and political analysts criticizing his lack of preparedness and inability to think quickly. The incident overshadowed any substantive policy discussions and undermined Perry's credibility as a serious candidate. Despite his efforts to recover from the blunder, Perry was unable to regain his standing in the race and ultimately withdrew following a weak showing in the Iowa caucuses.

ESTABLISH A NARRATIVE FOR EACH SUBJECT

To excel in a political debate, it is crucial to devise a set of concise and lucid talking points that support one's platform and policies while framing them within one's overarching narrative. In debates where the subjects are known beforehand, the talking points for each issue should be tailored to the specific audience being addressed, accentuating the candidate's strengths and exposing the opponent's weaknesses. Moreover, it is vital to ensure that the talking points are persuasive and memorable, leaving a lasting impression on the audience. In debates where the subjects are not disclosed in advance, the candidate should prepare by researching the moderators and host organization. Typically, moderators will pose questions related to their or the host organization's interests. Additionally, the candidate should be ready to discuss any subject that has garnered significant media attention or public debate. Host organizations' time and structural constraints often compel moderators to select engaging topics that resonate with the general voter population.

MESSAGE DISCIPLINE
AND BODY LANGUAGE

It is essential to present the candidate's arguments in a succinct and clear manner, with their delivery exuding confidence and expertise. Practicing body language and gestures that underscore crucial points can also help engage the audience and convey assurance. During the 2016 US presidential debates, Marco Rubio garnered accolades for his debate performances. Notably, in the New Hampshire debate, Rubio exhibited exemplary preparation and poise by repeatedly and effectively steering his responses back to his central message, the need for a "new American century." Despite facing criticism and attacks from his opponents, Rubio remained calm and composed, concentrating on his key talking points and delivering them with conviction. He also demonstrated a solid grasp of the issues, showcasing his knowledge of foreign policy, economic matters, and domestic policy.

Ultimately, Rubio's remarkable debate performance underscored the significance of thorough preparation and composure in debates and helped solidify his status as a rising star within the Republican party. Regrettably, a month later in Detroit, Michigan, Rubio unraveled his progress with voters (and his campaign efforts) by engaging in an unscripted and ill-advised exchange with Donald Trump. We will discuss this interaction and why it proved detrimental to Rubio's campaign later in this chapter.

THE SIGNIFICANCE OF BODY LANGUAGE IN DEBATES

During a debate, body language is as crucial as the words spoken. Maintaining an upright posture, making eye contact with the audience, and using hand gestures to emphasize key points are vital. Being mindful of facial expressions, avoiding appearing defensive or aggressive, and smiling when appropriate are essential in engaging the audience and conveying confidence.

In the US presidential debate between George H.W. Bush and Bill Clinton on October 15, 1992, at the University of Richmond in Richmond, Virginia, Bush's body language became a subject of discussion and critique. Viewers observed him checking his watch multiple times, which was perceived as boredom or impatience. This behavior was deemed disrespectful to both Clinton and the audience, and it reinforced the notion that Bush was disconnected from the concerns of everyday Americans. Additionally, Bush's overall demeanor during the debate was characterized as defensive and detached. His frequent crossing of arms and leaning back in his chair conveyed disengagement, contrasting starkly with Clinton's energetic and animated style, which bolstered the impression that Clinton was more in touch with Americans' concerns.

STAYING FOCUSED AND COMPOSED IN DEBATES

Remaining focused and composed during debates is crucial. Avoid being shaken by opponents' attacks or off-topic comments. Adhering to one's talking points and countering opponents' arguments with facts and evidence is key.

Utilizing body language and tone of voice to express confidence and conviction is necessary while steering clear of irrelevant issues or personal attacks.

Regardless of one's opinions on his politics and policies, an example of effective debate performance can be found in Barack Obama's conduct during the US Presidential debate on October 3, 2012, in Denver, Colorado. Throughout the debate, Romney aggressively challenged Obama on his policies and record, often interrupting and questioning his leadership (which also presented poor optics for Romney). Despite this, Obama remained calm and composed, focusing on the issues and calmly rebutting Romney's arguments with clear and concise responses. His demeanor reinforced the perception that President Obama was strong in the face of opposition.

A prime example of effective debate strategy unfolded when Romney accused Obama of cutting funding to Medicare during another US Presidential debate on October 16, 2012, at Hofstra University in Hempstead, New York. In response, Obama calmly noted that the savings from his healthcare reform law had, in fact, extended the life of Medicare. He then skillfully pivoted to criticize Romney's own proposals on healthcare, illustrating a brilliant execution of the PPC strategy—punch, pivot, communicate. Throughout the exchange, Obama maintained a measured and professional tone, avoiding any defensive or angry reactions that could have potentially undermined his credibility with the audience.

This example highlights the importance of maintaining composure, staying focused on the issues, and employing effective debate strategies to ensure a strong performance. Mastering the art of PPC can enable a candidate to effectively respond to attacks, emphasize their strengths, and leave a lasting impression on the audience. In doing so, candidates can build trust and credibility with voters, ultimately bolstering their chances of success.

THE ART OF DEFENDING AGAINST UNKNOWN ATTACKS AND MASTERING COUNTERPUNCHES

Debates are ever-changing, with candidates needing to be prepared for the unexpected—the unknowns. Opponents may attempt to unsettle a candidate with unforeseen questions or attacks—when unprepared, these are deemed "unknown unknowns" and can often be fatal. To transform these unknown attacks into "known unknowns," it is crucial to anticipate such possibilities and devise strategies to respond calmly and confidently. Candidates must be ready to defend their positions and records, avoiding being caught off guard. Identifying vulnerable areas in one's resume, voting record, or personal life that may be targeted by an opponent and developing counterarguments for each vulnerability is essential.

In the US presidential debate between Ronald Reagan and Walter Mondale, which took place on October 21, 1984 at the Municipal Auditorium in Kansas City, Missouri, Reagan's age was a significant topic of discussion. At 73 years old, he was the oldest president in US history at that time, and some voters expressed concerns about his ability to perform the duties of the presidency. Reagan brilliantly anticipated this issue and prepared accordingly. To defuse the matter, he humorously addressed his age by stating, "I want you to know that also I will not make age an issue of this campaign. I am not going to exploit, for political purposes, my opponent's youth and inexperience." The remark garnered laughter and applause from the audience, with Mondale, who was 56 at the time, joining in the laughter.

However, Mondale later confessed that he had been caught off guard by Reagan's comment and worried that it might effectively counterattack him, creating a perception of inexperience among voters unfamiliar with his electoral history. Mondale had first been elected to public office in 1962, to the US Senate in 1966, and had become the Vice President of the United States just eight years prior to his debate with Reagan. Reagan managed to throw Mondale off balance with an unexpected attack against what should have been a strength for Mondale. This helped defuse a potentially damaging issue for Reagan's campaign and led Mondale to question his campaign messaging.

CATERING TO THE AUDIENCE'S NEEDS AND DESIRES

As previously mentioned, it is imperative to understand the demographics and concerns of the audience watching the debate. Tailoring the messaging to cater to their needs and interests is crucial. Supporting arguments and proposals with data and statistics can bolster the candidate's credibility and expertise. Employing concrete examples to illustrate points and avoiding vague or unsupported claims is essential. Ultimately, the candidate's responses should align with the campaign's narrative arc, reinforcing the campaign's messaging while maintaining brand consistency and message continuity.

Conservatives have often struggled in this area. While they typically possess ample data to support their positions, they may fail to connect this information to voters in a meaningful way. If the message being conveyed is not received and understood by the audience, it loses its value. Candidates do not inherently possess the right to be "right" on the debate stage. Success in a debate must be earned, and even a candidate who may be wrong on certain issues can win the debate by connecting their message to the audience in a manner they can comprehend and appreciate. The goal of a debate is not to be "right" on the issues, but rather to sell one's ideas and positions and create buy-in from the voters. Debates are, in essence, a sales pitch, and people will not buy into what they do not understand or perceive as valuable.

The US Presidential debate on October 11, 1992, at the University of Richmond in Richmond, Virginia, featuring Bill Clinton, George H. W. Bush, and Ross Perot, was a turning point in the election campaign. Clinton's exceptional connection with the audience, stemming from his ability to articulate his vision for the country in a way that resonated with them, ultimately gave him an advantage over Bush and is widely recognized as a contributing factor in his election victory.

Clinton's ability to connect with the audience was due to his personable and relatable speaking style, which contrasted sharply with Bush's more formal and detached demeanor. Clinton used anecdotes and personal stories to emphasize his points, making his vision more tangible and accessible to the public. Additionally, he displayed empathy and a keen understanding of the struggles and concerns of the average American.

In contrast, Bush relied heavily on statistics and policy details, which alienated many voters. His seeming detachment from the concerns of everyday Americans further contributed to his eventual electoral loss. Meanwhile, Clinton demonstrated a deep understanding of the audience's fears and challenges during the debate. He shared his experiences growing up in a small town and witnessing the effects of economic hardship on families. For example, when an audience member asked him how he would create job opportunities for the American people, Clinton responded with a comprehensive plan emphasizing investments in education, infrastructure, and technology, and he connected these ideas to the listeners. His response resonated with the audience and earned him applause.

On the other hand, when Bush faced a similar question, he offered a detailed account of his administration's economic policies but failed to connect with the audience on a personal level. This approach permeated not only his debate performance but also his entire campaign, contributing to his eventual defeat.

Clinton's unrivaled ability to connect with the audience during the debate was instrumental in his election win. He appealed to a broader range of voters and conveyed a vision for the country that resonated with the American people. The University of Richmond Presidential debate in 1992 serves as a reminder of the importance of connecting with voters on a personal level and understanding their struggles and concerns in crafting one's responses.

MAINTAIN INTEGRITY AND FOCUS ON THE ISSUES

It is vital to concentrate on the issues and policies at hand rather than resorting to personal attacks on one's opponent. Candidates should steer clear of derogatory or inflammatory language, as it may backfire and portray them as unprofessional. Instead, emphasizing facts and issues, and employing research and data to substantiate one's stance is the preferred approach.

During the 2016 Republican primary debate in Detroit, Michigan, a heated exchange occurred between Donald Trump and Marco Rubio. Although Rubio had maintained discipline and focus in previous debates, he lost his composure and made a derogatory remark about Trump's "small hands," insinuating that he had a small penis. Trump retorted with a barrage of personal attacks, mocking Rubio as "Little Marco" and ridiculing his appearance and height.

This exchange deteriorated into a series of negative attacks and personal insults, overshadowing any meaningful discussion of policy issues. This negatively impacted Rubio's campaign and tarnished the overall Republican brand, providing the Democratic Party an opportunity to portray the entire Republican field as frivolous and juvenile. Prior to this debate, Rubio had been viewed as a rising star in the Republican Party. However, this altercation marred his image and eroded his credibility as a serious presidential candidate. The incident received widespread media coverage and social media attention, and many voters were put off by the acrimonious tone of the debate. Rubio's campaign struggled to recover from the fallout, and he eventually suspended his campaign following a string of primary losses. This episode underscores the importance of candidates maintaining composure and message discipline during debates.

ADDRESSING CHALLENGES AND COUNTERPUNCHING EFFECTIVELY

Preparing for tough questions that scrutinize one's platform or record is essential, as it allows for the development of clear and concise answers that emphasize strengths while addressing weaknesses. By utilizing research and data to support these responses and maintaining a calm and composed demeanor, the effectiveness of communication is enhanced. Furthermore, staying focused on the issues and avoiding distractions from personal attacks or irrelevant comments enables a smooth and coherent discussion, ultimately leading to a more persuasive argument.

During the first presidential debate of the 2008 US Presidential election, held on September 26, 2008, at the University of Mississippi in Oxford, Mississippi, Republican nominee John McCain faced challenges from his Democratic opponent, Barack Obama, on his support for the Iraq War and his national security record. In the debate, Obama questioned McCain's support for the Bush administration's decision to invade Iraq in 2003, despite the lack of evidence for weapons of mass destruction. McCain acknowledged his mistake in supporting the Iraq War but argued that the conflict was necessary to remove Saddam Hussein from power and prevent Iraq from becoming a terrorist breeding ground.

McCain then counterpunched, criticizing Obama's national security record and accusing him of advocating policies that would weaken the US military and compromise the nation's safety. He pivoted again, emphasizing his own experience as a war hero and a long-time advocate for a strong military, contrasting it with what he perceived as Obama's inexperience and naive approach to national security. Despite facing criticism for his Iraq War record, McCain's response was seen by many as a robust defense of his position, reassuring undecided voters of his ability to make tough decisions in the interest of national security.

APPEAR IMPECCABLE: PERCEPTION IS REALITY

A candidate's appearance is of utmost importance during televised or live debates. Dressing professionally and suitably for the occasion, ensuring comfort and a proper fit, and avoiding distracting accessories or attire, is crucial. This approach helps project an image of professionalism and confidence. The first televised debate between John F. Kennedy and Richard Nixon in 1960 serves as a prime example of how appearance can significantly impact public perception.

During the debate, Kennedy appeared tanned, well-rested, and confidently poised, while Nixon looked pale, exhausted, and somewhat uncomfortable.

This contrast in appearance influenced the way the audience perceived the candidates. Viewers who watched the debate on television tended to believe that Kennedy had won, as his polished appearance and confident demeanor projected the image of a capable leader. On the other hand, those who listened to the debate on the radio, focusing solely on the content of the candidates' arguments, often believed that Nixon had performed better.

This instance highlights how seemingly minor details, like clothing choices and overall appearance, can influence political criticism and shape voter perceptions. It underscores the importance of a candidate's visual presentation in addition to the substance of their arguments during debates, as it can significantly affect the audience's perception of their competence and leadership potential.

ACT SWIFTLY AND EFFECTIVELY

Debates provide abundant material for advertising, social media, text messaging campaigns, email campaigns, and earned media. Immediately following the debate, it is essential to follow up with supporters, the audience, and the press to reinforce the message and address any lingering concerns or questions. This strategy helps candidates remain top-of-mind and solidify their message. Additionally, leveraging social media to express gratitude to the audience and spotlight key debate moments, as well as scheduling interviews with media outlets to discuss the debate and platform in more detail, is crucial. A single 45-minute debate can yield countless 30-second content pieces that can be repurposed in various ways to benefit the campaign.

FINAL THOUGHTS

The preceding chapters of this book should have provided you with a comprehensive understanding of the overarching campaign process. Given the vast array of potential circumstances surrounding individual elections, this book has endeavored to offer as much detail as possible regarding the general structure of political campaigns. Politics is, at its core, a form of sales. The Dark Horse Political Method of campaign structure is modeled after proven political and sales methodologies that consistently work in every election cycle and within every political environment. What sets this methodology apart is the systematization of activities into a clear process that any conservative candidate can follow to achieve success in winnable districts.

The subsequent chapters of this book will delve deeper into the essential elements of the campaign process vital to securing victory. Specifically, we will examine fundraising, narrative building, coalition development, opposition research and the "The Dark Arts", and the creation of a campaign calendar that effectively organizes your master plan. While we have discussed each of these components to varying degrees throughout the book, it is crucial to emphasize the importance of thoroughly understanding how to execute each of these tasks properly.

With that said, let us embark on this journey.

CHAPTER 9

FUNDRAISING: BUILDING THE WAR CHEST

FUNDRAISING IS A VITAL ELEMENT of election success, but it is often misunderstood by new candidates. Many inexperienced contenders believe that announcing their candidacy and discussing the issues will attract donations, but this belief is far from reality. Effective fundraising requires a carefully planned and executed strategy. Although fundraising may seem intimidating to first-time candidates, this chapter aims to provide a comprehensive guide on organizing and carrying out a successful fundraising effort. Successful fundraising requires a strategic approach, taking into account each campaign's unique aspects and the ever-changing political and fundraising environment.

This chapter is divided into three distinct sections: fundamental principles, methods of internal fundraising, and methods of external fundraising. In the fundamental principles section, you'll discover the essential concepts that underpin successful fundraising efforts. In the methods of internal fundraising section, you'll explore various campaign income channels and how to maximize their effectiveness. In the methods of external fundraising section, you'll learn about different types of PACs (Political Action Committees) and their role in raising significant funds to support your candidacy or challenge your opponent. By following the principles and techniques outlined in this chapter, you can create a successful fundraising plan that helps your campaign achieve its goals and secure victory.

FUNDAMENTAL PRINCIPLES: BASIC CONCEPTS

When it comes to fundraising, it's essential to envision your endeavor as three distinct monetary figures: the total sum to be raised throughout the entire election cycle, the amount needed to carry out your primary election campaign, and the sum required for your general election campaign. This approach helps you plan your fundraising efforts accordingly and maximize their effectiveness.

During the primary election cycle, it is crucial to concentrate on building momentum and support among your core constituencies (your base). Your entire fundraising effort is sparked by your Top 200 List, and if those who know you best are unwilling to provide financial support, it is unlikely that you will persuade those less acquainted with you to do so. Beyond your Top 200 List, primary election fundraising targets the 3/4 and 4/4 conservative voters who oppose your opponent(s). This opposition does not necessarily imply hostility toward your opponent(s); it merely indicates that they do not support your opponent's candidacy for one reason or another. Raising funds from this group may involve engaging party officials and activists, grassroots supporters, and major donors. Crafting compelling messaging and fundraising appeals that resonate with these constituencies can help attract new donors and bolster fundraising efforts.

During the general election cycle, focus your fundraising efforts on reaching a broader audience and garnering support from swing voters. This may involve developing messaging and fundraising appeals that appeal to moderate and independent voters while maintaining fundraising initiatives among core constituencies. Additionally, consider targeting voters and organizations who are natural adversaries of your opponent. This can include those working in industries affected by your opponent's proposed policies or policies they supported while in office, as well as donors seeking to align themselves with your campaign for business reasons. Corporate SSFs (Separate Segregated Funds) can also contribute to federal campaigns in these cases. At the state level, each state has their own rules regarding contributions made by corporations. You would be wise to learn the contribution rules of your state if you are running a non-federal race. It should be noted that not all candidates embrace the idea of taking "corporate money" but it should also be understood that one or more of your opponents will likely accept this type of funding—especially if you are running against a Democrat or an incumbent establishment Republican—and the amounts they will raise from these sources are typically significant.

SETTING FUNDRAISING GOALS

A vital initial step in political fundraising is establishing fundraising goals that align with the campaign's overarching budget and strategy. Before embarking on any fundraising endeavors, it is imperative to have a lucid understanding of the required funds and the sources from which they will be procured. For non-federal races (state-level), the budgets vary extensively. To ascertain the appropriate budget for your race, review past budgets for both winning and losing candidates. This information can typically be found on your state's campaign financial public disclosure website. Once the required fundraising figure is determined, increase it by a minimum of 20% and use that number as your target.

For Congressional races, the average budget to win a seat has surged to between $3,500,000 and $5,500,000. Review past budgets for the winning candidate (the incumbent) to obtain a clear picture of the funds your opponent is likely to raise and their sources. This information can be found for federal candidates, past and present, at www.fec.gov. It is possible that the $3,500,000 to $5,500,000 range is actually too low; however, it is exceedingly improbable that you will win your election with less than $2,500,000 for the entire campaign cycle (especially if the incumbent is backed by outside money that will be spent against you).

The subsequent step is dividing the target number by the number of months you will be actively campaigning. For instance, if the target fundraising goal is $1,000,000 and the campaign lasts for 10 full months, the average target should be $100,000 per month in fundraising. Understand that contributions may not flow into the campaign consistently every month. Some months may be below average, while others may exceed it. However, you want your quarterly averages to approximate the monthly average mark. For example, if a campaign raises $50,000 in month one, $150,000 in month two, and $100,000 in month three, the three-month total is $300,000 raised divided by three months, which equals $100,000 raised per month on average.

The next step is determining the average amount *spent* (not raised) by the incumbent and challengers combined during their last three to four election cycles, focusing solely on the primary election, not the entire election cycle. Divide the average amount spent in the primary by the average total amount raised to obtain the percentage of the total budget spent during the primary election on average. The remaining balance would have been spent in the general election. For example, if the average dollars spent by the incumbent and the challenger combined is $2,000,000 during the primary election on average and the total amount raised for the entire election on average was $5,000,000, the equation would appear as follows:

$$\$2,000,000 \ / \ \$5,000,000 = 40\%$$

Next, multiply the percentage by the amount of money you determined is needed to win the entire campaign. For example, if you determined you will need to raise $5,500,000 for the entire campaign, multiply $5,500,000 by 40%, and your answer should be $2,200,000. Your spending budget for the primary should be $2,200,000, and your budget for the general election should be $3,300,000.

Now, ascertain the dollar figures and pertinent information necessary to complete the following exercise for your campaign. This exercise will clearly delineate exactly how much money needs to be raised and by when. Here is an example. The specifics of your race will vary:

Total Fundraising Target: $5,500,000

Total Months to Fundraise: 16 months

Primary Election Month: April

General Election Month: November

Campaign Starting Month: June of the year prior to the election

Total Months Campaigning in Primary: 10 months

Total Months Campaigning in General: 6 months

Average Monthly Fundraising Target:

$5,500,000 / 16 months = $343,750 per month target

Total Primary Fundraising Target:

$343,750 x 10 months = $3,437,500

Total General Fundraising Target:

$5,500,000 - $3,437,500 = $2,062,500

Primary Election Expected Spending: $2,200,000

General Election Expected Spending:

$5,500,000 Total - $2,200,000 Primary = $3,300,000

Average Monthly Primary Burn (Spending) Rate:

$2,200,000 / 10 months = $220,000 per month

Average Monthly General Burn Rate:

$3,300,000 / 6 months = $550,000 per month

Primary Election 90 in 30 Target:

$220,000 x 3 months (90 days) = $660,000

General Election 90 in 30 Target:

$550,000 x 3 months = $1,650,000

To be clear, these figures are presented as if in a perfect world. In practice, fundraising outcomes are almost never this neat (in fact, in my 26 years of involvement in politics, I cannot recall a single instance where the numbers aligned so cleanly in actuality). However, these numbers do provide a track to run on and serve as a guide to assess your progress in relation to the average required to hit your goal.

CULTIVATING DONOR RELATIONSHIPS

Cultivating strong relationships with donors is one of the most important aspects of running a successful political campaign. Donors are essential to funding a campaign and ensuring its success, so it's crucial to keep them engaged and motivated throughout the election cycle.

One of the key considerations for building and maintaining strong donor relationships is regular communication. Donors need to be kept informed about the campaign's progress, upcoming events, and policy initiatives. Regular email updates, newsletters, phone calls, and personal meetings can all be effective ways to keep donors informed and engaged. By staying in touch with donors throughout the election cycle, campaigns can build a strong sense of community and support around their cause.

Expressing gratitude is another crucial aspect of building strong donor relationships. Donors who feel appreciated and valued are more likely to continue supporting a campaign. Personalized thank-you notes, recognition on the campaign website, and invitations to special events are all effective ways to show donors that their contributions are appreciated. By taking the time to show donors that their support is valued, campaigns can foster a sense of loyalty and commitment among their supporters.

Sharing updates and progress on the campaign is also an important consideration for maintaining strong donor relationships. Donors want to know that their contributions are making a difference and that the campaign is making progress towards its goals. Regular updates on fundraising goals, campaign events, and policy initiatives can help keep donors informed and engaged. By keeping donors engaged with the campaign's progress, campaigns can inspire a sense of momentum and excitement around their cause.

Listening to donor feedback is another critical aspect of building strong donor relationships. Donors want to feel that their opinions and perspectives are valued, and campaigns that listen to their feedback are more likely to earn their continued support. Surveys, focus groups, and one-on-one conversations are all effective ways to gather feedback from donors and show them that their input is valued. By incorporating donor feedback into campaign strategies and initiatives, campaigns can build a sense of collaboration and partnership with their supporters.

Building trust is also essential to building long-term relationships with donors. Transparency and openness about the campaign's goals, strategies, and finances can help build trust with donors. By being transparent about how campaign funds are being used and the campaign's progress towards its goals, campaigns can build trust and earn the continued support of their donors. Being responsive is also crucial to show donors that their input is valued. Promptly responding to donor inquiries and concerns can help build trust and ensure that donors feel valued. Donors who feel that their input is valued are more likely to continue supporting a campaign.

Finally, personalizing donor interactions can help build stronger relationships with donors. Recognizing donors' interests and preferences, and providing tailored information and updates can help create a personal connection between the donor and the campaign. By personalizing donor interactions, campaigns can show donors that they are valued as individuals and not just as a source of funding.

FUNDRAISING PITFALLS TO AVOID OR MITIGATE

While fundraising is an essential aspect of running a successful political campaign, it is not without its challenges. There are several pitfalls that candidates must be aware of and avoid to maximize their fundraising efforts and increase their chances of success.

UNEXPECTED EVENTS AND CRISES

Unexpected events and crises can have a significant impact on fundraising efforts during election cycles. The COVID-19 pandemic, for example, forced campaigns to adapt quickly to the new realities of social distancing and virtual campaigning. Natural disasters, scandals, and other unforeseen events can also have a profound effect on the political landscape, and campaigns must be prepared to respond accordingly.

To mitigate the impact of unexpected events and crises, it is important to have a crisis management plan in place. This plan should outline how to respond to unexpected events, communicate with donors and supporters, and continue fundraising efforts in the face of adversity. In the case of the COVID-19 pandemic, campaigns shifted their fundraising efforts online, hosting virtual fundraisers, and using social media to engage with donors and supporters.

It is also worth noting that unexpected events can present fundraising opportunities. For example, during the COVID-19 pandemic and the heavy-handed authoritarian response from liberal (and a few Republican) state governors and the Trump administration led by Dr. Fauci, campaigns that championed issues such as individual freedom and liberty, medical freedom, and sane economic policy were able to rally support and donations around these issues. By being prepared to respond to unexpected events and crises, campaigns can minimize the impact on their fundraising efforts and even turn these events into opportunities to build support and momentum.

Another example of an unexpected event that can impact fundraising efforts is a scandal involving the campaign or candidate. Scandals can damage a campaign's reputation and erode donor trust, making it difficult to raise funds. Your general consultant and/or comms team should have the skills to develop a crisis management plan that addresses how to respond to scandals and rebuild trust with donors can help campaigns navigate these challenges.

Unexpected events and crises are an inevitable part of political campaigns. By being prepared with a crisis management plan, campaigns can minimize the impact of these events on their fundraising efforts and even turn them into opportunities to build support and momentum. Remember, campaigns that are flexible and responsive to changing circumstances are more likely to succeed, even in the face of unexpected events and crises.

MANAGING DONOR FATIGUE

In the course of extended election cycles, donor fatigue emerges as a prevalent obstacle. This phenomenon transpires when benefactors grow weary of incessant fundraising appeals, resulting in a diminished response to such solicitations. The judicious management of contact frequency proves crucial in circumventing donor fatigue. Campaigns that inundate their donor base with multiple daily emails may inadvertently exhaust their well of support. Such a tactic proves ineffective, leading to a swift exodus from the campaign's email list.

A more prudent strategy entails confining email correspondence to a range of 3 to 5 instances per week, while balancing the composition of email appeals by maintaining a ratio of 3 soft to 1 hard ask. Soft ask emails serve to inform recipients of campaign updates, share anecdotes involving the candidate, and accentuate pivotal campaign concerns, as illustrated in Chapter 5. In contrast, hard ask emails unambiguously solicit contributions from donors, fostering a more direct approach to fundraising.

Furthermore, curbing the frequency of fundraising appeals through text messages serves as an additional means to avert donor fatigue. Text messaging ought to be employed predominantly for disseminating information and extending invitations to events. Campaigns would be wise to restrict fundraising solicitations via text to month-end and quarter-end deadlines. This tactic diminishes the contact volume, ensuring that donors are not inundated with excessive fundraising appeals. By employing text messaging judiciously and with purpose, campaigns can circumvent donor fatigue and forge more robust relationships with their supporters.

STAYING COMPLIANT

Staying compliant with campaign finance laws and regulations is essential during election cycles. Violations of campaign finance laws can result in significant penalties and damage to the campaign's reputation. To stay compliant, campaigns must work with experienced compliance professionals, maintain accurate records, and report all contributions and expenditures in a timely and transparent manner. It is also important to stay up-to-date on changes to campaign finance laws and regulations, as these laws can change during election cycles. Compliance professionals can help campaigns navigate these changes and ensure that they are following all applicable laws and regulations. We will discuss compliance and treasury services later in this chapter.

FUNDRAISING JUDO

Crises and gaffes can be both a challenge and an opportunity. While unexpected events can create uncertainty and disrupt fundraising efforts, they can also present opportunities to mobilize supporters and raise money. The key is to be strategic, agile, and responsive to the situation. One of the most potent fundraising strategies is to use your opponents' mistakes and gaffes to your advantage. When your opponent makes mistakes or commits gaffes, their blunder can be leveraged as an opportunity to mobilize your supporters and raise funds for your campaign.

One example of using an opponent's mistake for fundraising is the case of Rick Santorum. In 2012, Santorum was running in the Republican presidential primary against Mitt Romney. During a campaign event, Santorum made a controversial statement about birth control, stating that it was not an essential medication, and that states should have the right to ban it. This comment created a firestorm of controversy and backlash. The Romney campaign quickly seized on the opportunity to raise funds and mobilize supporters by launching a fundraising campaign. The campaign sent out a fundraising email to supporters that said, "Rick Santorum just said birth control is not an essential medication. It's outrageous, and we need your help to fight back. Can you make a donation today to help us defeat Rick Santorum and his anti-woman agenda?" The email included a link to a donation page on the campaign website, and supporters responded generously.

This example illustrates how a gaffe or mistake by an opponent can be turned into a fundraising opportunity. By framing the opponent's mistake as a threat to a particular cause or group, campaigns can mobilize supporters and raise funds to counteract the impact of the mistake. One key consideration when using an opponent's mistakes and gaffes in fundraising appeals is timing. It is important to strike while the iron is hot and to mobilize supporters quickly in response to the situation. This can include sending out fundraising appeals immediately following a gaffe or mistake, while the news is still fresh in people's minds.

The quote "Never let a good crisis go to waste" is often attributed to Rahm Emanuel, who was serving as White House Chief of Staff to President Barack Obama at the time. Emanuel reportedly made the comment during a Wall Street Journal conference in November 2008, shortly after Obama's election victory. I will give you the same advice here. In the context of political fundraising, the phrase can be interpreted as encouraging campaigns to be agile, strategic, and responsive to unexpected events and crises in order to mobilize supporters and raise money.

THE ART OF CONSTRUCTING AND LEADING A FUNDRAISING TEAM

The creation and leadership of a powerful fundraising team is paramount for winning. To accomplish this objective, one must take into account several key aspects that will ultimately contribute to the team's success.

First and foremost, the delineation of roles and responsibilities is of utmost importance. Each team member must have a comprehensive understanding of their tasks and be fully aware of what is expected of them. This clarity will lead to efficient execution and foster an environment in which accountability thrives. A well-structured team will have individuals dedicated to donor prospect research, event planning, donor relations, and campaign finance compliance, among other responsibilities.

The recruitment of a skillful team is essential for success. Seek out individuals who possess experience in fundraising or those who demonstrate unwavering passion for the cause. Assembling a mixture of devoted volunteers and competent paid staff will ensure that the campaign has the necessary resources at its disposal. It is important to remember that a diverse team, including people with varied experience and perspectives, can bring innovative ideas and strategies to the table, further strengthening the fundraising efforts and avoiding group think.

For instance, Dark Horse Political frequently engages the expertise of professionals beyond the realm of politics. This approach has proven to be highly beneficial in areas such as prospecting, data mining, data analysis, digital marketing, and email fundraising. Moreover, these specialists have contributed significantly to the development of sales funnels, which have been ingeniously transformed into commitment funnels. These refined funnels are designed to guide potential voters through a journey that takes them from being intrigued prospects to devoted supporters, donors, and volunteers.

Investing in the growth of your fundraising team is crucial. Offer training and support to ensure that each member has the knowledge and abilities required to succeed in their respective roles. This may encompass instruction on fundraising techniques, such as live events, online campaigns, and major donor cultivation, as well as donor communication skills and legal and ethical considerations. By empowering your team, you create a force capable of overcoming obstacles and achieving remarkable results.

Additionally, consider implementing a mentorship program within your team, pairing experienced fundraisers with those new to the field. This will not only provide further support for team members but also create a sense of camaraderie and shared purpose, which can be highly motivating. Motivation is a powerful driving force. Set ambitious yet attainable goals for your team, and offer incentives for meeting or surpassing these targets. In doing so, you inspire individuals to strive for greatness, ultimately raising more money for the campaign. Encourage friendly competition among team members and celebrate milestones, both large and small, to maintain momentum and enthusiasm throughout the campaign.

Cultivate a positive team culture by promoting open communication, acknowledging the accomplishments of team members, and fostering a supportive and inclusive environment. When individuals feel valued and respected, they are more likely to invest their energy and talents in the campaign's success. Regular team meetings and opportunities for social interaction can help build trust and camaraderie, further strengthening the team's commitment to the cause. Collaboration with other campaign teams, such as communications and field operations, can also bolster the fundraising team's effectiveness. By working closely with these teams, fundraisers can ensure that the campaign's messaging and activities are aligned with donor interests, making the overall fundraising efforts more compelling and persuasive.

Lastly, never underestimate the power of evaluation and adaptation. Regularly assess your fundraising team's performance and modify strategies as needed to ensure progress towards the campaign's financial objectives. This may include analyzing the success of various fundraising tactics, surveying donors for feedback, and reviewing industry best practices to identify areas for improvement. By embracing change and learning from experience, the team will evolve and refine its methods, leading to an ever-improving fundraising machine.

THE SIGNIFICANCE OF COMPLIANCE AND TREASURY SERVICES

Strict adherence to campaign finance laws and ethical practices is vital for maintaining the trust of donors and preserving the integrity of the campaign. In this section, we briefly delve into the key aspects of compliance and ethical considerations for fundraising, emphasizing the importance of campaign finance laws and the roles of campaign treasurers and bookkeepers.

Acquiring a fundamental understanding of campaign finance laws is imperative for candidates. Grasping the rules of federal, state, and local regulations, such as contribution limits, reporting requirements, and disclosure requirements, is essential to ensure compliance. Contribution limits dictate the maximum sum an individual or entity can donate to a political campaign, while reporting requirements govern the declaration of campaign contributions and expenditures. Disclosure requirements, on the other hand, pertain to the rules surrounding the dissemination of information about campaign finances to the public. To maintain campaign finance compliance, accurate record-keeping is of paramount importance. Detailed records of contributions and expenditures, inclusive of donor information, contribution amounts, and dates of receipt, must be maintained. This involves tracking all contributions and expenditures, keeping meticulous records, regularly reconciling accounts, and adhering to reporting requirements.

The campaign treasurer and campaign bookkeeper both hold pivotal positions, responsible for overseeing the campaign's finances. The campaign treasurer, typically a designated individual, is tasked with managing the campaign's bank accounts, preparing and filing campaign finance reports, and ensuring proper documentation and reporting of all contributions and expenditures. In contrast, the campaign bookkeeper handles day-to-day accounting tasks, such as recording transactions, reconciling accounts, and preparing financial statements. While both the treasurer and bookkeeper are crucial to managing a campaign's finances, their roles and responsibilities differ distinctly. The treasurer assumes a broader oversight role, ensuring compliance with campaign finance laws and regulations, while the bookkeeper focuses on a more operational role, managing the campaign's financial records and transactions.

WARNING:

Under *no circumstances* should a candidate handle their own compliance and bookkeeping.

By establishing a strong foundation in compliance and treasury services, your campaign will create an environment of transparency and trust with donors and supporters. This commitment to ethical fundraising practices will not only protect the campaign from legal and reputational risks but also contribute to its overall success. Compliance and treasury services play an indispensable role in fundraising. By familiarizing themselves with campaign finance laws, developing internal compliance procedures, and maintaining accurate records, campaigns can ensure that their fundraising efforts remain within the bounds of the law and ethical standards. The campaign treasurer and bookkeeper, with their distinct yet complementary roles, work together to manage the campaign's finances and maintain its integrity throughout the fundraising process. Under no circumstances should a candidate handle their own compliance reporting and bookkeeping.

Strict compliance and reporting requirements are imposed by state and federal regulatory bodies, such as the Federal Election Commission (FEC). Navigating these complex and time-consuming regulations is challenging, and noncompliance can have severe repercussions for campaigns and political organizations (such as PACs). This is why employing professional treasury services to manage compliance and reporting requirements is vital. It is crucial for candidates and campaigns to avoid finding themselves on the wrong side of a compliance conversation or investigation by a regulatory body. The internal rule of the fundraising team should always be to err on the side of caution and never operate in gray areas. The risks involved in breaking the rules simply do not outweigh the benefits.

Professional treasury services offer numerous advantages to campaigns and political organizations. These benefits include proficiency in compliance and reporting. Staffed with experts well-versed in the intricate requirements of state and federal regulatory bodies, professional treasury services help ensure that campaigns and political organizations remain compliant with all relevant laws and regulations, reducing the risk of costly fines and penalties. Efficient reporting and record-keeping is another benefit of employing professional treasury services. These services utilize sophisticated software and tools to streamline the reporting and record-keeping process, saving time and money while guaranteeing the accuracy and timeliness of all financial reports.

The avoidance of conflicts of interest is also a significant advantage of using professional treasury services. As independent third-party organizations with no stake in the outcome of an election, their impartiality helps maintain the integrity of financial reporting. Moreover, professional treasury services prioritize the protection of donor information. Implementing state-of-the-art security measures and protocols, they ensure the safeguarding of donor data, reducing the risk of data breaches or other security incidents.

On the other hand, neglecting to use professional treasury services can result in serious consequences. Failure to comply with reporting requirements can lead to fines and penalties from state and federal regulatory bodies, and in extreme cases, even legal action against the candidate, campaign or political organization. A lack of transparency and accountability in financial reporting may also erode donor trust and confidence in the campaign, ultimately leading to decreased support and donations. Additionally, inadequate financial reporting can contribute to the perception of corruption within the organization, harming the candidate's reputation and undermining supporters' trust in the campaign.

CONSEQUENCES: A CAUTIONARY TALE

As clearly noted above, it is crucial to respect campaign finance laws and diligently report all contributions and expenses. A stark example that underscores the severity of this matter is the case of California Republican Congressman Duncan Hunter in 2018. He and his campaign faced accusations of violating federal campaign finance laws by misappropriating campaign funds for personal expenses, such as vacations, dental work, and even flights for his family's pet rabbit. The campaign was also suspected of failing to report expenditures accurately.

The Federal Election Commission embarked on a meticulous investigation into these allegations, leading to Hunter's indictment on charges of wire fraud, falsifying records, and campaign finance violations. In the end, he pleaded guilty to one count of conspiracy to misuse campaign funds and resigned from Congress in January 2020. After admitting guilt, the former California Republican Congressman was sentenced to 11 months in federal prison in March 2020, with an additional three years of supervised release following his prison term.

The ramifications of Congressman Hunter's inability to comply with campaign finance laws and accurately report his campaign's financial transactions were profound. He faced criminal charges, lost his seat in Congress, and damaged his reputation. This cautionary tale serves as a stern reminder of the paramount importance of abiding by campaign finance laws and meticulously reporting all contributions and expenditures to regulatory bodies such as the Federal Election Commission. Failure to do so can lead to grave legal and political consequences. As a fundamental principle, it is vital to avoid being on the wrong side of a conversation with a financial regulatory body at all costs. However, candidates should not anticipate receiving leniency if they are legitimately convicted of campaign finance violations.

In a surprising development, President Donald Trump granted a pardon to Duncan Hunter in December 2020, essentially absolving him of his conviction and eliminating any residual legal repercussions tied to the case. Furthermore, Trump extended pardons to other Republicans confronted with corruption allegations or convictions simultaneously, including former New York Republican Congressman Chris Collins, who was convicted of securities fraud and received a prison sentence of 26 months, and former Texas Republican Congressman Steve Stockman, who was convicted in 2018 for his involvement in a complex corruption scheme that included misusing charitable funds and was initially sentenced to 10 years in prison. These acts of clemency, which also included the commutation of the remainder of Stockman's sentence, were part of a broader series of pardons issued by President Trump during the final weeks of his tenure, sparking contentious discussions and debates.

These stories emphasize the importance of always operating within the boundaries of the law and maintaining transparency in financial dealings. The lesson learned from these cases is that the risks involved in breaking the rules simply do not outweigh the potential benefits. Once again, as a guiding principle, it is essential to never find oneself on the wrong side of a conversation with a financial regulatory body—**ever.**

THE CENTERPIECE OF
THE FUNDRAISING TEAM: THE CANDIDATE

Throughout this book, it has been emphasized that the candidate serves as the central figure in the fundraising effort. This is particularly true in the early stages of the campaign. Establishing a dedicated call time for the candidate each day, six days a week, forms the bedrock of the entire fundraising endeavor. At their core, candidates hold two primary roles within the campaign team: connecting with voters through personal interactions to win their support for the purpose of earning their vote and raising funds from them later, and making fundraising calls. As previously noted, politics is akin to sales, and candidates are expected to make sales calls to promote their campaign and foster both electoral and financial commitment from the voting public. A candidate must lead by example and cannot expect others on the team to invest their time, talent, and treasure into raising funds for the campaign if the candidate is unwilling to do the same.

Diligent candidates understand that they must allocate a significant portion of their time to fundraising efforts, even if it means sacrificing time that could be spent on other less important campaign-related activities. This relentless pursuit of financial support is a testament to the candidate's dedication and determination to see their campaign through to the end. Moreover, the candidate's unwavering commitment to fundraising serves as a source of inspiration for the entire campaign team. In the realm of fundraising, consistency is key. A candidate must not only commit to making fundraising calls but also maintain the discipline to follow through on a regular basis. This daily commitment to fundraising will not only build momentum but also generate a sense of urgency and importance among potential donors. By consistently engaging in fundraising efforts, the candidate reinforces the message that their campaign is a worthy investment and deserving of the electorate's support.

It is essential for candidates to recognize that each interaction with potential donors is an opportunity to build rapport and trust. By approaching these conversations with genuine interest and a listening ear, candidates can forge strong connections with their supporters. These connections, in turn, will serve as the foundation for future financial contributions and continued support throughout the campaign.

THE PHONE BANKING TEAM

The significance of a steadfast and proficient phone banking team cannot be overstated. These individuals function as an amplification of the candidate's own endeavors, laboring tirelessly to amass the essential financial backing for the triumph of the campaign. A masterfully coordinated phone banking team holds the power to magnify the campaign's reach exponentially, forging connections with prospective benefactors and reinforcing the candidate's message and vision.

The cardinal objective of a phone banking team lies in sparking discourse with potential patrons and advocates, methodically navigating through contact lists to elicit monetary pledges. As a crucial element of the fundraising journey, these dialogues strive to nurture and preserve relationships while also kindling

allegiance among established supporters. By transmitting the candidate's zeal and dedication to their mission, the phone banking team can engender a sense of urgency and significance, which may prompt potential contributors to invest financially in the campaign.

Moreover, the phone banking team's role extends to keeping supporters apprised of campaign progress, forthcoming events, and avenues to deepen their engagement with the campaign. This unceasing exchange not only fortifies the connection between the campaign and its advocates but also instills a sentiment of unity and fellowship. In its essence, the phone banking team operates as a nexus between the candidate and the voting populace, ensuring the campaign remains a prominent consideration in the minds of the electorate and fostering the indispensable financial support to propel the campaign toward a victorious outcome.

FUNDRAISING CONSULTANTS

In the competitive landscape of political campaigns, fundraising consultants play a crucial role in ensuring financial success. These professionals, often working independently or as part of a consulting firm, are engaged by clients to offer guidance and assistance in all aspects of fundraising. From crafting tailored fundraising strategies to implementing comprehensive fundraising programs, they provide invaluable expertise to candidates.

A successful fundraising consultant works closely with their clients to comprehend their financial goals, subsequently developing a customized plan to reach those objectives. They may furnish advice on various aspects of fundraising, including donor outreach, retention, compliance, and ethical considerations, among others.

The compensation structure for fundraising consultants varies depending on the project, with fees typically charged on an hourly, weekly, or monthly basis. They may be paid for their services on a project or retainer basis, and in addition to their fees, they might receive a commission or bonus contingent upon the amount of money raised.

The exact fees and compensation arrangements depend on factors such as the consultant's experience and expertise, the project's scope and complexity, and the consultant's individual preferences. Some consultants may charge a flat fee, while others may opt for a percentage of the funds raised. This commission-based fee structure, also known as a performance-based fee, typically ranges from 5% to 20% of the funds raised. Smaller campaigns or non-profit organizations with limited resources may agree to a higher percentage, while larger campaigns or organizations may use their size to negotiate a lower rate.

Fundraising consultants provide invaluable support to campaigns and political organizations in their pursuit of financial success. Their expertise and guidance can make all the difference in achieving their clients' goals, making them an indispensable resource in an increasingly competitive landscape.

BUNDLERS

The role of bundlers has grown increasingly significant, particularly as campaign finance reforms impose limitations on individual contributions. Bundlers, well-connected individuals with extensive networks, assist political candidates and organizations in raising money by aggregating donations from multiple donors. Their ability to leverage these networks enables campaigns and organizations to amass substantial funds while adhering to campaign finance laws and regulations.

Though bundlers are not financially compensated for their services, as it would breach campaign finance laws, they often receive non-monetary rewards such as exclusive access to the candidate or organization, invitations to special events, or meetings with key decision-makers. The amount raised by a bundler varies, with some managing to gather tens or even hundreds of thousands of dollars, while others raise smaller sums. The success of a bundler is frequently gauged by the amount raised, and this can determine their level of access and influence.

However, the practice of bundling brings forth several ethical considerations. One such issue is the influence and access that bundlers who successfully raise significant funds may gain with candidates or key decision-makers, potentially creating the perception of undue influence over the candidate or organization. Additionally, although campaign finance laws necessitate the disclosure of bundlers and their contributions, not all campaigns or organizations are transparent about their bundlers. This lack of transparency can create an appearance of impropriety and undermine public trust. The perception of quid pro quo is another concern when large sums of money are raised, as the relationship between a bundler and a candidate or organization may appear transactional.

Regarding bundlers, the merit of one's professional experience or abilities may not always be the sole determining factors for appointment to a prominent position. At times, the support rendered through political fundraising may unexpectedly elevate an individual to a role for which they might not possess the requisite qualifications. Such was the case with George Tsunis, a notable fundraiser for Barack Obama's 2012 re-election campaign.

Mr. Tsunis, having raised over half a million dollars, found himself nominated for the esteemed role of U.S. Ambassador to Norway. However, the subsequent Senate confirmation hearing unveiled a concerning lack of knowledge about the nation he was to represent. Missteps, such as referring to Norway's prime minister as a "president" and inaccurately labeling one of the country's major political parties as a "fringe" element, cast serious doubts on his qualifications for the ambassadorship.

This appointment garnered criticism across the political spectrum, with many asserting that the nomination was solely influenced by Tsunis's fundraising prowess rather than his genuine suitability for the position. The ensuing opposition in the Senate eventually led Mr. Tsunis to withdraw from consideration for the ambassadorship in December 2014.

FUNDRAISING TOOLS: MANAGING THE FUNDRAISING EFFORT USING SOFTWARE SOLUTIONS

Software solutions, like Aristotle 360, are designed to help campaigns and organizations manage their fundraising operations more efficiently. The advantages of using such a solution include effective donor relationship management, streamlined donation processes, and robust analytics and reporting tools that enable data-driven decision-making. These features can help campaigns be more strategic in their fundraising efforts, ultimately leading to better results. However, there can be drawbacks, such as a steep learning curve for unfamiliar users and potentially high costs. Moreover, some software solutions might be inflexible, requiring campaigns to adapt to the software's capabilities instead of catering to their unique needs.

Despite these potential disadvantages, the benefits of using a fundraising software solution generally outweigh the cons. By offering a comprehensive set of tools for managing donor relationships, processing donations, and tracking progress, fundraising software can help campaigns and organizations be more efficient and effective. In turn, this can help them achieve their fundraising goals.

CHOOSING A DONOR PORTAL

The importance of online donation processing in the realm of political fundraising cannot be overstated. In an increasingly digital world, user-friendly and secure platforms like WinRed and Anedot have become indispensable tools for campaigns and organizations looking to raise money more effectively.

Both platforms offer a host of unique benefits that cater to their users' needs, streamlining the donation process and enhancing donor engagement.

WinRed and Anedot share several key features, including customizable branding that allows campaigns to create a visually consistent and appealing donation page, mobile optimization to facilitate on-the-go donations, and automated compliance to ensure adherence to campaign finance laws and regulations. Additionally, these platforms offer features such as recurring donations, real-time notifications, and detailed reporting to help campaigns make data-driven decisions and refine their fundraising strategies.

The choice of platform should focus on fostering a sense of credibility and trust for potential donors. A visually appealing and professional-looking donor portal can inspire confidence in the campaign and its message, ultimately leading to increased donations. Conversely, an unpolished or untrustworthy appearance may deter potential donors, negatively impacting the campaign's fundraising efforts.

METHODS OF INTERNAL FUNDRAISING

THE ANATOMY OF A CANDIDATE CALL

As you already know, candidate donor calls are crucial for engaging potential donors and gaining their support. Creating an effective call script is vital for successful donor outreach, and a well-structured call script should consist of five key sections. In this section, we'll give you an introduction to the anatomy of a fundraising call. Focusing on the five sections - The Connection, The Transition, The Ask, The Close, and The Retargeting - can help candidates build trust, address donor concerns, and secure valuable financial support for their campaigns.

Firstly, The Connection section should start with a personal connection to the donor, establishing rapport and showing genuine interest in their concerns or interests. This can be done by asking about their family, job, or recent events or discussing shared experiences or acquaintances. Establishing a connection helps build trust and lays the foundation for a productive conversation.

Once a connection has been established, the candidate should smoothly transition into the purpose of the call, which is The Transition section. This might involve mentioning their campaign, discussing their goals, or identifying shared values and policy objectives. The transition should be natural and unforced, leading organically from the connection to the topic of fundraising.

The Ask section is the most crucial part of the call script, and the candidate should clearly and confidently request a specific donation amount. They should explain how the funds will be used and the impact they will have on the campaign. It is essential to be direct and **specific** in this request, as vagueness or hesitation may undermine the donor's confidence in the candidate.

After making the ask, the candidate should listen carefully to the donor's response and address any concerns or objections they may have in The Close section. The close should involve expressing gratitude for the donor's time and consideration. If the donor agrees to contribute, the candidate should thank them for their generosity and reiterate the impact their donation will have on the campaign. Finally, the candidate can either take a payment over the phone or inform the donor where they can donate online or mail a check.

If the donor declines the initial ask, the candidate should be prepared for The Retargeting section. This may involve asking for a smaller donation, offering alternative ways to support the campaign, or inviting the donor to an upcoming event. The retargeting should be tailored to the donor's specific concerns or objections and should demonstrate the candidate's persistence and dedication to their cause. By following these five sections, the candidate can make a compelling case for their campaign and successfully secure valuable financial support from donors.

CANDIDATE CALL SCRIPTS

The following sample call scripts are tailored for candidates reaching out to potential high dollar donors. While you are encouraged to adapt the script to fit your unique communication style and preferences, it is important to maintain the structure and flow of the call's key sections. Each section has been strategically designed to optimize the fundraising process, and altering them may compromise the effectiveness of your call. Utilize this script as a foundation to establish a connection with potential donors, confidently present your ask, and ultimately, secure their support for the campaign. Keep in mind that the outcome of each call will greatly depend on your ability to genuinely engage with the donor and address their concerns. Therefore, be prepared to actively listen and adjust your approach as needed.

YOUR 3:00 AM CALL SCRIPT

The initial call script to be at your disposal should be tailored for reaching out to family, close friends, and business associates with whom you share a strong bond. These individuals can be thought of as your "3:00 AM circle." They are the ones you would not hesitate to contact at 3:00 AM if you found yourself stranded on a desolate road, in need of assistance. This script should be used when calling your Top 200 List prior to you making any official announcement to the general public regarding your candidacy. Here is a sample of how to approach such a call.

Section 1 – The Connection

Hello [Name], it's [Your Name], how's it going?

Follow the conversation's natural course until the natural pause occurs—the pause that asks, "Why are you calling?"

Listen, the reason I'm calling is because I'd like to get your input on some really big news I'm sharing with close family and friends before I tell the public and also to ask for your help.

Then, share with them your rationale, story, and general narrative.

If you are using this script after you make your official announcement, modify the above verbiage accordingly.

Section 2 – The Transition

So, let me ask you this, do you think my logic on this makes sense?

Assuming your relationship is on good terms, they will likely say yes and follow with reasons of their own for you to run for public office.

I think so too and I appreciate your support.

Section 3 – The Ask

The other reason I'm calling is I need your help. We need to raise $[specific amount] by [specific date] to get our initial campaign efforts off the ground and make our race competitive. Are you able to contribute $[specific amount] to help us reach that goal?

<u>SHUT UP! DO NOT TALK.</u> Wait for them to respond (even if the silence is uncomfortable).

Section 4 – The Close

If yes:

Wow, thank you very much. I knew I could count on you and I am very grateful for your help. Would you like me to take a card right now over the phone or would you prefer I swing by and pick up a check (if they do not live close, ask if they'd like to mail a check)?

Section 4b – The Retargeting Close

If no, retarget your ask:

OK, no problem! I understand times are tough for all of us. How much are you able to give?

<u>SHUT UP! DO NOT TALK.</u> Wait for them to respond. Remember, they just told you they think this is a good idea and they support you. They aren't saying no to you. *They are saying no to the amount.* They will either respond with a dollar figure or tell you they cannot contribute. Either way, be gracious in your response and close the conversation accordingly.

YOUR WARM CALL SCRIPT

The next call script that you should have access to is for calling acquaintances or business associates whom you know and have a good relationship but not well enough to call them close friends or family. Although the sales process is the same, the verbiage should be slightly different. Here's an example of how to make this call.

Section 1 - The Connection

Hi, [Name], it's [Your Name]. How have you been? It's been a while since we last spoke.

Follow the conversation's natural course until the natural pause occurs—the pause that asks, "Why are you calling?"

Section 2 - The Transition

Listen, the reason I'm calling is because I'd like to get your input on some really big news I'm sharing with family and friends before I tell the public. I know you're busy, but I wanted to see if you had a few minutes to talk about my big decision and to ask for your help with something.

Share with them your rationale and story narrative and identify the key problems you'd like to address and your solutions.

So, let me ask you this, do you think my logic for running and my platform makes sense?

Assuming your relationship is on good terms and they hold similar conservative values, they will likely say yes.

Well, I agree and I appreciate your support.

Section 3 - The Ask

The other reason I'm calling is to ask for your help. Our campaign has a fundraising target of $[specific amount] that we need to raise by [specific date] to put us into a position to run a credible race. My question is, would you be willing to contribute $[specific amount] to help us meet our target?

<u>SHUT UP! DO NOT TALK.</u> Wait for them to respond.

Section 4 - The Close

If yes:

[Name], thank you so much for your support. It means a lot to me that you're willing to support my campaign with such a generous gift. Would you like me to take a card right now over the phone or would you prefer I swing by and pick up a check (if they do not live close, ask if they'd like to mail a check)?

Section 4b - The Retargeting

If no, retarget your ask:

Listen, I completely understand. Times are difficult right now for everyone. How much would you be able to contribute today to help us out?

SHUT UP. Wait for their response. Graciously receive any amount they tell you.

[Name], thank you so much for your support. It means a lot to me that you're willing to support my campaign with such a generous gift. Would you like me to take a card right now over the phone or would you prefer I swing by and pick up a check (if they do not live close, ask if they'd like to mail a check)?

If they say they cannot contribute anything at this time, be gracious and thank them very much for their support. Then follow with *another* retargeting ask.

[Name], I completely understand that now might not be a good time for you. Would it be ok if I reached out to you in a couple months to check in with you?

You want to get something from the call, even if it's only permission to call them again. If they completely shut you down by asking you not to call again, take them off your call list.

YOUR COLD CALL SCRIPT

The next call script that you should have access to is for calling known conservative donors whom you **do not** know. To be specific, these are cold calls to high dollar donors. Although the sales process is the same, the verbiage should be slightly different. Here's an example of how to make this call.

Section 1 - The Connection

Hi, my name is [Your Name], and I'm calling on behalf of my campaign for [enter specific office].

Section 2 - The Transition

I'm reaching out to conservative voters like you, and I wanted to talk to you about my campaign, why I think it's so important and to ask for your help. Do you have a moment to chat—I'll be brief?

Share with them your rationale and story narrative and identify the key problems you'd like to address and your solutions.

So, let me ask you this, do you think my logic for running and my platform makes sense?

They will likely say yes.

Well, I agree and I appreciate your support.

Section 3 - The Ask

The other reason I'm calling is to ask for your help. Our campaign has a fundraising target of $[specific amount] by [specific date] to put us into a position to run a credible race against [opponent's name]. My question is, would you be willing to contribute $[specific amount] to support our efforts and help us meet our target?

<u>SHUT UP! DO NOT TALK.</u> Wait for them to respond.

Section 4 - The Close

If yes:

[Name], thank you so much for your support. It means a lot to me that you're willing to support my campaign with such a generous gift. Would you like me to take a card right now over the phone or would you prefer to mail us a check?

Section 4b - The Retargeting

If no, retarget your ask:

Listen, I completely understand. Times are difficult right now for everyone. How much would you be able to contribute today to help us out?

<u>SHUT UP.</u> Wait for their response. Graciously receive any amount they tell you.

[Name], thank you so much for your support. It means a lot to me that you're willing to support my campaign with such a generous gift. Would you like me to take a card right now over the phone or would you prefer I swing by and pick up a check?

If they say they cannot contribute anything at this time, be gracious and thank them very much for their support. Then follow with another retargeting ask.

[Name], I completely understand that now might not be a good time for you. Would it be ok if I reached out to you in a couple months to check in with you (you can also invite them to a scheduled campaign event as your "special guest" if the potential donor lives close to you)?

You want to get something from the call, even if it's only permission to call them again. If they completely shut you down by asking you not to call again, take them off of your call list.

ASKING FOR REFERRALS

If the candidate wants to take their fundraising efforts to the next level, an optional sixth section can be added to each of these call scripts, which involves asking for referrals from prospects who have already contributed to the campaign. The key to this section is to express gratitude for the prospect's support and use positive language to encourage them to think of others who might be interested in supporting the candidate's campaign.

The script could be something like this:

[Name], before I let you go, I want to take a moment, once again, to express my sincere gratitude for your support. Your contribution means a lot to me and will go a long way towards helping me achieve my goals. As you know, fundraising is a critical part of any campaign, and I want to make sure that I reach as many people as possible who share our vision for the future.

So, let me ask you, do you happen to know at least two or three people who are like-minded and who you think would be interested in supporting my campaign or you believe I should contact? It could be friends, family, colleagues, or anyone you know who cares about the issues we're working on.

<u>SHUT UP!</u> Wait for a response.

If the prospect says yes, express your gratitude and ask for the contact information of the referral. Also, ask if it would be okay to mention their name when you reach out to the referral. Make sure to add the referral's information to your call list and follow up within the next two days.

If the prospect says no, be gracious and thank them for their support. Encourage them to keep your campaign in mind and let you know if they think of anyone who might be interested in supporting you. Remember that this is not the end of the conversation, and the prospect might think of referrals later on, so keep the door open for future communication.

ONE LAST THING

Finally, to make call scripts feel more natural and conversational, it's important to practice them regularly until you can work through a conversation without sounding rehearsed. The more you practice, the more comfortable you'll become with the script, allowing you to speak with ease and confidence. Over time, your script will become ingrained into your thinking and speech patterns, making it easier to use without sounding like you're following a script. It's important to note, however, that call scripts should still be used as a guide to ensure that you cover all the essential points during your conversation with a potential donor. By practicing your script regularly, you can increase your chances of success and make a lasting impression on your donors, which is essential for securing valuable financial support for your campaign.

DIALING FOR DOLLARS: CAMPAIGN PHONE BANKING

Volunteer phone banking stands as a potent technique for soliciting contributions from prospective supporters. This cost-effective method serves as an efficient means of reaching out to potential modest donors ($250 and below), while simultaneously forging a direct and personal bond between the campaign and its advocates. To guarantee the success of phone banking, it is imperative that campaigns equip volunteers with the skills necessary to effectively convey the campaign's message and address any donor hesitations.

This preparation ought to encompass providing volunteers with a script delineating the salient points of the campaign's message, alongside specific phrasing to tackle common donor reservations. Furthermore, volunteers must learn the art of active listening, attuning themselves to the concerns of donors and adapting their approach in a tailored manner. A well-drilled and equipped cadre of phone bankers possesses the power to maximize fundraising endeavors, thus generating invaluable backing for a campaign.

PHONE DIALER TECHNOLOGY FOR CAMPAIGN PHONE BANKING OPERATIONS

Phone dialer technology plays a crucial role in the effectiveness and efficiency of a campaign phone banking operation. This technology enables volunteers and staff to quickly connect with potential donors, saving time and maximizing outreach efforts. By automating the dialing process, phone dialer systems reduce manual effort, minimize the risk of misdialing numbers, and increase the number of successful connections. There are several vendors that offer phone dialer technology tailored to conservative campaigns. In this section, we will discuss the purpose and requirements of these technologies and provide three examples of vendors commonly used by conservative campaigns. We will also explore the features and benefits of auto dialer technology.

Phone dialer technology is designed to streamline the process of making calls to potential donors or voters. This technology can be used for various purposes, such as fundraising, voter engagement, and get-out-the-vote efforts. Some of the essential features of phone dialer technology include call automation, contact management, call recording, analytics, and reporting. These features enable campaigns to manage their contacts efficiently, monitor volunteer performance, and track the success of their phone banking efforts.

Auto dialer technology, a subset of phone dialer technology, offers several unique features and benefits that can significantly improve the productivity of phone banking operations. These include predictive dialing, which dials multiple numbers simultaneously and connects volunteers to live answers; progressive dialing, which dials numbers one at a time, allowing volunteers to preview information about the contact before the call; and call blending, which allows volunteers to switch between inbound and outbound calls. Auto dialers can also be integrated with CRM (customer resource management) systems, making it easier to track interactions with donors and voters.

Two vendors known for providing phone dialer technology to conservative campaigns include CallFire and Victory Solutions—Live Calls. Each of these vendors offers solutions tailored to political campaigns and has a track record of working with conservative candidates.

PHONE BANKING CALL SCRIPT

Phone banking cold calls are commonly directed toward identified voters who have previously supported one or more campaigns or causes. These calls should initially target the candidate's specific district or area of candidacy and progressively broaden outward. It is essential to bear in mind that all politics possess a local dimension.

To illustrate, a donor in Omaha, Nebraska, may have little incentive to care about or contribute to a school board race in Tyler, Texas. When reaching out to known donors beyond your district, it is crucial to contextualize the race within a broader scope, if feasible. For instance, if campaigning for the US Congress in Texas and contacting potential donors in Nebraska, the caller must emphasize the significance of gaining or maintaining the balance of power (the majority) in Congress and the crucial nature of every seat. Additionally, discussing the importance of electing Conservatives who align with the donor's values could aid the Republican majority in counteracting the radical agenda of the Democratic Party.

As such, the following phone banking script is intended to act as a foundation for your calling endeavors. Refrain from altering the script's structure; instead, tailor the language to effectively communicate the relevant details of your specific campaign.

Section 1 - The Connection

Hello [Donor's Name], this is [Volunteer's Name] calling on behalf of [Candidate's Name]'s campaign. How are you today?

Listen to their response and engage briefly in a personal conversation, e.g., about their day, family, or work.

Listen, I appreciate you taking the time to briefly chat with me.

Section 2 - The Transition

I wanted to speak with you today because I know you share our passion for [key issue(s) that the donor cares about]. [Candidate's Name] is committed to making a real difference in our community by [briefly describe candidate's solutions to identified problems]. Your support of candidates in the past has been invaluable, and we're reaching out to our dedicated conservatives to help us continue our mission.

Section 3 - The Ask

We're currently working towards our fundraising goal of $[specific amount] by [specific date] to help us [describe how the funds will be used, e.g., running ads, hiring staff, organizing events]. Would you consider making a generous contribution of $[specific suggested amount] to help [Candidate's Name] bring about the change we all want to see?

ın 4 - The Close

ϳ you so much for your generous support, [Donor's Name]! Your contribution will have

ᵢfıcant impact on [Candidate's Name]'s campaign and our shared goals. We truly

ᵢciate your dedication to our cause. Would you allow me to take a card right now over

ϳone so we can lock in that contribution?

rain from suggesting that the donor send a check by mail unless they

ϳlicitly express their preference to do so. Frequently, donors may

intentionally neglect to post the check, leaving the campaign to pursue the

ntribution at a later date. It is invariably more advantageous to secure the

ϳnation during the phone conversation with the donor.

ϳection 4b - The Retargeting

If no, retarget your ask:

I completely understand, [Donor's Name]. Would you consider a smaller donation of

$[reduced suggested amount] instead? Every dollar helps us move closer to our goal.

Alternatively, you could also [offer other ways to support, e.g., volunteering, attending events,

sharing information on social media]. We appreciate any support you can provide.

If the donor has concerns or objections.

I understand your concerns, [Donor's Name]. [Address their specific concerns or objections].

Your support means a lot to us, and we hope you'll reconsider your decision.

EMAIL FUNDRAISING

In the modern era of political campaigning, email has emerged as a powerful instrument for fundraising, particularly for conservative candidates. As a medium of communication, email allows campaigns to reach a broad audience swiftly and efficiently, delivering their message with both clarity and impact. Crafting an effective fundraising email requires the perfect blend of inspiration and motivation. Just as a compelling vision can propel an individual towards personal success, so too can a well-articulated campaign message inspire potential donors to contribute to a cause they believe in. The key lies in striking a balance between the candidate's aspirations and the urgency of their financial needs.

An email campaign must be thoughtfully designed and executed, taking care to avoid overwhelming potential donors with excessive requests. By providing timely updates on the campaign's progress, sharing stories that resonate with the target audience, and expressing sincere gratitude for every contribution, a conservative candidate can cultivate a sense of trust and loyalty among their supporters. Additionally, campaigns should alternate between soft ask and hard ask emails as described previously by utilizing a ratio that works best for your campaign. This, in turn, can serve as the bedrock for a robust fundraising campaign, fueling a dedicated and passionate base of donors.

One must also recognize the growing challenges faced by political campaigns in the realm of email communication. Due to the misuse of email by numerous national campaigns, many email providers have implemented measures to throttle the delivery of political messages. This often results in political emails being undelivered or directed straight to the recipient's spam folder. Email providers such as Gmail, Outlook, Yahoo Mail, Hotmail, iCloud, AOL Mail, Proton Mail, and others use an algorithm to detect spam trigger words. If the algorithm detects these words in your email copy it automatically flags them as spam and either does not deliver the message or it sends it to the recipient's spam folder.

Additionally, bulk mailers such as Constant Contact, Mailchimp, and GetResponse monitor your bounce rate, spam rate, etc. If a significant number of your emails are flagged as spam, your account will be suspended or, worse, your domain could be blacklisted (which effectively shuts down your entire email operation). Sending mail flagged as spam is a waste of time and resources. To circumvent such obstacles, it is essential to check your email copy for spam trigger words. To do this, I recommend the free email spam checker tool on the Blogiestools website (https://blogiestools.com/email-spam-trigger-words-checker-tool/). Another free spam checker tool can be found at Mailmeteor (https://mailmeteor.com/spam-checker). Both tools are indispensable for making sure your email copy passes the spam protocols set by email providers.

ONLINE FUNDRAISING

Online fundraising has gained significant traction, emerging as both cost-effective and efficient. This approach encompasses the solicitation of donations via social media, digital advertising, email, and dedicated fundraising landing pages. To fully capitalize on the potential of online fundraising, campaigns must devise compelling appeals that resonate with their target audience and inspire them to contribute. A crucial aspect of successful online fundraising is the development of a user-friendly donation platform (as discussed earlier in this chapter), which facilitates a seamless and straightforward experience for donors (Anedot makes this particularly simple).

This ease of use encourages potential contributors to follow through with their donations, ensuring that the campaign garners the financial support it requires.

Furthermore, the strategic utilization of social media is indispensable in the modern fundraising landscape. By harnessing the power of various platforms, campaigns can significantly broaden their reach, engaging a diverse audience and fostering a sense of connection with potential donors both inside and outside of your campaign's target area. Through consistent and engaging content, as well as targeted ads, social media can amplify a campaign's message and facilitate the acquisition of vital contributions.

SHORTCODES

Shortcodes are short numerical codes that campaigns can utilize for fundraising and communication purposes. Typically consisting of 5 to 6 digits, these codes provide an efficient and convenient way for supporters to donate or engage with a campaign via text messaging. By texting a designated keyword to the shortcode, supporters can quickly contribute funds, sign up for updates, or join a campaign's contact list. Often, you will see campaign advertisements or signs that read, "Text [keyword] to 12345 to Donate." These are shortcodes.

Campaigns effectively use shortcodes for fundraising by promoting them through various channels such as social media, email, and direct mail. By providing an easy-to-remember code and a simple call-to-action, campaigns can encourage supporters to make impulsive donations or opt-in for regular updates. Shortcodes can also be used during events or debates, enabling instant contributions and capturing potential supporters' interest at the height of their enthusiasm.

In addition to raising funds, shortcodes help campaigns build their contact lists, as donors are required to provide their contact information when making a donation or opting in for updates. This information can be used for future communication and engagement, increasing the likelihood of further donations and strengthening the relationship between the campaign and its supporters. This information can also be used during your GOTV efforts in Phase 5 to make sure your known supporters participate in the election.

MERCHANDISE

Merchandise presents a unique opportunity to generate contributions while simultaneously engaging supporters and augmenting visibility. This approach entails offering campaign-related items for purchase, including T-shirts, hats, and stickers, which not only serve as a source of financial support but also foster a sense of camaraderie among the campaign's advocates. To optimize the impact of merchandise fundraising, campaigns must thoughtfully select items that harmonize with the campaign's message and resonate with the target audience. These products should be both visually appealing and emblematic of the candidate's core values, ensuring that supporters are proud to don the items and showcase their allegiance. Winred has a seamless online store solution for candidates that handles the donation, online store with customizable products, order fulfilment, and 100% automation. For campaigns large and small, this is an effective solution for providing merchandise.

Moreover, the strategic use of high-quality merchandise can cultivate brand recognition, which may lead to organic promotion as supporters sport the items in public settings. This increased visibility can pique the interest of potential donors and voters, ultimately expanding the campaign's reach and bolstering its financial resources.

TEXTING

Texting has emerged as an increasingly popular instrument for political fundraising, as campaigns and organizations leverage text messages to connect with potential donors and solicit contributions. One key application of texting in fundraising involves direct solicitation of donations from prior contributors. This can entail sending personalized messages requesting specific amounts or providing links to user-friendly mobile donation platforms. It is generally advisable to utilize texting for fundraising during end-of-month and end-of-quarter pushes.

Text messages can also serve to remind donors to contribute or follow up on previous donation requests. Personalized reminders or automated follow-up messages can be sent to donors who have yet to donate or have expressed interest in doing so. Additionally, texting can be employed to share campaign or organizational updates, keeping donors engaged and invested in the cause. Mobilizing supporters around specific events or initiatives, such as rallies or canvassing efforts, is another way texting can bolster campaign activities. Text messages can also facilitate the conduction of surveys and gathering of feedback from donors and supporters, enabling campaigns and organizations to tailor their fundraising and outreach efforts accordingly. Furthermore, texting can foster and maintain strong relationships with donors, expressing gratitude and offering opportunities for involvement in the campaign or cause.

EVENTS

Fundraising events, including rallies, dinners, and receptions, have proven to be an effective means of soliciting donations and engaging donors for conservative candidates. These gatherings not only facilitate the generation of sizable contributions but also foster the development of lasting relationships with donors, which can prove invaluable for the campaign's success.

To maximize the impact of such events, campaigns must carefully plan gatherings that resonate with the campaign's message and captivate the target audience. This involves selecting suitable themes, speakers, and locations, all of which should reflect the candidate's values and objectives. Offering opportunities for donors to interact with the candidate and campaign staff during these events is essential, as it fosters a sense of connection and inspires continued support.

Moreover, a well-executed event can instill a sense of camaraderie among attendees, providing a platform for the exchange of ideas and insights. Such interactions can lead to the formation of a dedicated network of supporters, who may then act as ambassadors for the campaign within their respective circles, broadening the reach and influence of the candidate's message.

values could aid the Republican majority in counteracting the radical agenda of the Democratic Party.

As such, the following phone banking script is intended to act as a foundation for your calling endeavors. Refrain from altering the script's structure; instead, tailor the language to effectively communicate the relevant details of your specific campaign.

Section 1 - The Connection

Hello [Donor's Name], this is [Volunteer's Name] calling on behalf of [Candidate's Name]'s campaign. How are you today?

Listen to their response and engage briefly in a personal conversation, e.g., about their day, family, or work.

Listen, I appreciate you taking the time to briefly chat with me.

Section 2 - The Transition

I wanted to speak with you today because I know you share our passion for [key issue(s) that the donor cares about]. [Candidate's Name] is committed to making a real difference in our community by [briefly describe candidate's solutions to identified problems]. Your support of candidates in the past has been invaluable, and we're reaching out to our dedicated conservatives to help us continue our mission.

Section 3 - The Ask

We're currently working towards our fundraising goal of $[specific amount] by [specific date] to help us [describe how the funds will be used, e.g., running ads, hiring staff, organizing events]. Would you consider making a generous contribution of $[specific suggested amount] to help [Candidate's Name] bring about the change we all want to see?

multiple numbers simultaneously and connects volunteers to live answers; progressive dialing, which dials numbers one at a time, allowing volunteers to preview information about the contact before the call; and call blending, which allows volunteers to switch between inbound and outbound calls. Auto dialers can also be integrated with CRM (customer resource management) systems, making it easier to track interactions with donors and voters.

Two vendors known for providing phone dialer technology to conservative campaigns include CallFire and Victory Solutions—Live Calls. Each of these vendors offers solutions tailored to political campaigns and has a track record of working with conservative candidates.

PHONE BANKING CALL SCRIPT

Phone banking cold calls are commonly directed toward identified voters who have previously supported one or more campaigns or causes. These calls should initially target the candidate's specific district or area of candidacy and progressively broaden outward. It is essential to bear in mind that all politics possess a local dimension.

To illustrate, a donor in Omaha, Nebraska, may have little incentive to care about or contribute to a school board race in Tyler, Texas. When reaching out to known donors beyond your district, it is crucial to contextualize the race within a broader scope, if feasible. For instance, if campaigning for the US Congress in Texas and contacting potential donors in Nebraska, the caller must emphasize the significance of gaining or maintaining the balance of power (the majority) in Congress and the crucial nature of every seat. Additionally, discussing the importance of electing Conservatives who align with the donor's

METHODS OF EXTERNAL FUNDRAISING

OUTSIDE SPENDING AND SUPER PACS

A Super PAC, or Independent Expenditure Only Committee as it is officially called by the FEC, is an independent political organization that can raise unlimited amounts of money from individuals, corporations, unions, and other groups to support or oppose political candidates or issues. Super PACs operate independently from political candidates and campaigns, meaning that they cannot coordinate directly with candidates or their campaigns. However, Super PACs can spend unlimited amounts of money on political advertisements, such as TV and radio ads, mailers, and online ads, to influence the outcome of an election. Super PACs can also engage in other forms of political activity, such as voter mobilization efforts, issue advocacy, and research.

Super PACs were created following the U.S. Supreme Court's 2010 Citizens United v. FEC decision, which removed limits on independent spending by corporations and unions in political campaigns. This decision opened the door for the creation of Super PACs, which are able to raise and spend unlimited amounts of money to influence elections. While Super PACs are not allowed to coordinate directly with political candidates or their campaigns, they can still have significant influence on the political process. The ability to raise and spend unlimited amounts of money allows Super PACs to fund large-scale media campaigns and other political activities that can sway public opinion and influence election outcomes.

The decision to support a particular political candidate is generally made by the leadership of a Super PAC. The leaders of the Super PAC, which can include donors, political strategists, and other influential individuals, decide which candidates to support based on a variety of factors, such as the candidate's political ideology, record, and electability. Super PACs may also focus their support on candidates who are seen as more likely to win or who are in competitive races. In some cases, Super PACs may also support multiple candidates from the same political party or even candidates from opposing parties if they share similar policy positions.

The decision to support a candidate may also be influenced by the interests of the donors who contribute to the Super PAC. Donors may have particular issues or policies that they want to support, and the Super PAC leadership may choose candidates who align with those interests. It's important to note that while Super PACs can raise and spend unlimited amounts of money to support political candidates, they are not permitted to coordinate directly with those candidates or their campaigns. This means that candidates have no control over the messaging or strategies used by Super PACs, which can sometimes lead to negative or controversial ads that candidates may not agree with.

One example of a Republican candidate who was supported by a Super PAC is Mitt Romney during the 2012 presidential election. The Super PAC supporting Romney, called Restore Our Future, spent more than $142 million on advertising and other activities in support of his candidacy. An example of a Democrat who was supported by a Super PAC is Barack Obama during the 2012 presidential election. The Super PAC supporting Obama, called Priorities USA Action, spent more than $65 million on advertising and other activities in support of his candidacy.

During the 2016 presidential election, a Super PAC called Great America PAC supported Donald Trump's campaign. This Super PAC was primarily funded by small-dollar donations from Trump supporters and spent more than $23 million on advertising, voter outreach, and other activities to support his candidacy. Specifically, Great America PAC ran ads in swing states such as Ohio, Pennsylvania, and Florida to promote Trump's positions on issues such as immigration, national security, and job creation.

On the other hand, a Super PAC called Priorities USA Action—the same Super PAC that supported Obama in 2012—supported Hillary Clinton's campaign during the 2016 election. This Super PAC was primarily funded by large donations from wealthy donors, labor unions, and other interest groups and spent more than $126 million on advertising, voter outreach, and other activities to support her candidacy. Specifically, Priorities USA Action ran ads targeting key demographics such as women, minorities, and young voters in swing states such as Florida, Ohio, and Pennsylvania. The ads promoted Clinton's positions on issues such as healthcare, gun control, and reproductive rights, while also attacking Trump's record and statements on various issues.

HOW TO SEEK SUPER PAC ENDORSEMENTS

As a candidate seeking the coveted endorsement and support from Super PACs, it is of utmost importance to engage in diligent outreach and relationship-building endeavors. Remember, politics is sales. Your focus as a candidate seeking the support of Super PACs is to create buy-in and close the deal by getting their commitment to support your campaign. This meticulous process will enable you to present a compelling case for your candidacy, ultimately increasing the likelihood of garnering the support you desire. In this detailed section, the crucial steps for seeking Super PAC endorsements are thoroughly explored.

During Phase 1 of the primary election, begin with thorough research, identifying Super PACs that closely align with your values and policy positions. Delve into their history, analyzing the candidates and issues they have previously supported. This assessment will help you pinpoint Super PACs that have a proven record of endorsing candidates who share your vision and principles. Once you have discerned the Super PACs that seem to be a suitable match, make an effort to obtain contact information for the organization or those individuals responsible for making endorsement and funding decisions. This may involve visiting the Super PAC's website, consulting campaign finance treasurers, or networking with political consultants who have established relationships with the Super PAC in question.

Upon making contact with your target Super PAC, concentrate on cultivating relationships with decision-makers. One way or another, you want to set a meeting with the representatives of the Super PAC. These meetings typically occur in their offices in Washington DC (the majority of large Super PACs are headquartered in or around the Washington DC area) or other location. Attend events or fundraisers where representatives of the Super PAC are likely to be present, engage in meaningful one-on-one conversations with key individuals, and extend invitations to Super PAC representatives to meet with you and your campaign team.

When the opportunity arises to present your case to a Super PAC, be well-prepared to communicate a clear and persuasive vision for your candidacy and policy platform. Remember, scared money, don't make money. That is to say, if you show fear or uncertainty in this meeting, the representatives of the Super PAC will sense it and typically will not support you. You need to be professional, bold (but not obnoxious), and confident (but not arrogant) in your delivery. You want to give them a reason to say yes. Emphasize your accomplishments and credentials, elucidating how your values resonate with those of the Super PAC. In order to effectively present your case to a Super PAC for endorsement, it is crucial to supply them with a comprehensive understanding of your campaign and platform.

Furnish a succinct biography outlining your political experience (if any), accomplishments, and policy positions, ensuring clarity regarding your platform and policy priorities. Detail your campaign strategy and elucidate how you intend to secure victory in your election. Be candid about your fundraising strategy and goals, and depict the political landscape of your district or state and delineate how you plan to navigate it. Prepare an analysis of your opponents, highlighting their strengths and weaknesses. Realize, the Super PAC will verify your information. Therefore, it is important to be truthful, thorough, and forthright in your assessment.

Super PACs are eager to comprehend who you are and what you represent. They seek candidates who embody their values and policy objectives and are inclined to support candidates who possess a well-defined path to victory. Keep in mind, Super PACs see numerous—many times, over 100 different candidates seeking their support. You must give them a reason to say yes. To accomplish this, you must give them the information they are looking for in a format they can digest and understand clearly. Super PACs favor candidates who demonstrate a serious commitment to fundraising and have devised a plan to acquire the necessary resources for a successful campaign. They prefer candidates in winnable districts who possess a profound understanding of the political climate and are well-positioned to succeed. Super PACs are drawn to candidates who can articulate a clear path to victory and expound on their strategy for overcoming their opponents.

Lastly, after making your case, be sure to ask for the sale. That is, ask for their support directly. Make them tell you "yes," "not yet" (this is a conditional yes, as it may be too early for them to give you formal support, or they may want to see how your fundraising performs in the early phases of the campaign), or "no." In high-stakes meetings like these, you want a "yes," "not yet," or "no" and you want to avoid a "maybe" at all costs. Super PACs that say "maybe" are politely telling you "no." If you get told "maybe," follow up immediately and say, "Obviously, I haven't given you the information you need to come to a clear 'yes' or 'no' decision. What further information or details can I provide today that will help us get to a clear decision for your support?" Regardless of the outcome of the meeting—whether they supported you or not—be sure to follow up with the Super PAC and express your gratitude for their time and consideration. Keep the lines of communication open and continue to build the relationship over time. Remember, a strong relationship with Super PACs can be invaluable in bolstering your campaign's success.

FINAL THOUGHTS

Let us reflect on the pivotal role that fundraising plays in the lifeblood of any political campaign. The life force of a campaign is undoubtedly its financial resources, fueling every aspect of its operations, from voter outreach to the dissemination of the candidate's message. It is the cornerstone upon which a campaign's success or failure often hinges, and as such, demands the utmost attention and dedication from all involved, particularly the candidate.

A candidate's personal involvement and leadership in fundraising efforts are of paramount importance. When the candidate themselves takes the helm in orchestrating the campaign's fundraising strategy, it sends a powerful message to potential donors and supporters. It is a testament to the candidate's unwavering commitment to their cause and their determination to triumph in the face of adversity. Through diligent calling efforts and attendance at live events, the candidate is able to forge strong connections with donors, cultivating relationships that may prove invaluable in the long run. In essence, the candidate's active participation in fundraising serves as a rallying cry, galvanizing supporters and inspiring them to invest in the campaign's success.

To maximize the impact of fundraising efforts, a campaign must be well-organized and utilize multiple streams of revenue. A diverse fundraising portfolio not only provides financial stability but also enables the campaign to reach a wider audience of potential donors. By employing a multi-faceted approach that encompasses direct mail, online fundraising, merchandise sales, events, and endorsements from Super PACs (to name but a few), a campaign can tap into a vast reservoir of resources. This strategic diversity in fundraising efforts ensures that the campaign can weather the ebbs and flows of the political landscape and remain steadfast in its mission.

In our final thoughts, let us not forget the immense responsibility that falls upon the candidate and their campaign team in navigating the complex realm of fundraising. It is a journey that requires unwavering dedication, adaptability, and an unyielding drive for success. By heeding the lessons imparted in this chapter, the candidate and their campaign team will be well-equipped to conquer the challenges that lie ahead and ultimately achieve the ultimate victory – the realization of their political aspirations.

As you embark on this noble quest, remember that the foundation of a successful campaign is built upon the relationships you nurture, the values you champion, and the financial support you garner from those who believe in your cause. Your steadfast commitment to fundraising will not only empower your campaign but will also serve as a beacon of hope, inspiring others to join you in your pursuit of a brighter future for all.

CHAPTER 10

TELLING YOUR STORY: THE ART OF THE NARRATIVE

STORYTELLING HAS LONG HELD an esteemed place in the annals of campaigning, functioning as an indispensable instrument for conveying ideas, values, and policy propositions in a manner that is both relatable and memorable. The potency of a masterfully woven narrative has the capacity to be transformative, empowering candidates to establish connections with the electorate, inspire allegiance, and ultimately secure victory. In the realm of conservative campaigns, the crafting of enthralling narratives is particularly vital for resonating with the voting populace and communicating the significance of time-honored values and principles in contemporary society. In this chapter, we shall unravel the complexities of storytelling as they pertain to the conservative political narrative. We shall delve into the six elements of a story— identifying a threat or an opportunity, eliciting fear or hope, pinpointing a victim of a threat or denied opportunity, unmasking a villain, offering a resolution, and celebrating a hero—and examine how each component may be adeptly employed to fabricate a captivating narrative that strikes a chord with conservative and moderate voters.

To comprehend the importance of storytelling in conservative campaigns, one must be cognizant of the broader historical and cultural milieu in which these narratives are embedded. Conservatism, as a political philosophy, frequently accentuates the value of tradition, stability, and continuity, advocating a vision of society that endeavors to safeguard individual liberty and cherished values. Consequently, the narratives woven by conservative candidates must not only engage and persuade voters but also furnish a sense of reassurance and familiarity amidst a rapidly evolving world that is increasingly hostile to conservative values. In an environment where information is copious and attention spans are increasingly fragmented, the prowess to narrate a gripping tale has become paramount for political campaigns. Voters are incessantly assailed by news, opinions, and rival narratives, making it all the more essential for candidates to craft stories that captivate and leave an indelible mark. For conservative campaigns, this entails constructing narratives that not only encapsulate the core tenets of their ideology but also proffer a lucid and persuasive vision of the future that voters can place their faith in.

The six elements of a story offer a valuable blueprint for building such narratives, enabling campaign strategists to meticulously ponder each facet of the story and its contribution to the overarching message. By pinpointing a threat or an opportunity, for instance, conservatives can connect with the apprehensions and aspirations of their target demographic, demonstrating a comprehension of the issues that hold paramount importance for voters. Similarly, by invoking fear or hope, campaigns can instill a sense of urgency, galvanizing voters to spring into action and rally behind the conservative cause. The act of identifying a victim within the narrative serves to humanize the issues at stake, rendering them more relatable and tangible for the audience. This is particularly crucial in conservative narratives, which frequently underscore the impact of policy decisions on ordinary individuals and communities. By illuminating the experiences of these victims, campaigns can engender empathy and illustrate the real-world ramifications of the threats or denied opportunities they endeavor to address. The villain, meanwhile, assumes a pivotal role in erecting a discernible antagonist within the narrative. In campaigns, villains may adopt various guises, from rival politicians and activist factions to foreign menaces and ideological foes. By pinpointing a shared adversary, conservative narratives can rally voters around a common sense of purpose and engender unity in the face of tribulation.

The resolution represents the linchpin of any political narrative, as it proposes the solution to the problem at hand. Within the context of conservative campaigns, the resolution often entails championing conservative principles and policy suggestions as the most efficacious means of addressing the identified threat or opportunity. By proffering a lucid and actionable resolution, conservatives can manifest the practicality and feasibility of their ideas, bolstering confidence in their capacity to effect meaningful change. Lastly, the hero emerges as the central figure in the narrative, embodying the values, experience, and qualities requisite for implementing the proposed resolution. In all campaigns, the hero is customarily the candidate themselves, with the narrative striving to position them as the ideal standard-bearer for the conservative cause. By showcasing the candidate's background, personal values, and devotion to traditional principles, the narrative can foster trust and credibility with voters, convincing them that the candidate is the most fitting leader to steer the nation in the face of the identified threats or opportunities.

As we delve into each of these six elements in depth throughout this chapter, it is paramount to bear in mind that the most effective narratives are those that are both genuine and emotionally evocative. Authenticity is crucial, as voters can rapidly grow disenchanted with campaigns that appear insincere or manipulative. In crafting their narratives, conservative campaigns should endeavor to remain faithful to their core values and principles, while concurrently acknowledging the complexities and subtleties of the issues they seek to address. Emotional resonance, on the other hand, is the very attribute that ultimately permits a narrative to forge profound connections with voters. By skillfully interweaving the six elements of a story—threat or opportunity, fear or hope, victim, villain, resolution, and hero—campaigns can concoct narratives that elicit potent emotional reactions, inspiring voters to not only endorse the candidate but also become champions of their campaign.

In a world that is evolving at breakneck speed, the mastery of crafting compelling narratives has assumed unparalleled importance for political campaigns. For candidates, comprehending and adeptly employing the six elements of a story can make all the difference in resonating with voters, communicating the significance of America First values, and ultimately, securing electoral victory. As we probe deeper into each of these elements in the ensuing sections, you will glean valuable insights into the art and science of storytelling within the realm of political campaigns, learning to create mesmerizing narratives that captivate their target audience and withstand the test of time.

PINPOINTING A THREAT OR AN OPPORTUNITY

A threat or an opportunity lays the bedrock for any political narrative, furnishing the driving force for the unfolding tale and setting the stage for the impending conflict and resolution. Within the purview of campaigns, pinpointing a threat or an opportunity is particularly vital, as it constructs the central issue around which the narrative shall be woven. For campaigns, threats frequently pertain to matters such as national security, economic stability, and cultural values, while opportunities might concentrate on economic expansion, job creation, or the preservation of traditional values. To craft an enthralling narrative, it is imperative to meticulously contemplate the nature of the threat or opportunity to be presented and its alignment with the core values and priorities of the conservative target demographic. This process commences with an exhaustive analysis of the political terrain, factoring in elements such as the prevailing economic conditions, the geopolitical state of affairs, societal trends, and the concerns of the electorate.

By scrutinizing these factors, campaigns can discern potential threats or opportunities that strike a chord with their target audience. For instance, amid economic uncertainty, a campaign may emphasize the threat of unemployment and the erosion of the middle class, underscoring the necessity for pro-growth policies and an unwavering commitment to job creation. Conversely, in the face of burgeoning cultural or demographic shifts, a campaign might accentuate the significance of safeguarding traditional values and institutions, proffering an opportunity to rally voters around a mutual vision of society.

Once a broadly common threat or opportunity has been pinpointed, it is crucial for campaigns to devise a lucid and coherent narrative that effectively conveys the issue to voters. This entails not only presenting the threat or. opportunity in an easily comprehensible manner but also framing it within the broader context of the campaign's message and objectives. By connecting the identified threat or opportunity to the campaign's overarching themes and values, campaigns can create a cohesive and captivating narrative that resonates with their target audience on a macro and micro level.

A prime example of this approach is exemplified by the 1980 United States presidential election when Ronald Reagan's campaign spotlighted the threat of economic stagnation and the opportunity for economic growth through free-market policies. During that period, the United States grappled with high inflation, high unemployment, and low economic growth, leading a multitude of voters to feel disenchanted and apprehensive about the nation's future. Reagan's campaign capitalized on these concerns, framing the election as a critical juncture wherein voters possessed the opportunity to choose between two disparate visions for the future: one characterized by continued stagnation under the Carter administration, and another defined by revitalized prosperity and growth through the implementation of conservative, free-market policies. By juxtaposing the threat of economic stagnation with the opportunity for economic growth, Reagan's campaign skillfully crafted a potent narrative that resonated with voters and ultimately contributed to his win.

In addition to pinpointing threats or opportunities that align with the concerns of the target audience, it is equally crucial for campaigns to ponder the wider ramifications of their chosen narrative. This encompasses assessing the potential risks and benefits of concentrating on a specific issue, as well as contemplating how the narrative might be received by diverse segments of the population. By judiciously evaluating these factors, campaigns can forge narratives that not only resonate with their core supporters but also possess the potential to sway undecided voters and broaden their base of support. For instance, a campaign opting to focus on the threat of illegal immigration through our southern border might run the risk of estranging certain demographic groups or being perceived (or accused by the left) as divisive. In such scenarios, it might be more fruitful for the campaign to frame the issue of illegal immigration in terms of national security, human rights tragedies or economic stability, emphasizing the necessity for responsible immigration policies such as building a border wall that safeguard the interests of citizens, hamper the business of the cartels, and uphold the rule of law, while protecting immigrants who entered the country legally.

IDENTIFYING FEAR OR HOPE

Fear and hope are potent emotions that play a pivotal role in shaping political narratives, serving to create a sense of urgency and drive action among voters. In the context of campaigns, skillful use of fear and hope is vital for resonating with the target audience and garnering support for the campaign's proposed solutions. Fear is often employed to underscore the consequences of inaction, spotlighting the potential hazards and adverse outcomes that could arise from failing to address the identified threats or opportunities. Conversely, hope is harnessed to inspire confidence in the proposed solutions, offering a vision of a brighter future achievable through the implementation of conservative policies and principles.

To craft captivating narratives, campaigns must pinpoint fears or hopes that resonate with their target audience, tapping into the concerns, aspirations, and values that underlie the conservative worldview. This process commences with a comprehensive understanding of the campaign's target audience, encompassing an analysis of their demographic characteristics, political leanings, and the issues that matter most to them. By gaining insights into the fears and hopes that drive their audience, campaigns can tailor their narratives to address these emotions and forge a powerful emotional connection with voters.

One example of a campaign that effectively utilized fear and hope in its narrative is the Brexit campaign in the United Kingdom. In the lead-up to the referendum on whether the UK should leave the European Union, the pro-Brexit campaign tapped into widespread fears of unbridled immigration, loss of sovereignty, and the perceived adverse impact of EU regulations on the British economy. Simultaneously, the campaign offered the hope of heightened national independence, the potential for new trade opportunities, and the promise of a more prosperous and self-determined future outside the EU. The Brexit campaign's success in mobilizing voters around these fears and hopes exemplifies the potential of fear and hope as powerful narrative tools in conservative campaigns. By identifying and addressing the emotions underpinning their audience's beliefs and attitudes, campaigns can create a sense of urgency and inspire action among voters, ultimately contributing to their electoral success.

To effectively weave fear or hope into their narratives, campaigns should consider the following guidelines:

Be Specific and Relatable: To connect with voters on an emotional level, the fears and hopes presented in a narrative must be specific and relatable. Rather than relying on abstract concepts or generalized statements, offer concrete examples and anecdotes that illustrate the potential consequences of inaction and/or the benefits of the proposed solutions. By rendering the fears and hopes tangible and relatable, campaigns can establish a stronger emotional connection with their audience.

Balancing Fear and Hope: For campaigns to flourish, they must acknowledge the potent influence of fear while skillfully interweaving hope. Overemphasizing fear alone could plunge voters into despondency and skepticism (for example, the "It's Rigged" narrative that was pervasive during the 2022 election cycle), causing them to not participate in the election. When campaigns infuse hope in the guise of attainable, practical solutions, they ignite optimism and self-assurance among voters, inspiring them to rally behind the candidate's campaign.

Align With the Campaign's Essential Values and Aims: The fears and hopes entwined in a narrative must synchronize with the campaign's essential values and objectives, fortifying the overarching message and crafting a unified narrative. For instance, a campaign accentuating national security could underscore the dread of foreign adversaries or the threat of nuclear war, whilst offering the promise of a secure future through the enforcement of robust defense strategies and the opportunity for peace. By aligning fears and hopes with the campaign's primary themes, campaigns can devise narratives that reverberate with their target audience and reinforce their pivotal messages.

Steer Clear of Fearmongering and Unfounded Pledges: In their pursuit to elicit fear and hope among voters, campaigns ought to refrain from fearmongering or unfounded promises. Overblown statements or deceitful information can erode a campaign's credibility and estrange voters. Rather, campaigns must endeavor to present precise, equitable information that underlines legitimate concerns voters harbor, while also proffering well-founded, viable solutions. Upholding honesty and integrity within narratives enables the candidate to forge trust with their audience, guaranteeing long-term success in their messaging.

Adapt to the Shifting Tides: As the political landscape undergoes transformation, so too must the fears and hopes that captivate voters. Campaigns ought to remain flexible, adapting narratives to the evolving circumstances and pinpointing new or emergent fears and hopes that mirror their audience's apprehensions and ambitions. This may call for reevaluating campaign messages, perpetually engaging in research and analysis, and consistently modifying the narrative to ensure sustained relevance and resonance with voters.

Master the Art of Storytelling: To effectively invoke fear and hope, campaigns must hone their storytelling prowess. This entails utilizing vibrant imagery, persuasive language, and emotionally charged anecdotes that breathe life into the fears and hopes. By wielding effective storytelling techniques, campaigns can weave narratives that ensnare voters' imaginations, allowing them to undergo the emotional journey of fear and hope, and ultimately impelling them to act.

To summarize, the identification and adept utilization of fear and hope are indispensable elements of any efficacious political narrative, particularly for conservative campaigns. By discerning the fears and hopes that drive their audience, and by deftly interlacing these emotions into their narratives, campaigns can fabricate potent, emotionally charged stories that incite action among voters, leading to victory. By adhering to the principles delineated above, campaigns can channel the energy of fear and hope to construct compelling narratives that resonate with their target audience and promote their policy objectives and ideological tenets.

DISCERNING THE PLIGHT OF THE AFFLICTED AND DISADVANTAGED

Cultivating empathy and involvement within a political narrative frequently hinges on recognizing those who suffer from adversity or missed opportunities due to the action or inaction of the government. By sharing the ordeals of these individuals, campaigns can render the issues at hand more personal, eliciting compassion and comprehension from voters, thus inspiring them to endorse the proposed resolutions. Victims may embody individuals, groups, or even entire communities, and their accounts can serve to exemplify the real-world ramifications of the dangers or opportunities the campaign aspires to confront. This represents a facet of storytelling in which candidates from the Democratic Party have customarily demonstrated proficiency. In the realm of conservative campaigns, pinpointing those afflicted by adversity or deprived opportunities can prove particularly potent in inciting a sense of urgency and marshaling support for conservative principles and policies. By displaying the experiences of those detrimentally impacted by the issues at hand, conservative campaigns can underscore the indispensability of their suggested remedies and create an irresistible call to action for voters.

To proficiently weave the stories of victims into their narratives, conservative campaigns should contemplate the following principles:

Select Identifiable and Compassionate Victims: The victims chosen for a narrative should be identifiable and evoke compassion from the target audience, arousing empathy and concern for their misfortune. This may involve selecting victims who possess similar demographic traits, values, or experiences as the target audience or who have confronted challenges that reverberate with the audience's own apprehensions and worries.

Offer Precise and Comprehensive Accounts: To forge a potent emotional bond with voters, victims' stories should be explicit and comprehensive, enabling the audience to grasp the full scope of their anguish or loss. This may involve providing background details on the victim's personal history, delineating the circumstances that precipitated their victimization, and spotlighting the repercussions of the adversity or denied opportunity on their lives.

Connect the Victim's Ordeal to the Campaign's Overarching Themes and Objectives: The experiences of the victims should be connected to the campaign's all-encompassing themes and objectives, reinforcing the overall narrative and illustrating the pertinence of the proposed solutions. For instance, a campaign centered on economic expansion might exhibit the stories of small business proprietors negatively affected by excessive regulation, utilizing their experiences to demonstrate the need for pro-growth policies and the reduction of bureaucratic constraints.

Employ the Victim's Narrative to Generate Urgency and a Call to Action: The portrayal of the victim's narrative should evoke a sense of urgency and a call to action among voters, motivating them to support the campaign's suggested solutions to avert further anguish or loss. This may involve accentuating the potential consequences of inaction, the prospects for positive transformation, and the necessity for collective endeavor to tackle the identified perils or opportunities.

Exercising Tact and Sensitivity: When sharing the accounts of victims, it is paramount for conservative campaigns to treat the subject matter with respect and consideration. The experiences of victims can be profoundly personal and distressing, and it is crucial to ensure their stories are conveyed in a way that upholds their dignity and privacy. This may entail acquiring consent from the victims or their families, while also avoiding sensationalism or exploitation.

Emphasize Resilience and Fortitude: Alongside illustrating the challenges victims face, campaigns should underscore their resilience and strength amid adversity. By showcasing victims' ability to surmount obstacles and reconstruct their lives, campaigns can foster hope and optimism among voters, bolstering the potential for positive change through the realization of conservative policies and principles.

Offer a Stage for Victims' Narratives: To further personalize the issues and foster a deeper bond with voters, your campaign might contemplate providing a platform for victims to directly share their stories with the public. This could encompass public speeches, interviews, or testimonials, enabling victims to express their experiences and the influence of the identified threats or opportunities on their lives in their own words. By granting victims a voice and empowering them to tell their stories, candidates can create an authentic and emotionally poignant narrative that resonates with voters.

Employ Diverse Channels to Disseminate Victims' Stories: To engage a broad range of voters and maximize the impact of their narratives, campaigns should employ diverse mediums to disseminate victims' stories. This may include traditional communication methods, such as print and broadcast media, as well as digital platforms like websites, social media, podcasts, and video content. By utilizing multiple channels to share victims' stories, campaigns can ensure their message reaches the largest possible audience, fostering empathy and engagement among voters. An excellent example of a campaign adeptly utilizing victims in its narrative is Donald Trump's 2016 United States presidential campaign. In this campaign, Donald Trump identified victims of globalization and economic shifts, such as blue-collar workers who lost their jobs due to outsourcing or the decline of manufacturing industries. By accentuating these victims' stories, Trump's campaign generated empathy and understanding among voters who harbored similar concerns about the repercussions of economic change on their own lives and communities.

The campaign's emphasis on the experiences of these victims also served to reinforce its wider themes of economic nationalism, trade protectionism, and the necessity for resolute leadership to rejuvenate American prosperity. By connecting victims' stories to these overarching themes, the campaign constructed a cohesive and emotionally evocative narrative that resonated with a vast array of voters, ultimately contributing to Trump's victory.

To summarize, the adept identification and incorporation of victims into a political narrative can be a potent instrument for cultivating empathy and engagement among voters. By demonstrating the tangible consequences of threats or missed opportunities, campaigns can humanize the issues at hand, generate a sense of urgency, and rally support for their suggested solutions. By adhering to the guidelines delineated above, candidates can create emotionally captivating narratives that resonate with their target audience, leading to electoral success and ultimately advancing their policy objectives and ideological tenets.

IDENTIFYING A VILLAIN

A clear antagonist is essential for establishing conflict within a political narrative, as it fosters a sense of opposition and urgency. For campaigns, antagonists can take various forms, such as rival politicians, activist groups, or foreign threats. By pinpointing an antagonist, campaigns can effectively position themselves as the champions of their constituents' values and interests, rallying support for their policies and principles.

Identifying a villain in a campaign involves several key considerations:

Select a Pertinent and Credible Villain: To engage their target audience effectively, campaigns should identify an antagonist that is both pertinent and credible. The chosen adversary should represent a genuine threat or challenge to the audience's values, interests, or well-being and be perceived as having the power or influence to cause harm or enact change. By selecting a relevant and credible antagonist, campaigns can create a sense of urgency and motivate voters to support their proposed solutions.

Refrain From Caricaturing or Demonizing Opponents: While it might be tempting for campaigns to caricature or demonize their opponents to generate a stronger sense of conflict, this approach can ultimately backfire by alienating moderate voters and undermining the credibility of the campaign's narrative. Instead, campaigns should strive for a balanced and nuanced portrayal of their chosen antagonist, acknowledging their legitimate concerns or perspectives while emphasizing the areas of disagreement and opposition.

The remarkable success of Donald Trump in the 2016 election can be attributed to his distinctive approach to campaigning, which deviated from conventional political strategies. Although it is generally inadvisable for candidates to caricature and demonize their opponents, Trump managed to connect with the electorate in a unique way. By tapping into the emotions of the populace, he employed an unorthodox method that resonated with many voters who sought a change in the political landscape. Trump's campaign capitalized on the desire for a non-traditional leader, one who could challenge the status quo and bring about transformative change. In doing so, he demonstrated an uncanny ability to understand the mindset of the disenchanted voter, speaking to their aspirations and fears. This connection allowed him to circumvent the pitfalls associated with a more aggressive approach to portraying his opponents.

Ultimately, Trump's success in the 2016 election can be viewed as a testament to the power of an individual who knows how to harness the emotions of the masses and transform them into a driving force for change, even when employing methods that defy conventional wisdom. Although the distinctive approach employed by Donald Trump's campaign proved fruitful in his particular case, the unique circumstances surrounding his election must be acknowledged. Ordinarily, it is wise to refrain from resorting to caricaturing or vilifying one's opponent in order to intensify conflict, as it may not yield the desired outcome and will likely backfire.

Connect the Antagonist to the Identified Threats or Opportunities: To create a cohesive narrative, the chosen antagonist should be directly linked to the identified threats or opportunities. This connection should be clear and explicit, demonstrating how the antagonist's actions or policies have contributed to the negative outcomes experienced by the victims or have the potential to do so in the future. Establishing a direct link between the antagonist and the identified threats or opportunities allows candidates to create a more compelling and persuasive narrative that resonates with voters.

Be Adaptable and Responsive to Changing Circumstances: In the ever-changing world of politics, it is vital to remain flexible and adapt to shifting circumstances. As villains that resonate with voters evolve, campaigns must be prepared to adjust their narratives accordingly, identifying new or emerging adversaries that align with their audience's concerns and interests. This may involve reevaluating key messages, conducting ongoing research and analysis, and fine-tuning the narrative to ensure it remains relevant and resonant with voters.

Create a Clear Contrast Between the Villain and the Campaign's Proposed Hero: When identifying a villain, establish a clear contrast between the antagonist and the campaign's proposed hero or solution. Highlight the differences in values, beliefs, or policy proposals, illustrating how the campaign's hero or solution is better suited to address the identified threats or opportunities. A stark contrast will underscore the importance of the campaign's policies and principles, garnering further support from the target audience.

Use The Villain as a Rallying Point for Collective Action: Encourage voters to unite and cooperate against the identified villain, emphasizing shared values and interests. This sense of unity and shared purpose can drive support for the campaign's policies and principles.

Be Mindful of Potential Backlash: While identifying a villain can generate support, be cautious of potential backlash, especially if the chosen villain is well-liked, controversial or polarizing. To mitigate backlash risks, present a balanced and nuanced portrayal of the villain, avoiding inflammatory or divisive rhetoric that could alienate moderate voters or fuel counter-narratives. By being mindful of potential backlash, campaigns can ensure their narrative remains credible and persuasive to a broad audience.

Finally, successfully identifying and portraying a villain is a crucial component of any political narrative, particularly for conservative campaigns. By understanding the villains that resonate with their target audience and following the guidelines outlined above, candidates can craft compelling narratives that effectively position themselves as defenders of their constituents' values and interests. This approach can help generate support for their policies and principles, leading to electoral success and the advancement of their ideological objectives.

CRAFTING A SOLUTION

In a political narrative, the solution to the problem presented is vital, as it demonstrates the effectiveness of conservative principles and policies. When constructing a narrative, it is crucial to offer a clear and actionable solution that addresses the identified challenges or opportunities. By providing an enticing solution, candidates can position themselves as the best choice for voters, garnering support for their policies and principles. In this section, we will outline the essential considerations for crafting a solution within the context of a campaign.

Align The Solution with Conservative Principles: For the solution to be effective, it must align with the foundational principles and values of the conservative ideology. These principles may include limited government, individual liberty, free-market capitalism, and traditional values. By ensuring that the solution aligns with these and other conservative principles, campaigns can create a cohesive narrative that resonates with their target audience and underscores the importance of their ideological beliefs.

Make the Solution Specific and Actionable: To persuade voters, the proposed solution must be specific and actionable, offering a clear understanding of the steps that will be taken to address the identified challenges or opportunities. This may involve outlining particular policy proposals, legislative initiatives, or organizational strategies that will be implemented if the campaign is successful. By providing a specific and actionable solution, campaigns can create a sense of urgency and momentum, motivating voters to support their policies and principles.

For instance, in the 2010 United States midterm elections, the Tea Party movement proposed solutions such as limited government, lower taxes, and strict adherence to the Constitution to address the perceived threats of government overreach and fiscal irresponsibility. By presenting specific policy proposals that aligned with their core principles, the Tea Party garnered significant support and achieved victory.

Illustrate the Effectiveness of the Solution: To further enhance the persuasiveness of the proposed solution, conservative campaigns should showcase its effectiveness in addressing the identified challenges or opportunities. This can be done by providing evidence from historical examples, case studies, or expert testimonials that demonstrate how similar solutions have succeeded in the past. By illustrating the effectiveness of their proposed solutions, conservative campaigns can build credibility and trust among voters, increasing the likelihood that they will support their policies and principles.

Address Potential Objections or Concerns: In order to create a persuasive narrative, campaigns must address potential objections or concerns that may arise from their target audience or political opponents. This involves acknowledging potential drawbacks or trade-offs associated with the proposed solution while emphasizing the benefits and advantages that outweigh these concerns. By tackling potential objections, campaigns can craft a more balanced and credible narrative, increasing the likelihood that voters will be persuaded by their proposed solutions.

Allow us to consider an example where the principle of addressing potential objections or concerns has been put into practice with notable success. During the 1960 presidential campaign, John F. Kennedy, the Democratic candidate, faced the challenge of addressing concerns surrounding his youth and inexperience, as well as the fact that he was the first Catholic candidate for the presidency. Kennedy astutely recognized that these concerns had the potential to deter voters from supporting his bid for the highest office in the land.

Kennedy confronted these objections head-on, presenting a compelling counter-narrative that emphasized his commitment to the values of the American people and his ability to bring a fresh perspective to the presidency. He successfully highlighted the advantages of his youth, framing it as a source of energy and innovation, while assuring voters that his religious beliefs would not interfere with his commitment to respecting the values of all Americans. In doing so, Kennedy demonstrated the importance of directly addressing potential objections or concerns, crafting a persuasive narrative that ultimately secured him a narrow victory in the 1960 election.

Present the Solution as an Alternative to the Villain's Methods: To further emphasize the contrast between the campaign's narrative and the identified villain, campaigns should showcase their proposed solution as a clear alternative to the villain's methods. This involves underlining the differences in values, beliefs, or policy proposals and demonstrating how the campaign's proposed solution is better equipped to address the identified challenges or opportunities. By creating a stark contrast between the solution and the villain's approach, conservative campaigns can reinforce the significance of their own policies and principles, garnering support from their target audience.

Adapt the Solution to Shifting Circumstances: As the political landscape evolves, so too do the challenges, opportunities, and concerns that resonate with voters. Campaigns must be prepared to adapt their solutions to changing circumstances, ensuring that their proposed remedies remain relevant and effective in addressing the needs and concerns of their target audience. This may involve reassessing the campaign's key messages, conducting ongoing research and analysis, and adjusting the solution as needed to maintain relevance and resonance with voters.

Communicate the Advantages of the Solution to the Identified Victims: To foster empathy and engagement with the political narrative, it is essential to communicate the benefits of the proposed solution to the identified victims of the threat or denied opportunity. This involves outlining how the solution will directly address the negative outcomes experienced by these individuals or groups or how it will help prevent future harm or loss. By clearly communicating the advantages of the solution to the identified victims, campaigns can create a more persuasive and impactful narrative that resonates with voters.

Present the Resolution as a Rallying Point for Collective Action: One of the paramount objectives of presenting a resolution is to forge a rallying point for collective action, inspiring voters to unite in support of the campaign's proposed solutions. To accomplish this, campaigns ought to emphasize the necessity for unity and collaboration in the face of the identified challenges or opportunities, underscoring the common values and interests that unite the target audience. By showcasing the resolution as a rallying point, campaigns can cultivate a sense of camaraderie and shared purpose among voters, propelling support for their policies and principles.

Exercise Caution to Avoid Potential Backlash: While proposing a resolution can be a potent strategy for garnering support, it is crucial for campaigns to remain aware of potential backlash, particularly if the proposed solution is controversial or polarizing. To mitigate the risk of backlash, campaigns ought to present a balanced and nuanced portrayal of the resolution, steering clear of overly inflammatory or divisive rhetoric that could alienate moderate voters or fuel counter-narratives. By remaining vigilant of potential backlash, candidates can ensure that their narrative retains credibility and persuasiveness for the broadest possible audience.

In closing, the identification and presentation of a resolution are vital elements of any fruitful political narrative, especially in the context of conservative campaigns. By understanding the challenges and opportunities that resonate with their target audience and adhering to the guidelines delineated above, candidates can craft compelling narratives that effectively position themselves as the optimal choice for voters. This approach, in turn, can aid in generating support for their policies and principles, contributing to their overall electoral success and the advancement of their ideological objectives. By providing clear, actionable, and efficacious resolutions, campaigns can demonstrate the merit of their principles and policies to voters, fostering support and nurturing a sense of unity and shared purpose.

WE SAY/THEY SAY

In the realm of strategic communication, especially in the world of political campaigns, lies the indispensable tool known as the "we say/they say" concept. This invaluable method assists in crafting and defining persuasive narratives while foreseeing and addressing the narratives presented by one's opponent.

Initiate the "we say/they say" exercise by formulating a clear and concise statement representing the position you wish to advocate or uphold. With a lucid understanding of your own narrative, proceed to anticipate the probable arguments, claims, or messages your rival may convey. This step may involve investigating their prior declarations, studying their policy stances, or scrutinizing the general trends and attitudes within their political party or ideology.

Upon identifying the expected counterarguments, it becomes crucial to devise well-reasoned and convincing responses that tackle the opponent's concerns while bolstering your own narrative. This may entail presenting facts, figures, anecdotes, or logical reasoning that corroborate your standpoint while debunking or refuting the opposing argument. Maintain respect and professionalism throughout the exercise, as the objective is to sway undecided or neutral individuals rather than estrange potential supporters.

The "we say/they say" method holds particular utility in campaigns for several reasons. Firstly, it equips candidates and their teams to face debates, interviews, and public appearances with confidence and poise, ready to tackle any challenge or critique. Secondly, by predicting and addressing the opposition's arguments, candidates can demonstrate a profound comprehension of the issues at hand and exhibit their capacity for engaging in constructive discourse. This quality can be especially enticing to undecided voters who appreciate problem-solving and collaboration.

USING WE SAY/THEY SAY IN STORYTELLING

Within the context of political storytelling, a candidate can skillfully utilize the "we say/they say" instrument to weave their story, incorporating the six elements of a story into their messaging while concurrently addressing their opponent's narrative. Each element can be seamlessly integrated within the "we say/they say" framework as follows:

The identification of a threat or an opportunity is the first element. In the "we say" portion of the story, the candidate must concentrate on recognizing a pressing issue or opportunity requiring attention, such as unemployment, climate change, or healthcare reform. In the "they say" segment, the candidate should anticipate their opponent's perspective on the same issue or opportunity and prepare to counter their arguments.

The second element involves eliciting fear or hope. The candidate should provoke emotions in their narrative. In the "we say" portion, they can emphasize the potential negative consequences if the issue remains unaddressed or the opportunity is not seized. Alternatively, they can create a sense of hope by illustrating how their proposed solutions can improve people's lives. In the "they say" segment, they should prepare to counter any fearmongering or false hope propagated by the opponent.

Pinpointing a victim of a threat or denied opportunity constitutes the third element. In the "we say" portion, the candidate should humanize the issue by spotlighting real-life examples of individuals affected by the problem or those who could benefit from the proposed solution. In the "they say" segment, the candidate should be ready to counter any attempts by the opponent to divert focus away from the victims or blame them for their predicament.

The fourth element is unmasking a villain. In the "we say" portion, the candidate should identify the forces, systems, or individuals responsible for the problem or the denial of opportunities. In the "they say" segment, the candidate should anticipate how the opponent might deflect responsibility or attempt to pin the blame on others, and prepare to challenge these claims.

Offering a resolution is the fifth element. In the "we say" portion, the candidate should present a clear and practical solution to the problem or a plan to capitalize on the opportunity. In the "they say" segment, the candidate should be ready to counter any criticisms of their proposed solution or alternative proposals by the opponent.

Lastly, the sixth element is celebrating a hero. In the "we say" portion, the candidate should position themselves as the hero — the individual capable of effectively addressing the issue, seizing the opportunity, and creating positive change. In the "they say" segment, the candidate should be prepared to counter any attempts by the opponent to undermine their credibility or present themselves as a more suitable hero.

CASTING THE HERO:
THE CENTRAL FIGURE OF TRIUMPH

The hero stands as the pivotal character in any political narrative. Within the context of political campaigns, this role is customarily filled by the candidate. By exhibiting the candidate's attributes, values, and experiences, the narrative positions them as the ideal individual to execute the proposed resolution. In this section, we will delve into the crucial aspects of identifying a hero, using examples from victorious campaigns to illustrate the process.

Emphasize the Candidate's Values and Principles: To position the candidate as the hero of the narrative, it is imperative to showcase their dedication to conservative values and principles. This may involve highlighting their policy stances, voting record, or personal beliefs, demonstrating their alignment with the core principles of the conservative ideology. By emphasizing the candidate's values and principles, campaigns can forge a strong connection with their target audience, situating the candidate as a defender of their mutual beliefs.

For instance, in the 1984 United States presidential election, Ronald Reagan was depicted as the hero who would guide the nation toward economic prosperity and robust national defense. His commitment to conservative values, such as limited government, free-market capitalism, and a powerful military, solidified this image in the minds of voters.

Illuminate the Candidate's Personal Qualities: Beyond their values and principles, campaigns should also spotlight the candidate's personal qualities, such as their leadership prowess, charisma, or integrity. These attributes can humanize the candidate and establish a sense of trust and rapport with voters, positioning them as a relatable and inspiring figure. By illuminating the candidate's personal qualities, campaigns can create a more engaging and memorable portrayal of the hero, generating support and enthusiasm among voters. For instance, Reagan's charismatic communication style, often dubbed the "Great Communicator," enabled him to connect with voters on a personal level, further enhancing his image as the hero who would steer the nation toward a brighter future (which he did).

Exhibit The Candidate's Experience and Qualifications: To establish credibility and trust among voters, campaigns should display the candidate's experience and qualifications, showcasing their ability to effectively implement the proposed resolution. The rationale and story statement established during Phase 1 of the primary contest shall adequately satisfy this prerequisite. This may involve highlighting their previous roles in government, business, or civic organizations, as well as their accomplishments and successes in these positions. By exhibiting the candidate's experience and qualifications, conservative campaigns can cultivate confidence in the hero's ability to tackle the identified challenges or opportunities. For instance, Reagan's experience as governor of California demonstrated his capacity to govern effectively and helped solidify his credibility as a potential president.

Position the Candidate as a Contrast to the Villain: To further strengthen the tension between the campaign's narrative and the identified villain, campaigns should present the candidate as a contrast to the villain's approach. This may involve highlighting the differences in values, beliefs, or policy proposals, demonstrating how the candidate's approach is better equipped to address the identified challenges or opportunities. By creating a clear contrast between the hero and the villain, campaigns can reinforce the importance of their own policies and principles, further driving support from their target audience.

During the height of the COVID-19 pandemic, Governor DeSantis faced adversaries who advocated for rigorous lockdown measures and far-reaching mandates, ostensibly to contain the spread of the virus. In contrast, Governor DeSantis staunchly defended the principles of individual liberty and personal responsibility, opting for a more measured approach that prioritized the economic and personal well-being of Florida's citizens over blind obedience to Dr. Fauci's big government solutions of unfettered governmental control. While his opponents sought to impose extensive restrictions and mandates, Governor DeSantis highlighted the potential negative consequences of such actions, such as economic downturns and a loss of personal freedoms. Instead, he proposed targeted measures that emphasized personal choice and risk assessment, allowing businesses to remain open and individuals to make informed decisions about their own health and safety.

By clearly contrasting his own approach with that of his adversaries, Governor DeSantis showcased his commitment to preserving liberty and prosperity in the face of challenges. This unmistakable contrast between the hero, Governor DeSantis, and the antagonists who favored a more stringent response to the crisis, exemplified by the Trump administration and Dr. Fauci, underscored the significance of his conservative principles, attracting backing from individuals who cherished liberty and personal choice amidst the pandemic. Governor DeSantis went on to win reelection as Florida's Governor by the widest margin in 40 years.

Establish the Hero's Connection to The Identified Victims: To foster empathy and engagement within the political narrative, campaigns ought to emphasize the hero's bond with the identified victims of the threat or denied opportunity. This could involve underlining the candidate's personal experiences or relationships with impacted individuals, groups, or communities, manifesting their comprehension of the hardships faced by these victims and their dedication to addressing their needs. By illustrating the hero's connection to the identified victims, campaigns can render a more relatable and empathetic portrayal of the candidate, inciting support and enthusiasm among the electorate. For instance, during the 2016 United States presidential election, Donald Trump resonated with blue-collar workers who had lost their jobs due to outsourcing or the decline of manufacturing industries by underscoring his commitment to repatriate jobs to America and rejuvenate these struggling communities.

Exhibit the Hero's Persistence and Fortitude: To create an inspiring and enthralling portrayal of the hero, campaigns should display the candidate's persistence and fortitude in the face of adversity. This could entail sharing accounts of personal challenges or setbacks that the candidate has surmounted or emphasizing their capacity to persevere despite opposition or criticism. By presenting the hero's persistence and fortitude, campaigns can craft a more inspiring and memorable representation of the candidate, stimulating support and enthusiasm among the voters. For instance, during the 2016 United States presidential election, Donald Trump's campaign underscored his fortitude in the face of various controversies and setbacks, positioning him as a combatant who would never abandon his mission to "Make America Great Again."

Employ Endorsements and Testimonials to Bolster the Hero's Credibility: Endorsements and testimonials from esteemed individuals or organizations can serve to fortify the hero's credibility and augment their image in the minds of the electorate. By showcasing the backing of key figures within the conservative movement, as well as distinguished members of the community, campaigns can foster a sense of legitimacy and trust in the hero's capacity to tackle the identified threats or opportunities. For instance, during the 1980 United States presidential election, Ronald Reagan secured the endorsement of several influential conservative organizations and individuals, such as the National Rifle Association and evangelical leader Jerry Falwell, which bolstered his credibility among conservative evangelical voters.

Adapt the Depiction of the Hero to the Shifting Political Landscape: As the political landscape transforms, campaigns must be prepared to modify the depiction of the hero to ensure continued pertinence and resonance with the electorate. This could involve reassessing the campaign's core messages, adjusting the candidate's image or policy proposals, or altering the hero's journey to reflect evolving circumstances. By demonstrating adaptability and responsiveness to the shifting political landscape, conservative campaigns can guarantee that their portrayal of the hero remains persuasive and credible to the broadest possible audience.

A prudent reminder is in order at this juncture. During the 2016 Presidential election, the Clinton campaign endeavored to soften Hillary Clinton's stern public image, casting her as an amiable, grandmotherly figure. Regrettably for the campaign, this attempt utterly failed, only serving to intensify the public's aversion to Clinton. The campaign neglected to consider that individuals, when under pressure, invariably revert to their true personality rather than maintain a fabricated persona. Each instance of Mrs. Clinton displaying anger, a loss of self-control, or arrogance served to undermine the portrayal the campaign sought to convey. The portrayal simply lacked authenticity, and voters could sense the disingenuousness.

In the process of adapting a candidate to the fluctuating political terrain, it is of utmost importance to ascertain that any transformation corresponds with their authentic nature. Presenting a candidate as someone they are not should be avoided at all costs. Instead of endeavoring to portray Mrs. Clinton in a gentler manner, the campaign should have crafted a narrative where she could be presented as a resilient female leader, tempered by the trials of a male-dominated Washington D.C. political sphere. This approach would have been congruous with her disposition, granting voters a rationale for tolerating Mrs. Clinton's less endearing characteristics.

During the early 1930s, the United States found itself in the throes of the Great Depression, a period of profound economic turmoil and widespread despair. As the political climate evolved, so too did the public's priorities and concerns. Recognizing the opportunity for decisive action and transformative policies, Franklin D. Roosevelt crafted his presidential campaign around the New Deal, a series of ambitious socialist programs designed to address the nation's most pressing issues (an example of never allowing a good crisis to go to waste).

Throughout his campaign and subsequent tenure in office, Roosevelt persistently modified his depiction as the hero to harmonize with the ever-evolving political landscape. As new challenges surfaced, he tailored his policies and messages to maintain continued pertinence and connection with the electorate. For instance, he broadened the scope of the New Deal to encompass not only economic revival but also social reform and financial regulation, responding to the fluid public sentiment and the transforming needs of the nation. As World War II ignited in Europe and the US economy faced stagnation despite (or as a consequence of) his progressive reforms, Roosevelt adeptly adapted his image as the valiant hero who confronted the menacing forces of the Nazis and the Empire of Japan.

In summation, identifying and depicting a hero are essential elements of any efficacious political narrative, particularly concerning conservative campaigns. By grasping the significance of values, personal attributes, experience, and storytelling techniques, and adhering to the guidelines delineated above, campaigns can create captivating narratives that effectively position their candidate as the quintessential individual to implement the proposed resolution. This approach, consequently, can help to garner support for their policies and principles, contributing to their overall electoral victory and the advancement of their ideological goals. By presenting a robust and inspiring hero, campaigns can reverberate with voters and foster a sense of trust, enthusiasm, and backing for their candidate.

CASE STUDY:
THE 1980 PRESIDENTIAL ELECTION PRESIDENT JIMMY CARTER VS. RONALD REAGAN

In this case study, we will examine the 1980 United States presidential race between Ronald Reagan, the Republican candidate, and Jimmy Carter, the incumbent Democratic president. This campaign provides a prime example of how Reagan effectively utilized the six elements of a story to create a compelling narrative that resonated with the American electorate and ultimately contributed to his electoral victory. The following paragraphs will provide a detailed account of how each element was employed by Reagan and his campaign team.

Identifying a Threat or an Opportunity: The foundation of Reagan's campaign narrative was the recognition of several key threats and opportunities. The United States was experiencing a period of economic stagnation, characterized by high inflation, high unemployment, and slow economic growth. Reagan emphasized these economic challenges as a significant threat to the American way of life, underscoring the need for a new approach to governance. In addition to the economic threats, Reagan also focused on the perceived decline of American global influence, particularly concerning the Soviet Union. The opportunity Reagan presented was a vision of economic growth and renewed global leadership, which he argued could be achieved through the implementation of free-market policies, tax cuts, and a robust national defense.

Eliciting Fear or Hope: Reagan's campaign masterfully evoked both fear and hope in the American electorate. He kindled fears about the consequences of continued economic stagnation, asserting that the nation was at a critical juncture and that decisive action was needed to prevent further decline. The slogan "Are you better off than you were four years ago?" encapsulated this sentiment and effectively framed the election as a referendum on Carter's handling of the economy. On the other hand, Reagan's campaign also offered hope, presenting a vision of a prosperous and strong America. His optimistic rhetoric and the idea of "Morning in America" inspired confidence in the proposed solutions and the belief that the nation could overcome its challenges.

Pinpointing a Victim of a Threat or Denied Opportunity: Reagan's campaign successfully humanized the economic issues at stake by identifying the victims of the economic stagnation. These victims included small business owners struggling with high taxes and regulations, blue-collar workers facing unemployment due to factory closures, and families grappling with the rising cost of living. By highlighting the experiences of these individuals and groups, Reagan's campaign was able to create empathy and engagement with the American electorate, making the consequences of the economic challenges more tangible and relatable.

Unmasking a Villain: The antagonists within the campaign narrative appeared in dual forms, both internal and external. Internally, Reagan aimed his sights at the Carter administration and its policies, holding them responsible for the nation's economic woes, and asserting that their approach to governance had proven ineffective. Externally, Reagan pinpointed the Soviet Union as a primary adversary, emphasizing the necessity of a robust national defense and a resolute stance against the proliferation of communism and the prospect of nuclear war. By presenting clear villains, Reagan's campaign generated a sense of urgency and accentuated the importance of electing a leader who could competently address these threats.

Offering a Resolution: Reagan's campaign offered a lucid and actionable resolution to the identified threats and opportunities. The proposed economic plan, often referred to as "Reaganomics," focused on reducing taxes, deregulation, and minimizing government intervention in the economy. These policies, Reagan argued, would stimulate economic growth, create jobs, and reduce inflation (which it did). In terms of foreign policy, Reagan championed a powerful military and a more assertive approach to global leadership, pledging to confront the Soviet Union and safeguard American interests abroad. By presenting specific policy proposals, the campaign inspired confidence in Reagan's ability to tackle the nation's challenges.

Celebrating a Hero: Lastly, Ronald Reagan was portrayed as the hero of his campaign narrative. His experience as Governor of California, his background as an actor, and his charismatic communication style solidified this image in the minds of voters. Reagan was depicted as a strong, decisive leader who possessed the experience, values, and vision necessary to enact the proposed resolutions and steer the nation toward a brighter future. His optimistic outlook and ability to connect with the American people on a personal level further reinforced his role as the hero in his campaign's narrative.

Throughout the 1980 presidential campaign, Reagan and his team adeptly employed the six elements of a story to create a cohesive and enthralling narrative that resonated with the American electorate. This narrative played a crucial role in shaping the perception of Ronald Reagan as a strong, visionary leader who could address the nation's economic challenges and restore its global standing. The solution proffered by the campaign showcased the efficacy of conservative tenets and strategies, while positioning Reagan as the protagonist solidified the perception of the ideal individual to bring forth the desired changes. Throughout the unfolding narrative, the campaign maintained a congruous tone and message that harmonized with Reagan's overarching objectives and principles, adeptly conveying their ideas and aspirations to the populace.

Ultimately, the potency of the captivating narrative, coupled with the frailties of the Carter administration and a faltering economy, culminated in a resounding triumph for Ronald Reagan in the 1980 presidential race. This victory not only signified a notable political transition within the country but also bore witness to the paramount importance of storytelling in the political sphere. This case study highlights the necessity of devising a persuasive narrative that resonates with the electorate and effectively conveys the candidate's concepts, principles, and vision. By achieving this, America First candidates can garner support and ultimately attain victory, thereby molding the trajectory of the nation's destiny.

FINAL THOUGHTS

In closing, the six components of a story offer a powerful structure for developing captivating narratives within America First campaigns. By pinpointing a relevant threat or opportunity, invoking fear or hope, making the issue personal through affected individuals, introducing a distinct villain, proposing a solution, and positioning the candidate as the protagonist, campaigns can create enthralling stories that connect with voters and ultimately contribute to victory. By mastering these components, America First campaigns can effectively convey their ideas and principles, inspiring support and initiating meaningful transformation in the United States.

CHAPTER 11

BUILDING COALITIONS: THE ART OF UNITING FORCES

IN THE REALM OF POLITICAL ENDEAVORS, the mastery of forging alliances is paramount to triumph. As the political landscape grows ever more diverse in thought and divided, the capacity to gather various factions and individuals with aligned goals and/or values is vital. Through nurturing relationships, recognizing mutual interests, and crafting a unified message, one can bolster the impact and reach of a campaign. The art of uniting forces not only fortifies the foundation of a political candidate but also paves the way for extending their circle of influence. This proves particularly significant for those facing staunch opposition or those whose agendas may not align with the national party. By fostering cooperation and coordination among different groups, they can merge resources, wisdom, and skills to realize a shared purpose. Consequently, the resulting collaboration forges a robust and unified message that resonates with the electorate.

Moreover, alliances can offer candidates invaluable endorsements and connections. By joining forces with key stakeholders and influencers, campaigns can tap into previously uncharted networks, extending their reach and bolstering their chances of winning the hearts and minds of undecided voters. For conservative candidates, the art of uniting forces holds a particularly crucial role in achieving victory. As political landscapes evolve and demographics shift, it becomes increasingly imperative for conservatives to engage with diverse communities and showcase the relevance of their core principles. Building wide-reaching alliances enables conservative candidates to expand beyond their traditional base, mobilize fresh support, and secure electoral wins.

One of the key challenges for conservative candidates lies in addressing the concerns of various factions within the conservative movement itself, including fiscal conservatives, social conservatives, and national security conservatives, among others. By uniting these diverse groups, they ensure a comprehensive representation of conservative values, thereby reinforcing the overall campaign message. Another vital aspect of alliance-building for conservative candidates is reaching out to non-traditional conservative groups. Engaging moderate and independent voters, single-issue voters, and minority communities can expand the conservative support base and provide a more multi-dimensional representation of conservative values. By doing so, conservative candidates present themselves as attractive options to a wider range of voters.

Alliances can also aid conservative candidates in navigating complex policy issues by drawing upon the expertise of various partner organizations. This collaboration empowers the candidate to develop well-informed and comprehensive policy proposals, contributing to increased credibility and support among the electorate. Furthermore, alliances can assist in refining campaign messaging and strategy. By incorporating input from diverse partners, conservative candidates can develop tailored messaging that addresses the concerns and priorities of different constituents. This targeted approach enhances the campaign's effectiveness in reaching and persuading undecided voters.

The art of uniting forces is of utmost importance in political campaigns, particularly for conservative candidates. Traditionally, alliance building has not been an activity at which conservative candidates and organizations have been particularly skilled. By gathering diverse groups and individuals under a common set of values and goals, they can build far-reaching support networks that elevate their chances of winning elections. As demographics and political landscapes continue to transform, the ability to form and maintain alliances will remain a crucial factor in the success of conservative campaigns.

THE PILLARS OF ALLIANCE-BUILDING

The process of forging successful alliances is indispensable for political candidates seeking to unite various groups and individuals under a common set of values and/or goals. By adhering to a series of fundamental principles, candidates can create solid, unified alliances that effectively amplify their message and broaden their support base. One of the foundational pillars of alliance-building is the identification of shared values and/or goals among potential partners. This involves understanding the priorities, motivations, and concerns of each group, and discovering common ground that can serve as the basis for collaboration. By focusing on these shared values and/or goals, a campaign can create a strong foundation for cooperation and coordination. Identifying these commonalities can also help bridge gaps between groups with seemingly divergent interests, allowing them to work together towards a common objective.

Another vital pillar is placing emphasis on common ground rather than differences. While alliance partners may hold differing opinions on certain matters, it is crucial to concentrate on what unites them in the campaign. By directing attention to shared values and/or goals, the alliance can forge a cohesive message that resonates with voters and fortifies the overall campaign. This approach also helps minimize internal conflicts and disagreements, ensuring that the alliance remains focused on the collective objective of winning the election.

Maintaining open lines of communication stands as another fundamental pillar in the formation of successful alliances. Effective communication guarantees that all partners remain informed, engaged, and actively contributing to the alliance's endeavors. This includes regular meetings, updates, and feedback sessions that provide opportunities for alliance members to voice their concerns, share ideas, and discuss strategies. Open communication also enables the campaign to address any issues or challenges that may arise, allowing for timely resolution and minimizing the potential for misunderstandings or conflicts.

Finally, ensuring representation is a pivotal pillar in forging successful alliances. By inviting input from all alliance partners and respecting their perspectives, a campaign can create a representative alliance that accurately reflects the interests and priorities of the various groups involved. This approach not only strengthens the alliance's message and credibility but also fosters a sense of unity and shared purpose among alliance members.

The art of uniting forces is an indispensable skill for political candidates, particularly for those with conservative views. By gathering diverse groups of ideas and individuals under a shared set of values and goals, candidates can build expansive support networks that increase their chances of victory. As demographics and political landscapes continue to evolve, the ability to create and maintain alliances will remain a vital factor in the success of political campaigns. By adhering to the fundamental principles of alliance-building, candidates can create strong, unified alliances that effectively amplify their message and broaden their support base.

In the quest for electoral success, representation necessitates engaging with traditionally underrepresented groups, such as minority communities, and integrating their perspectives and concerns into the campaign's vision and message. By demonstrating a genuine commitment to addressing the needs of all constituents, trust and support can be cultivated among a wider range of voters. Historically, conservative candidates and the Republican Party have struggled to connect with these communities, despite the presence of shared values and common ground. Campaigns that sincerely reach out to these groups have the opportunity to build bridges where none existed, particularly at the county, state, and national party levels.

Constructing ironclad coalitions is a multifaceted process, rooted in several key principles. By pinpointing shared values and objectives, emphasizing common ground, fostering trust and transparency, maintaining open channels of communication, and ensuring representation, a campaign can develop a robust and unified coalition, maximizing its chances of winning an election. As the political landscape evolves and diversifies, the capacity to form and maintain successful coalitions will remain crucial in determining the outcomes of political campaigns.

Recognizing that building successful coalitions demands time and effort is crucial. Fostering collaboration among groups with divergent interests is not an instantaneous process; it requires patience, persistence, and a sincere commitment to the shared objectives of the coalition. By investing the necessary time and resources into forging strong relationships, a campaign can establish a resilient and effective coalition capable of weathering the inevitable challenges and setbacks that arise during a political campaign.

The principles of building successful coalitions are vital for political candidates seeking to unite diverse groups of thought and individuals in pursuit of a common goal. By identifying shared values and objectives, emphasizing common ground, fostering trust, maintaining open channels of communication, and ensuring representation, candidates can form powerful and effective coalitions that bolster their chances of winning elections. By adhering to these principles and diligently working to build and maintain strong, unified coalitions, candidates can harness the collective power of their supporters to achieve their goals and ultimately secure victory at the polls.

THE ESSENCE OF COALITION BUILDING: IDENTIFYING POTENTIAL ALLIES

In the pursuit of victory, cultivating a potent coalition is indispensable, especially for conservative candidates aiming to unite diverse groups of ideas and individuals under shared values and/or goals. The crucial first step in this process is identifying potential coalition partners to lay the groundwork for cooperation and collaboration. Candidates must consider engaging with an array of partners, encompassing traditional conservative groups, non-traditional conservative groups, and influential stakeholders.

Traditional conservative groups often form the foundation of conservative coalitions, as they typically share core values and policy objectives. These groups can be classified into three principal factions: fiscal conservatives, social conservatives, and national security conservatives. Fiscal conservatives champion limited government intervention in the lives of citizens, free market principles, and lower taxes, while social conservatives value traditional family structures and moral values. National security conservatives, on the other hand, emphasize a strong military and robust foreign policy.

To build a victorious coalition, it is also essential to engage with non-traditional conservative groups, which can offer valuable perspectives and broaden the candidate's support base. These groups include moderate and independent voters, single-issue voters, and minority communities. By addressing their concerns and demonstrating alignment with their interests, candidates can forge alliances with these vital voting blocs. Influential stakeholders play a significant role in a campaign's success. Business owners, industry leaders, religious and community leaders, and issue advocates can provide valuable resources, endorsements, and connections, bolstering a candidate's credibility and reach.

Identifying potential coalition partners is a critical first step in building a formidable coalition. By engaging with a diverse range of partners and forging alliances with various groups and individuals, conservative candidates can construct a winning coalition that maximizes their chances of victory. As political landscapes continue to evolve, the ability to form and maintain strong coalitions will remain a key determinant of success for conservative campaigns. By adhering to these principles and diligently working to identify and engage potential coalition partners, candidates can ensure their campaigns are well-positioned for victory and lasting impact.

FORMING ALLIANCES: STRENGTHENING YOUR CAMPAIGN

Conservative political campaigns often depend on alliances with diverse partners to create strong coalitions and expand their reach. To establish these alliances, candidates must focus on identifying collaboration points, addressing concerns, fostering mutual respect, aligning campaign messaging with partners' priorities, and developing a shared vision and strategy.

Discovering collaboration points is vital for building alliances. This requires researching partners' priorities, values, and goals, and pinpointing where interests align with the candidate. Establishing common ground lays a foundation for cooperation. Addressing concerns and reservations is crucial, as potential partners may be hesitant about working with a conservative campaign. Candidates should openly address concerns and demonstrate a willingness to listen, learn, and adapt. Developing mutual trust and respect involves ongoing dialogue and collaboration. Candidates must invest in building relationships with potential partners by attending meetings, events, and demonstrating their commitment. Aligning campaign messaging with partners' priorities ensures the campaign resonates with a broad range of voters. Candidates should work closely with partners to develop messaging that advances shared objectives. Creating a shared vision and strategy involves developing a campaign vision that incorporates partners' goals and aspirations.

By focusing on collaboration, addressing concerns, fostering trust, aligning messaging, and developing a shared vision, candidates can create powerful partnerships that amplify their message and expand their reach. In a polarized political environment, alliances demonstrate commitment to collaboration, helping candidates stand out as pragmatic and solutions-oriented leaders. By maintaining strong partnerships, conservative candidates can contribute to a more representative and responsive political landscape, benefiting all Americans.

MAXIMIZING CAMPAIGN SUCCESS THROUGH COALITION PARTNERSHIPS

Leveraging coalition partnerships is crucial for campaign success, especially for conservative candidates aiming to build diverse support bases. To optimize the impact of campaign efforts, candidates must focus on coordinated messaging and communication, joint events and activities, voter outreach and mobilization, sharing resources and expertise, and coordinated fundraising. Coordinated messaging and communication are vital in creating a unified narrative that resonates with various voters. Candidates should collaborate with partners to align messaging, develop talking points, and leverage each partner's unique channels and networks for maximum reach. Joint events and activities showcase commitment to collaboration and the strength of alliances. Pooling resources and expertise for events like rallies, town halls, or community service projects can attract larger audiences and generate media attention.

Voter outreach and mobilization are essential for campaign success. Candidates should work with partners to tap into existing networks of supporters and volunteers, coordinate phone banking, door-to-door canvassing, and voter registration drives, and develop targeted digital and social media campaigns. Sharing resources and expertise creates synergies, helping candidates achieve shared goals more efficiently. This may include sharing policy research, data analysis, media production expertise, office space, equipment, or voter databases. Collaborative fundraising and financial support are essential for campaign success. Candidates and partners can collaborate on fundraising efforts, expand donor networks, and maximize financial support through joint fundraising events, online campaigns, or sharing donor lists.

Ultimately, the success of a campaign depends on the strength and diversity of coalitions built and leveraged. By actively forging strong partnerships, candidates can create powerful coalitions that increase success and help achieve policy objectives once in office, contributing to a more representative and responsive political landscape for all conservative voters. Continued success in coalition partnerships hinges on maintaining strong alliances and adapting to the evolving political landscape. As conservative candidates work to maximize campaign success, ongoing engagement, communication, and collaboration are essential in sustaining fruitful partnerships.

Candidates should be prepared to invest time and effort in nurturing relationships with coalition partners by attending regular meetings and staying in close contact throughout the campaign. Flexibility and adaptability are critical as new issues emerge and political dynamics shift, requiring candidates and their partners to reassess strategies and priorities. Openness to change on flexible issues ensures that alliances remain strong and effective, even amid rapidly changing political circumstances. Commitment to accountability is also crucial in leveraging coalition partnerships. Open and honest communication about goals, strategies, and progress builds trust and goodwill among partners, fostering a culture of accountability within the coalition.

Ultimately, the strength and diversity of the coalition conservatives can build and leverage determine its success. By focusing on the strategies outlined above, conservatives can create powerful, unified coalitions that not only increase their chances of electoral success but also help them achieve policy objectives once in office. In doing so, they contribute to a more representative and responsive political landscape that serves the needs and aspirations of coalition partners. Embracing the power of coalition partnerships and diligently building and maintaining strong alliances enables candidates to navigate the complexities of the modern political landscape and achieve lasting success. Collaborative messaging, joint events, targeted outreach, resource-sharing, and collaborative fundraising forge powerful coalitions that resonate with a broad range of voters and lay the foundation for impactful and transformative policy change. By leveraging coalition partnerships effectively, conservatives can advance their cause and promote a more responsive republic.

NAVIGATING CHALLENGES IN COALITION-BUILDING

Navigating the intricacies of coalition-building is an essential yet challenging aspect of running a successful political campaign. Coalition-building allows candidates to expand their support base and unite diverse groups of thought and individuals with shared goals and values. However, addressing the challenges that arise while building and maintaining coalitions can be a complex and demanding endeavor. Key challenges include balancing competing interests and priorities, managing internal conflicts and disagreements, overcoming ideological differences, and maintaining a unified front despite occasional setbacks.

One significant challenge in coalition-building is balancing competing interests and priorities. As coalitions bring together diverse groups and individuals, each partner may have unique priorities and objectives that do not always perfectly align with those of others. It is vital for coalition partners to find common ground, compromise on flexible issues, and collaborate to achieve shared goals. This process often involves open and honest discussions, making concessions on flexible issues when necessary, and focusing on the coalition's broader vision and purpose. By addressing competing interests and priorities, coalition partners can create a more cohesive and effective alliance better equipped to achieve collective objectives.

Another critical challenge in coalition-building is managing internal conflicts and disagreements. Conflicts and disagreements are inevitable due to the diverse nature of coalitions. The key to addressing these conflicts is to foster an environment where all partners feel heard, respected, and valued. This approach involves open and honest communication, active listening to the concerns and grievances of all partners, and working together to find mutually acceptable solutions. Conflict resolution skills, such as negotiation, mediation, and facilitation, can be instrumental in helping coalition partners navigate internal disputes and maintain positive and productive working relationships.

A third challenge in coalition-building, especially in today's polarized political landscape, is overcoming ideological differences. Although coalition partners may share common goals and/or values, they may still have significant ideological differences on specific issues. To overcome these differences, it is crucial for coalition partners to focus on areas of agreement and common ground, rather than fixating on disagreements. This strategy may involve emphasizing shared values, such as fiscal responsibility, family values, or national security, and collaborating on policy initiatives reflecting these shared principles. By bridging ideological divides and working together on shared goals, coalition partners can create a stronger and more unified alliance better prepared to navigate the political environment's challenges.

A fourth challenge in coalition-building is maintaining a unified front despite occasional setbacks. Coalitions will inevitably face disappointments, such as electoral losses, policy defeats, or unanticipated shifts in public opinion.

In these situations, it is essential for coalition partners to remain committed to their shared vision and/or goals, even when the path forward is uncertain or challenging. This commitment involves focusing on the coalition's long-term objectives, learning from setbacks and adjusting strategies as needed, and maintaining unity and solidarity among partners. By staying united in adversity, coalition partners can demonstrate resilience and determination to voters and opponents alike, ultimately increasing their chances of achieving shared goals.

Navigating coalition-building challenges is a complex and demanding task, but it is also vital for running a large successful political campaign. By focusing on balancing competing interests and priorities, managing internal conflicts and disagreements, overcoming ideological differences, and maintaining a unified front despite occasional setbacks, coalition partners can create a more cohesive and effective alliance better positioned to achieve collective objectives. As the political landscape continues to evolve, building and navigating strong coalitions will remain a key determinant of success for conservatives and all political campaigns seeking to create lasting change and make a meaningful impact on the citizens they represent.

CASE STUDIES:
SUCCESSFUL CONSERVATIVE COALITIONS

Examining successful conservative coalition campaigns can offer valuable insights into effective strategies, tactics, and best practices. In these case studies, we will explore historical examples of winning conservative coalitions, the strategies and tactics employed, and the lessons learned from these campaigns.

One notable historical example of a successful conservative coalition campaign is the election of President Ronald Reagan in 1980. Reagan's campaign brought together a broad and diverse coalition of supporters, including fiscal conservatives, social conservatives, national security hawks, and disaffected Democrats known as "Reagan Democrats." This coalition played a significant role in propelling Reagan to a decisive victory over incumbent President Jimmy Carter. Reagan's campaign employed several key strategies and tactics to build and maintain this coalition. First, Reagan focused on communicating a clear and consistent message that resonated with various factions within the conservative movement. This message centered on themes such as smaller government, lower taxes, strong national defense, and traditional family values. By emphasizing these shared principles, Reagan was able to unite disparate groups under a common banner.

Second, the Reagan campaign actively sought to engage and mobilize its coalition partners, leveraging their resources and networks to reach a broader range of voters. This involved coordinating with various conservative organizations, such as the Moral Majority and the National Rifle Association, as well as working closely with influential conservative media figures and commentators. Through these partnerships, the Reagan campaign was able to amplify its message and galvanize support among key voter groups.

The Reagan campaign skillfully addressed the concerns and priorities of different segments within the coalition, fostering trust and support among a diverse array of groups. For example, Reagan's strong anti-communist stance and commitment to rebuilding the military appealed to national security conservatives, while his stance on issues like abortion and school prayer resonated with social conservatives. By demonstrating a genuine understanding of and commitment to the issues that mattered most to different coalition partners, Reagan was able to build trust and support among a diverse array of groups.

One crucial component of Reagan's coalition was the Reagan Democrats, a group of traditionally Democratic voters who supported the Republican candidate in the 1980 and 1984 presidential elections. The concerns of these voters were wide-ranging and included economic, national defense, social, law and order, and leadership issues.

During the late 1970s, under President Jimmy Carter's administration, the United States faced economic stagnation, high inflation, and high unemployment. Reagan's pro-growth policies, such as tax cuts, deregulation, and a focus on free-market principles, appealed to working-class voters concerned about their financial well-being. His strong stance against the Soviet Union, advocating for a robust national defense and a more assertive American presence on the global stage, attracted blue-collar workers with a strong sense of patriotism.

Reagan also embraced conservative social values, such as opposition to abortion and support for traditional family structures. This resonated with many Reagan Democrats who felt that the Democratic Party had become too liberal on social issues. Additionally, the 1970s saw a surge in crime rates in the United States, and Reagan's tough-on-crime rhetoric and support for law enforcement struck a chord with those worried about the safety of their communities.

Reagan's charismatic leadership style and optimistic vision of a prosperous and strong America appealed to voters disillusioned with the perceived weakness and indecisiveness of the Carter administration. By addressing the diverse concerns of the various segments within his coalition, Reagan was able to forge a strong and unified political force, ultimately contributing to his success in the 1980 and 1984 presidential elections.

Another example of a successful conservative coalition campaign is the 1994 Republican Revolution, which saw the Republican Party capture both houses of Congress for the first time in 40 years. The success of this campaign can be attributed in large part to the "Contract with America," a policy document that outlined a clear and concise set of conservative principles and policy proposals. This document served as a rallying point for various factions within the conservative movement, helping to unite them around a shared agenda.

A key figure in crafting the Contract with America was Newt Gingrich, then-Speaker of the House. Gingrich recognized the importance of presenting a united front and a coherent policy platform to the American public. By working closely with fellow Republicans and conservative thinkers, he helped develop a document that not only addressed the concerns of diverse conservative factions but also resonated with a broad swath of the American electorate.

The strategies and tactics employed by the Republican candidates during the 1994 campaign included a focus on grassroots organizing and mobilization, leveraging the support and resources of various conservative organizations, and maintaining a relentless focus on the Contract with America. By effectively communicating their policy agenda and demonstrating a commitment to conservative principles, Republican candidates were able to build a broad and diverse coalition of support that propelled them to victory.

Under Gingrich's leadership, the Contract with America became a powerful symbol of the Republican Party's dedication to America First values and reform. Its success in unifying various conservative factions and capturing the attention of the American public at-large makes Speaker Gingrich one of the most consequential conservative figures in the last 100 years of Republican politics and serves as a testament to the importance of clear messaging, strategic alliance-building, and unwavering commitment to core principles in the realm of political campaigning.

Regrettably, in the years following Speaker Gingrich's historic tenure as the leader of the House of Representatives, Republicans lost sight of their agreement—their contract—with America, and their hard-earned coalition began to crumble under the weight and distraction of the new reality brought to bear by the September 11 attacks and the Global War on Terror. The domestic focus that had built the Contract with America coalition was overshadowed by pressing foreign concerns and a deep recession at home during the early 2000s.

It is important to remember that coalitions require constant nurturing and attention. The needs of the coalition members must be met; otherwise, they may perceive no value in maintaining their allegiance and may seek new alliances. As the Republican Party shifted its focus to address the emerging international challenges and the ensuing economic downturn, the diverse factions that had been united under the Contract with America began to drift apart.

This underscores the critical importance of maintaining a consistent focus on the priorities and concerns of the various groups within a coalition. Even as new challenges arise, it is essential for political leaders to remain attentive to the needs of their constituents and ensure that their policy agendas continue to reflect the values and interests of the broad array of supporters who helped bring them to power. In doing so, they can foster a sense of unity and commitment that strengthens the coalition and ensures its continued relevance and effectiveness in the ever-changing political landscape.

The 2016 election of President Donald Trump showcased the power of building a conservative coalition that included not only traditional conservative groups but also disaffected Democrat working-class voters and individuals concerned about globalization and its effects on the economy. Trump's campaign tapped into a populist sentiment that resonated with many Americans who felt left behind by the political establishment—many of whom were Democrats, swing voters, and left-leaning independent voters. The Trump campaign employed several key strategies and tactics to build and maintain this coalition. First, Trump utilized social media and non-traditional media outlets to communicate directly with voters, bypassing traditional gatekeepers and crafting a unique and distinctive campaign message. This message centered on themes such as immigration control, trade protectionism, and "draining the swamp" of political corruption in Washington, D.C.

Second, the Trump campaign focused on energizing and mobilizing its base of supporters, using large-scale rallies and targeted digital advertising to engage and activate key voter groups. By effectively leveraging the enthusiasm of his supporters, Trump was able to generate significant grassroots momentum and build a powerful coalition of voters who were dissatisfied with the status quo.

An additional example of a successful conservative coalition campaign is the election of Senator Ted Cruz in Texas in 2012. Cruz's campaign managed to build a coalition between unlikely allies, such as Tea Party activists, libertarians, and traditional conservatives. His coalition was instrumental in defeating the establishment-backed candidate, Lieutenant Governor David Dewhurst, in the Republican primary. Cruz's campaign employed several key strategies and tactics to build and maintain this diverse coalition. First, he focused on a message centered around limited government, constitutionalism, and individual liberty, which resonated with various factions within the conservative movement. This message allowed him to bridge the gap between different groups and unite them under a common vision.

Second, the Cruz campaign actively engaged with grassroots activists, leveraging their energy and commitment to build a powerful ground game. By connecting with these activists and empowering them to take an active role in the campaign, Cruz was able to tap into a passionate and motivated base of supporters who played a critical role in his primary victory.

From the Cruz campaign, we can derive several important lessons and best practices for building successful conservative coalitions. First, the ability to find a unifying message that resonates with various factions within the conservative movement is essential for bringing together unlikely allies. Second, grassroots engagement and empowerment are crucial for building a strong and motivated coalition of supporters, particularly when attempting to challenge establishment-backed candidates.

Examining historical examples of successful conservative coalition campaigns, such as the elections of President Ronald Reagan, the 1994 Republican Revolution led by Speaker Newt Gingrich, President Donald Trump, and Senator Ted Cruz, can provide valuable insights into effective strategies, tactics, and best practices for building and maintaining winning coalitions. Key lessons learned include the importance of clear and consistent messaging, active engagement and coordination with coalition partners, grassroots organizing and mobilization, addressing the concerns and priorities of different coalition partners, and leveraging non-traditional media and messaging to reach a broader range of voters. As the political landscape continues to evolve, the ability to build and navigate strong coalitions will remain a key determinant of success for conservatives and, indeed, for all political campaigns seeking to create lasting change and make a meaningful impact on the lives of the citizens they represent.

FINAL THOUGHTS

In this chapter, we have delved into the significance of coalition-building in campaigns, examining various strategies, tactics, and best practices for establishing successful and diverse coalitions. As the political environment grows increasingly polarized and complex, the capacity to create and sustain robust coalitions becomes ever more critical for candidates aspiring to win elections and create a lasting impact on their constituents' lives.

We commenced by exploring the principles of constructing successful coalitions, encompassing the identification of shared values and goals, emphasizing common ground rather than differences, prioritizing trust and transparency, maintaining open communication channels, and ensuring inclusivity and representation. These principles lay the groundwork for forging alliances that are not only extensive in scope but also firm in commitment and purpose.

Subsequently, we addressed the process of pinpointing potential coalition partners, spanning from traditional conservative factions like fiscal conservatives, social conservatives, and national security conservatives, to non-traditional conservative groups such as moderate and independent voters, single-issue voters, and minority communities. We also stressed the significance of engaging influential stakeholders like business owners, religious and community leaders, and issue advocates to further reinforce the coalition.

Cultivating partnerships with potential allies involves determining key collaboration points, addressing concerns and reservations, fostering mutual trust and respect, aligning campaign messaging with partners' priorities, and devising a shared vision and strategy. We investigated examples of how conservatives could construct coalitions with minority communities, such as Black and Latino communities, by engaging with them, addressing their unique concerns and priorities, and emphasizing shared values like family, faith, and hard work.

Once coalitions are established, capitalizing on these partnerships for campaign success is crucial. Synchronized messaging and communication, joint events and activities, voter outreach and mobilization efforts, sharing resources and expertise, and coordinated fundraising and financial support are all vital elements of effectively leveraging coalition partnerships. Addressing the challenges associated with coalition-building is a critical aspect of preserving successful alliances. Managing competing interests and priorities, resolving internal conflicts and disagreements, overcoming ideological differences, and maintaining a unified front despite occasional setbacks are all hurdles that must be tackled to ensure the coalition's strength and longevity.

By examining historical case studies, we underscored successful conservative coalition campaigns, such as the elections of President Ronald Reagan, the 1994 Republican Revolution led by Speaker Newt Gingrich, and President Donald Trump. These examples demonstrated the importance of clear and consistent messaging, grassroots organizing and mobilization, and leveraging non-traditional media and messaging to engage a wider range of voters.

Coalition-building is a vital component of executing and winning a campaign. By comprehending and applying the principles, strategies, and tactics discussed in this chapter, conservatives can effectively establish broad and diverse coalitions that not only enhance their chances of electoral success but also pave the way for impactful and transformative policy changes. As the political landscape continues to evolve, the ability to build and navigate strong coalitions will remain a key determinant of success for conservative campaigns, and indeed, for all political campaigns.

Ultimately, the success of America First candidates rests on their ability to forge diverse coalitions that reflect the varied interests, values, and priorities of their constituents. By embracing the lessons and best practices outlined in this chapter, conservatives can ensure that their campaigns are well-positioned to achieve victory and drive significant, transformative change for the communities they serve.

CHAPTER 12

OPPOSITION RESEARCH AND THE DARK ARTS

IN THE REALM OF POLITICAL COMBAT, the battle of ideas and ideals is waged on a grand scale, where the victors emerge as leaders, shaping the destiny of nations. Amidst this struggle, a subtle yet potent weapon is employed to gain the upper hand - the art of opposition research, often dubbed as "oppo research." In this chapter, we shall explore the diverse methods and techniques employed by campaigns in their pursuit of opposition research, ranging from scrutinizing public records and media archives to conducting interviews and field research. We shall also examine the ethical considerations that must guide opposition research, emphasizing the importance of accuracy, privacy, and eschewing unnecessary personal attacks. Lastly, we shall venture into the darker side of opposition research - the infamous "Dark Arts" - and the potential repercussions of engaging in unethical tactics. By offering a comprehensive overview of opposition research, this chapter aims to illuminate a vital aspect of modern political campaigns, providing insights into the strategies and considerations that shape the electoral landscape and ultimately determine the outcome of elections.

In the intricate world of politics, where the fickle winds of fortune can turn in an instant, opposition research has become an indispensable tool for the astute campaigner. By meticulously compiling information about an opponent's history, statements, and associations, a candidate can anticipate their adversary's tactics and devise countering strategies. Moreover, opposition research allows campaigns to craft a compelling narrative about their opponent, influencing the messaging and tactics deployed in various arenas, such as advertising, debates, interviews, and social media engagement.

The roots of opposition research trace back to the dawn of political power; however, its scope and significance have swelled exponentially in the digital era and the 24-hour news cycle. Today, campaign operatives have a vast repository of information at their disposal, sifting through extensive data to pinpoint the most pertinent and influential details about their rival. This endeavor demands not only a comprehensive understanding of the political landscape and the issues that resonate with the electorate but also adherence to ethical guidelines that ensure responsible use of information in the electoral process.

A critical aspect of opposition research is striking a delicate balance between highlighting an opponent's shortcomings and promoting a positive vision for the candidate. While negative advertising and attack ads may effectively erode an opponent's support, they should be employed judiciously, alongside a clear and inspiring message from the candidate. This approach helps maintain focus on the issues that matter to the electorate, preventing the campaign from descending into a vitriolic exchange that may alienate voters.

INOCULATION RESEARCH: THE ART OF SELF DEFENSE

In the high-stakes game of political campaigns, inoculation research emerges as a proactive tactic, turning the spotlight inward to scrutinize one's own candidate rather than the adversary. This method entails an exhaustive examination of the candidate's background, policy positions, voting record, financial transactions, and personal history. The primary objective of inoculation research is to foresee potential critiques and assaults the opposition may deploy and devise efficacious countermeasures, thereby "inoculating" the candidate against such onslaughts. In contrast, opposition research centers on collecting intelligence about the rival to pinpoint vulnerabilities, inconsistencies, or controversies, which can then be leveraged to devise targeted messaging and strategies. While both opposition and inoculation research strive to confer a strategic edge to a campaign, they diverge in focus and goals.

A key distinction between the two lies in their respective targets. Opposition research zeroes in on the opposing candidate, whereas inoculation research revolves around one's own candidate. This variation in focus engenders divergent outcomes: while opposition research seeks to capitalize on an opponent's frailties, inoculation research endeavors to shield and fortify the candidate against potential offensives. Another dissimilarity between the two arises from their approaches. Opposition research often adopts a more pugnacious stance, aiming to unearth detrimental information about the opponent to erode their credibility. Inoculation research, conversely, is more self-reflective, assisting a campaign in comprehending its own candidate's susceptibilities and preparing accordingly.

Inoculation research serves as a linchpin in guaranteeing that a campaign is primed to counter any attacks or allegations that may surface during a political contest. By recognizing and addressing their own shortcomings, candidates can develop cogent responses to potential censures and retain command over their campaign narrative. This preemptive strategy enables candidates to concentrate on their messaging, connect with the electorate on pressing issues, and ultimately, construct a robust and resilient campaign.

While both opposition research and inoculation research constitute indispensable facets of a triumphant political campaign, they fulfill distinct roles and necessitate different approaches. By engaging in both forms of research, campaigns can not only capitalize on their opponent's weaknesses but also ensure that their own candidate is well-equipped to confront any hurdles that may materialize during the course of an intensely competitive political race.

THE ESSENCE OF OPPOSITION RESEARCH

A profound comprehension of an opponent's strengths and weaknesses is indispensable for any candidate aspiring to secure electoral victory. Through opposition research, candidates can pinpoint salient issues that reverberate with the electorate and, more crucially, capitalize on their adversaries' frailties. By amassing intelligence on an opponent's political trajectory, voting records, financial transactions, and personal background, a campaign can devise targeted stratagems to weaken their opponent's credibility and allure to the voting public. Furthermore, opposition research empowers candidates to anticipate and brace for potential offensives from their rivals. By discerning areas of vulnerability, candidates can formulate responses to mitigate potential controversies or scandals before they enter the public domain. This preemptive approach enables candidates to retain control over their campaign narrative, ensuring that their messaging remains consistent and focused.

Beyond strategic benefits, opposition research can also offer invaluable insights for sculpting campaign messages. By scrutinizing an opponent's policy stances, past declarations, and voting records, candidates can mold messages that accentuate the disparities between themselves and their adversaries, underscoring their strengths and juxtaposing their values against those of their rivals. This process aids in clarifying the choice for voters, facilitating their understanding of the election's stakes and the ramifications of their vote. Moreover, opposition research is instrumental in preparing for debates and interviews. By foreseeing the arguments and critiques an opponent may proffer, candidates can devise compelling counter-arguments and rebuttals. This preparation instills candidates with confidence and knowledge, bolstering their credibility and enhancing the probability of a successful performance in these high-stakes settings.

It is noteworthy that opposition research is not exclusively fixated on uncovering negative facets of an opponent's background or record. In certain cases, comprehending an opponent's strengths can be equally invaluable, enabling a campaign to acknowledge and adapt to areas where their rival may possess an edge. By recognizing these strengths, a campaign can devise tactics to neutralize them or even transform them into potential weaknesses.

Opposition research also plays a pivotal role in discerning potential coalitions and voter segments that may be swayed by the campaign's messaging. By grasping an opponent's support base and the issues that galvanize them, a campaign can customize its outreach to specific demographics or interest groups, augmenting the likelihood of winning over undecided or swing voters.

In the era of digital communication and social media, opposition research has gained paramount importance for monitoring an opponent's online presence and activities. By tracking an opponent's social media accounts, blog posts, and online interactions, a campaign can glean insights into their rival's messaging strategies, policy positions, and affiliations with various groups and individuals. This information can be harnessed to inform a campaign's own digital strategy, ensuring that they remain competitive in the rapidly evolving realm of online political communication.

Finally, the objective of opposition research is to furnish a comprehensive comprehension of an opponent's background, record, strengths, and weaknesses, empowering a campaign to devise efficacious strategies for winning. By assembling and scrutinizing this intelligence, candidates can create targeted messages, foresee and prepare for onslaughts, and retain control over their campaign narrative. In this endeavor, opposition research functions as a critical instrument for any candidate pursuing electoral success, aiding in ensuring that their campaign remains concentrated, adaptable, and responsive to the ever-shifting dynamics of contemporary politics.

UNDERTAKING OPPOSITION RESEARCH

Numerous methods exist for undertaking opposition research, encompassing the exploration of public records to personal interviews with individuals acquainted with the opponent. One prevalent approach is to examine public records and documents, such as voting records, financial disclosures, and legal documents. These sources can disclose crucial information about an opponent's policy inclinations, financial transactions, and any previous legal issues that may have transpired. Media archives constitute another invaluable resource for opposition researchers. By assessing news articles, interviews, and editorials, campaigns can acquire insights into an opponent's past declarations, controversies, and stances on pivotal issues. Furthermore, an opponent's social media presence and digital footprint can offer a wealth of information, particularly when it comes to measuring public opinion and pinpointing potential areas of dispute.

Personal and professional networks can also yield valuable insights into an opponent's character, work history, and associations. Interviews with acquaintances, colleagues, and former staff members can reveal information that may not be accessible through public records or media sources. Moreover, examining an opponent's endorsements and affiliations can help to identify potential conflicts of interest or ideological incongruities. Field research and surveillance represent more dynamic approaches to opposition research, entailing the direct observation and monitoring of an opponent's public events, speeches, and appearances. A common tactic employed by rival campaigns is the deployment of "trackers" who shadow candidates at various events. These trackers attend rallies, speeches, and other public gatherings with the primary objective of capturing any potentially damaging statements, policy shifts, or moments of vulnerability that can be leveraged by their respective campaigns.

Through trackers, campaigns can acquire first-hand knowledge of an opponent's messaging, policy proposals, and areas of weakness. This intelligence can then be harnessed to inform campaign strategies and tactics, ensuring that a candidate's messaging is both reactive and proactive. Trackers are also indispensable for detecting any inconsistencies in an opponent's policy stances, which can be highlighted to voters and utilized to undermine their credibility. Furthermore, the presence of trackers can serve as a disincentive for candidates, rendering them more cautious in their public statements and appearances. This, in turn, may yield a more disciplined and focused campaign, as candidates endeavor to avoid furnishing their opponents with any ammunition that could be employed against them. It is vital to emphasize that the use of trackers should be conducted ethically and within the parameters of the law. For instance, trackers should not engage in intrusive activities, such as stalking or harassment, nor should they obtain information through illicit means, such as hacking or unauthorized access to private records.

The engagement of trackers as part of field research and surveillance is an essential component of opposition research. By meticulously monitoring opponents' public events and appearances, trackers can collect invaluable information that can be utilized to inform campaign strategies and tactics, while also ensuring that candidates remain vigilant and disciplined in their messaging. Provided these activities are conducted ethically and within the confines of the law, they can contribute to a more informed and competitive electoral process.

Another technique for conducting opposition research involves analyzing an opponent's legislative and political history. This encompasses examining their voting records, sponsored legislation, and committee memberships. By comprehending an opponent's legislative priorities and achievements, a campaign can devise targeted messages that accentuate differences in policy positions and values. Besides reviewing past records and statements, opposition research also entails monitoring an opponent's current activities and declarations. By closely observing an opponent's campaign activities, speeches, and policy proposals, researchers can stay informed about potential shifts in strategy or messaging. This real-time information can be crucial for developing effective counter-strategies and maintaining a competitive edge.

When conducting opposition research, it is vital to be thorough, methodical, and objective. Researchers must sort through copious amounts of information to pinpoint the most relevant and impactful details, often drawing on multiple sources and cross-referencing their findings to ensure accuracy. In addition to traditional research methods, contemporary opposition research teams may also utilize advanced data analytics tools and techniques to help them analyze and synthesize information more effectively.

A key challenge in opposition research is the need to discern between reliable and unreliable information. Given the vast amount of data available online and the prevalence of misinformation, researchers must be diligent in verifying the accuracy of their findings. This may involve checking multiple sources, consulting with experts, and relying on reputable databases and archives. Moreover, it is crucial to maintain a high level of ethical conduct when conducting opposition research. This includes respecting the privacy of opponents and their families and avoiding the use of unsubstantiated rumors or personal attacks. By adhering to ethical guidelines and concentrating on relevant, verifiable information, opposition researchers can contribute to a fair electoral process. Opposition research is not a one-size-fits-all endeavor. Different campaigns have varying needs and priorities, and researchers must tailor their approach to the specific context in which they are operating. This may involve focusing on local or regional issues, prioritizing certain policy areas, or targeting specific voter demographics.

Conducting opposition research is a multifaceted and dynamic process that demands a combination of traditional research methods, advanced analytics tools, and a commitment to ethical conduct. Generally, it is not recommended for campaigns or candidates to conduct their own opposition research. Many firms specialize in working with conservative candidates, and finding one will not be difficult. A recommended firm for conservative candidates is Capitol City Research, owned by my friend Willis Jones, a veteran in the oppo space and political trenches for over 20 years, actively championing conservative values. More information about the firm can be found at www.capitolcityresearch.com.

Ultimately, it is essential to recognize that opposition research is not an inherently negative or malicious practice. While often associated with the so-called "Dark Arts" of politics, opposition research can contribute to a more informed and engaged electorate by illuminating the differences between candidates and their respective policy positions. In this sense, opposition research can be viewed as a valuable instrument for promoting transparency, accountability, and informed decision-making in the electoral process.

UTILIZING OPPOSITION RESEARCH

Equipped with the information procured through opposition research, campaigns can create targeted messages and strategies that accentuate their candidate's strengths and exploit their opponent's weaknesses. One prevalent application of opposition research is in the development of negative advertising and attack ads. These ads, which often concentrate on an opponent's policy positions, personal history, or controversies, can be highly effective in swaying public opinion and undermining an opponent's credibility. Nonetheless, it is vital for campaigns to balance negative ads with positive messaging that highlights the candidate's qualifications, values, and vision for the future.

Besides its role in shaping campaign messages, opposition research is also crucial for debate and interview preparation. By anticipating the arguments and critiques an opponent is likely to raise, candidates can develop counter-arguments and refutations that effectively neutralize these attacks. This preparation not only assists candidates in appearing knowledgeable and confident, but it also ensures they can stay on message and articulate their positions clearly.

Opposition research is invaluable for rapid response and crisis management as well. When confronted with unexpected attacks or allegations, a campaign that has conducted thorough opposition research will be better prepared to respond swiftly and decisively. This ability to manage crises can help to mitigate potential scandals and controversies, allowing the candidate to maintain control over the campaign narrative and stay focused on the issues important to voters.

Another method of utilizing opposition research is by incorporating it into the campaign's overall messaging strategy. This may involve emphasizing specific policy differences between the candidates, stressing an opponent's inconsistencies, or highlighting instances where the opponent has changed their position on key issues. By drawing attention to these discrepancies, campaigns can create a clear contrast between their candidate and the opponent, assisting voters in better understanding the election's stakes. Furthermore, opposition research can be used to inform targeted voter outreach efforts. By understanding an opponent's policy positions and vulnerabilities, campaigns can tailor their canvassing and phone banking scripts to address the concerns of specific voter demographics. For example, if opposition research discloses that an opponent has a weak record on free speech and censorship issues, a campaign might target voters with customized messaging that emphasizes their candidate's dedication to protecting the First Amendment.

In some instances, the information discovered through opposition research may be used to influence third-party groups, such as political action committees (PACs) or issue advocacy organizations. However, before sharing any information with third-party groups, consult with legal counsel to ensure the information being shared does not violate any campaign laws. By sharing opposition research findings with these groups, campaigns can encourage them to create their own ads or materials that focus on the opponent's weaknesses, further amplifying the campaign's message.

It is also crucial to consider the timing of releasing opposition research findings, as campaigns must strategically decide when to deploy certain information to maximize its impact. This includes the concept of the "October Surprise," a term used to describe a significant event or revelation deliberately timed to occur shortly before an election, with the intention of influencing the outcome. By releasing a damaging piece of information at this critical juncture, campaigns aim to catch their opponents off guard, limiting their ability to effectively respond and recover before Election Day. However, the timing of an October Surprise can be a double-edged sword. Releasing a damaging piece of information too early in the campaign might allow the opponent time to recover and respond, while waiting too long might result in the information being overshadowed by other events or issues. Moreover, an October Surprise can also backfire if the information is perceived as a desperate political maneuver, potentially damaging the credibility of the campaign that released it.

Ultimately, the effective utilization of opposition research findings, including the timing of an October Surprise, necessitates careful planning and strategic thinking. Campaigns must evaluate the potential benefits and risks of releasing damaging information at various stages of the election cycle, taking into account the specific context and dynamics of each race. By doing so, they can maximize the impact of their opposition research efforts and increase the likelihood of a successful outcome for their candidate. However, it is crucial for campaigns to exercise caution and discretion when utilizing opposition research. Releasing information that is unverified, misleading, or of dubious relevance can backfire and damage a candidate's credibility. Additionally, campaigns should be mindful of the potential for negative ads or attacks to alienate voters, particularly if they are seen as overly personal or harsh. A successful campaign must strike the right balance between highlighting an opponent's weaknesses and promoting the candidate's own strengths and vision.

Ethical considerations also play a significant role in determining how opposition research is deployed. Campaigns should avoid engaging in unnecessary or untrue personal attacks or relying on unsubstantiated rumors, focusing instead on the opponent's policy positions, voting record, and relevant personal history. By adhering to ethical guidelines and using opposition research responsibly, campaigns can contribute to a more informed electoral process.

Lastly, it is important for campaigns to recognize the potential risks and pitfalls associated with utilizing opposition research. Overreliance on negative tactics or the dissemination of misleading or unverified information can ultimately undermine a candidate's credibility and diminish the effectiveness of their campaign. To avoid these pitfalls, campaigns should ensure that their opposition research efforts are grounded in accuracy, relevance, and ethical considerations.

CASE STUDIES

BARACK OBAMA VS. MITT ROMNEY
(2012 U.S. PRESIDENTIAL ELECTION)

During the 2012 presidential election, opposition research played a significant role in shaping the narrative around Republican nominee Mitt Romney. One of the most notable instances was the release of a video in which Romney, speaking at a private fundraiser, claimed that 47% of Americans were dependent on the government and would vote for Obama regardless of policy positions. The video, leaked by an anonymous source, quickly went viral and contributed to the perception of Romney as an out-of-touch elitist. This instance of opposition research was deemed ethical, as it focused on Romney's policy views and public statements (private fundraisers are still public campaign events. Candidates must always assume their comments are being recorded).

GARY HART VS. MICHAEL DUKAKIS
(1988 U.S. DEMOCRATIC PRIMARY)

In the 1988 Democratic primary, Gary Hart was considered a frontrunner for the nomination. However, his campaign was derailed by a scandal involving an extramarital affair with a woman named Donna Rice. The story initially emerged due to investigative journalism, and it was later revealed that some opposition research had been conducted by rival campaigns. Although the focus on Hart's personal life raises ethical questions, the scandal effectively ended his presidential aspirations, and Michael Dukakis eventually secured the Democratic nomination.

BILL CLINTON VS. GEORGE H. W. BUSH (1992 U.S. PRESIDENTIAL ELECTION)

During the 1992 presidential election, the Clinton campaign effectively utilized opposition research to highlight the economic struggles faced by many Americans under the administration of President George H. W. Bush. The Clinton campaign focused on Bush's broken promise not to raise taxes, which had been a key part of his 1988 election platform. By honing in on this issue, the Clinton campaign was able to frame the election around the economy, which proved to be a winning strategy. This instance of opposition research was ethical, as it centered on policy positions and campaign promises, ultimately contributing to Bill Clinton's victory.

LYNDON B. JOHNSON VS. BARRY GOLDWATER (1964 U.S. PRESIDENTIAL ELECTION)

In the 1964 presidential election, Lyndon B. Johnson's campaign conducted extensive opposition research on Republican nominee Barry Goldwater. They found that Goldwater had made numerous controversial statements over the years, including advocating for the use of nuclear weapons in Vietnam. The Johnson campaign used this information to create the famous "Daisy" ad, which depicted a young girl picking petals from a daisy as a countdown to a nuclear explosion played in the background. The ad effectively portrayed Goldwater as a dangerous and reckless candidate, and it is considered one of the most successful political ads in history.

HILLARY CLINTON VS. BERNIE SANDERS
(2016 U.S. DEMOCRATIC PRIMARY)

During the 2016 Democratic primary, opposition research played a role in shaping the narrative around Vermont Senator Bernie Sanders. The Clinton campaign highlighted Sanders' past positions on issues such as gun control, which were seen as more moderate than his current progressive stance. By doing so, the campaign sought to portray Sanders as inconsistent and less committed to progressive values than Hillary Clinton. This use of opposition research was ethical, as it focused on policy positions and voting records, helping to differentiate the candidates and clarify their respective policy stances for voters.

DOUG JONES VS. ROY MOORE
(2017 U.S. SENATE SPECIAL ELECTION IN ALABAMA)

In the 2017 special election for the U.S. Senate seat in Alabama, opposition research played a significant role in Democrat Doug Jones' surprising victory. During the campaign, reports emerged that Republican nominee Roy Moore had been accused of inappropriate conduct with underage girls several decades earlier. The allegations, which were supported by multiple accusers and corroborated by witnesses, effectively derailed Moore's campaign and contributed to Jones' narrow win.

The allegations against Roy Moore were never definitively proven to be true or false. Multiple women came forward to accuse Moore of inappropriate conduct and sexual misconduct, some of which occurred when they were teenagers and he was in his 30s. These allegations were supported by witnesses and contemporaneous accounts. However, Moore denied the allegations and claimed they were politically motivated. While the focus on Moore's personal life raises ethical questions, the serious nature of the allegations and their relevance to his fitness for office made this information pertinent to the election, if true.

THE ETHICS OF OPPOSITION RESEARCH

The significance of ethics within political campaigns, particularly in relation to opposition research, is a matter of great importance. The quest for information regarding an adversary is both legitimate and essential in the election process. However, it is crucial that campaigns adhere to ethical principles which promote fairness, responsibility, and respect for the election process. A fundamental ethical tenet is the dedication to accuracy and truth. Opposition research should rely on verifiable facts, steering clear of the manipulation or distortion of information. Deceptive or false assertions not only impair the campaign's credibility but also erode the integrity of the electoral process as a whole. The onus lies upon campaign staff and researchers to ascertain the accuracy, relevance, and fair presentation of gathered information. Upholding truthfulness is vital for preserving the sanctity of the political process and maintaining public trust in the electoral system.

Equally significant is the ethical consideration of privacy. While probing an opponent's public actions and statements is justified, campaigns must exercise caution when delving into purely personal matters unrelated to a candidate's suitability for office. Striking the delicate balance between public and private information demands sound judgment and dedication to respecting the dignity of one's adversaries. For instance, examining an opponent's family life or private relationships may be deemed inappropriate, unless there is an explicit and direct link to their professional conduct or policy stance. At Dark Horse Political, the guiding principle is that publicly available information about an opponent is fair game, while attacks on an opponent's spouse, children, or family are off-limits, unless they are directly involved in the political process or employed by or engaged in business with the government or politically inclined media.

Alongside privacy concerns, campaigns must remain vigilant of the potential legal ramifications of their opposition research endeavors. This encompasses adherence to copyright laws when utilizing or disseminating materials, as well as compliance with rules and regulations governing campaign finance and coordination with third-party organizations. Engaging in unlawful activities in pursuit of opposition research not only exposes the campaign to potential legal consequences but also jeopardizes the ethical foundation upon which the campaign is built. The Watergate scandal leading to President Nixon's resignation serves as a prime example, which we shall discuss later. Moreover, campaigns ought to contemplate the potential harm resulting from the release of opposition research findings. While exposing an opponent's weaknesses and inconsistencies is crucial, it is also imperative to weigh the potential adverse consequences of divulging certain information, both for the opponent and the broader public. In some instances, revealing sensitive or damaging information may have unforeseen consequences, such as harming innocent third parties or exacerbating societal divisions. Campaigns must thoroughly assess the potential repercussions of their actions and make decisions that prioritize the overall well-being of the electoral process.

Ultimately, campaigns should abstain from resorting to personal attacks centered on an adversary's character or private life, as opposed to their policy stances or aptitude for office. While unveiling inconsistencies and weaknesses is crucial, campaigns ought to concentrate on the issues that matter to the electorate, avoiding personal vilification. Adherence to this principle fosters civility within the electoral process and ensures that the campaign remains dedicated to substantial policy discourse. It is crucial to acknowledge that in today's social media-driven culture, this endeavor has become increasingly challenging. Even so, it is paramount to recognize that the ethical guidelines encompassing opposition research also pertain to the manner in which the information is employed by a campaign. This necessitates resisting the allure of smear tactics or the distortion of truth for political advantage. By maintaining an emphasis on policy positions and qualifications for office, campaigns can ensure that their utilization of opposition research is both strategic and ethically sound.

THE DARK ARTS: UNETHICAL PRACTICES IN OPPOSITION RESEARCH

Despite the significance of upholding ethical guidelines, some campaigns engage in what is often referred to as "The Dark Arts," employing unscrupulous tactics in their opposition research efforts and campaign activities. Such tactics may involve manipulating and distorting information to fabricate false narratives or invading an opponent's privacy through illicit activities such as hacking or stalking. In certain instances, campaigns may resort to smear campaigns and character assassination, attempting to tarnish an opponent's reputation and credibility through baseless allegations and insinuation. Engaging in the dark arts can have severe consequences for a campaign and a candidate. Apart from undermining its credibility and eroding public trust, a campaign utilizing unethical tactics may also confront legal repercussions if found engaging in illegal activities. Ultimately, the risks associated with the dark arts far surpass the potential benefits, and campaigns prioritizing integrity are more likely to prevail in the long run.

During the 2004 U.S. Senate race in Illinois, Republican candidate Jack Ryan faced allegations that he had pressured his then-wife, actress Jeri Ryan, to engage in sexual acts at public clubs. The allegations, based on sealed court documents from the couple's divorce proceedings, were leaked to the press and inflicted significant damage to Ryan's reputation. Although the veracity of the allegations was never conclusively proven, Ryan eventually withdrew from the race, enabling Democratic candidate Barack Obama to win the election by a substantial margin. Just four years later, Obama would become President of the United States.

A notorious example of the Dark Arts backfiring is the Watergate scandal during the 1972 U.S. presidential election. In an attempt to gather intelligence on their Democratic opponents, operatives from President Richard Nixon's re-election campaign broke into the Democratic National Committee's headquarters at the Watergate complex in Washington, D.C. The resulting scandal, which implicated high-ranking members of the Nixon administration, led to Nixon's resignation and a widespread loss of public trust in the political system.

Certain opposition research firms have garnered notoriety for their engagement in such underhanded tactics, employing unethical methods to collect information on adversaries and construct damaging narratives. One such firm, Fusion GPS, gained infamy for its role in the creation of the contentious "Steele dossier" during the 2016 U.S. presidential election. This dossier, laden with salacious and completely fabricated allegations against then-candidate Donald Trump, was later exposed as having been concocted and financed by the Democratic National Committee and the Clinton campaign.

Another firm known for its engagement in these dark practices is Cambridge Analytica, a British political consulting firm that contributed to numerous political campaigns, such as the 2016 U.S. presidential election and the Brexit campaign. The company faced widespread criticism for its unethical data mining activities, which involved obtaining the personal data of millions of Facebook users without their consent. This data was subsequently employed to develop targeted political advertisements designed to sway voter behavior in favor of Hillary Clinton and the Democratic Party. Cambridge Analytica's actions led to extensive backlash, multiple investigations, and ultimately the company's dissolution.

The employment of dark practices in opposition research can yield significant consequences not only for individual campaigns, but also for the overall health of the electoral process. When campaigns resort to such unethical tactics, they erode public trust in the electoral system, foster a toxic political atmosphere, and risk legal repercussions. Therefore, it is crucial for campaigns to prioritize ethics, accuracy, and fairness in their opposition research endeavors to ensure that elections remain an accurate representation of the people's will. However, it is vital to recognize that some campaigns may still opt for these tactics, lured by the potential short-term benefits. It is possible that your adversaries will employ these methods against your campaign, hence the reason for this chapter. In highly competitive races where every advantage is crucial, a win-at-all-costs mentality can be alluring. But history has demonstrated that campaigns relying on unethical tactics often face exposure, resulting in long-term damage to their reputations and the election process as a whole.

FINAL THOUGHTS

The significance of opposition research in the realm of political campaigns cannot be overstated, as it equips candidates with a thorough comprehension of their adversaries, allowing them to craft strategic plans that resonate with the voting populace. By delving into their rivals' political pasts, voting records, financial dealings, and personal histories, campaigns can identify critical issues that matter to the electorate and capitalize on their opponents' vulnerabilities. This practice aids in formulating campaign messages, preparing for debates and interviews, and managing crises through the anticipation of potential controversies.

A critical component of opposition research lies in adhering to ethical principles that champion fairness, responsibility, and respect for the election process. Accurate and truthful information serves as the foundation of effective opposition research. Deceptive or false claims not only damage a campaign's credibility but also threaten the very fabric of our republic. Honoring privacy is another ethical consideration, as it is essential to distinguish between public actions and purely personal matters that bear no relevance to a candidate's suitability for office. Campaigns must exercise discretion and sound judgment in this regard. Moreover, concentrating on an opponent's policy stances and qualifications, rather than succumbing to personal attacks and mudslinging, ensures that the debate remains focused on the issues that matter to voters.

Although capitalizing on an opponent's shortcomings is necessary, striking a balance between negative ads and positive messaging is vital for a campaign's credibility and rapport with the electorate. By offering a clear choice and an inspiring vision for the future, campaigns can spark enthusiasm and boost voter turnout. In the end, reverence for and the integrity of the electoral process yield far-reaching benefits for individual candidates and our republican system as a whole. By conducting opposition research ethically and responsibly, campaigns can contribute to an informed and vigorous debate on the issues most relevant to voters. This, in turn, guarantees that the electoral process remains dynamic, engaging, and responsive to the needs and aspirations of the electorate. By valuing fairness, responsibility, and respect for our republic, campaigns can cultivate an environment in which the finest ideas and candidates rise to prominence, and our Constitutional republic can once again flourish.

CHAPTER 13

THE CAMPAIGN CALENDAR: YOUR MASTER PLAN

HOW YOU DO ANYTHING, is how you do everything. Within the vast array of invaluable wisdom contained within these pages, no element holds greater significance than the meticulous orchestration and rational formulation of a plan, embodied in the campaign calendar. Candidates vying for victory in winnable districts, equipped with campaign calendars, often outperform their opponents who neglect to devise written strategies—even outperforming those who hold the mantle of incumbency. This singular aspect of assembling your campaign effort distinguishes the novices from the masters. In essence, your master plan constitutes the very fabric that constitutes victorious campaign tactics.

Your attention to detail, coupled with the capacity to marshal these elements into a tangible blueprint, establishes the benchmark that your entire campaign team shall strive towards, for the speed of the leader dictates the speed of the pack. A superior candidate will assemble a team of exceptional caliber, who shall, in turn, consistently yield a result of the utmost quality. Such is the method through which victory is secured across all pursuits, transcending the realm of politics alone because, as mentioned in the open of this chapter, *how you do anything is how you do everything.*

The creation of a campaign calendar is the stage at which most campaigns and candidates falter. Neglecting the minutiae of execution often leads to the collapse of their campaigns. If you overlook the details of a well-executed campaign before your campaign's launch, the entire endeavor will be plagued by disarray, preventing it from ever gaining traction. The details matter—do not ignore them.

The process of crafting your campaign calendar bestows the added advantage of compelling the candidate and the campaign team to meticulously contemplate the entire campaign process and strategy. In my experience, numerous conservative candidates aspiring for public office neglect to devote the necessary time and attention to detail essential for victory in their campaigns before announcing their candidacy. While it is true that smaller campaigns with modest budgets and limited voter participation may not necessitate an intricate level of detail to succeed, federal and statewide elections do demand such thoroughness. The explanation for conservatives losing elections to corrupt or incompetent incumbents who ought to be unseated lies in their consultants, campaign managers, and advisors failing to invest the effort required to effectively execute a winning strategy.

To be explicit, if you are a federal or statewide candidate (or even a state legislative candidate) and your consultant or campaign manager does not develop a campaign calendar outlining the specific metrics involved in securing your election, you have engaged an amateur while possibly compensating them as a professional. That being said, employing professionals—among whom there are numerous exceptional and highly skilled individuals—comes at a high cost. If you anticipate procuring top-tier staff and consultants for a mere pittance, be prepared for a spectacle. Retaining high-quality professionals necessitates meeting their established fees. Nonetheless, higher fees demand a degree of accountability; specifically, you can (and should) anticipate exceptional results. While no one can guarantee victory, if the professional fails to deliver as agreed upon, seek an alternative.

Be warned, a disconcerting trend has emerged in the political consulting and management spheres. Namely, a low threshold for entry has resulted in a massive influx of political operators with minimal knowledge or comprehension of securing an election victory. Instead, they establish professional networks and social media followings to fabricate social proof, captivating unsuspecting candidates who genuinely wish to serve their communities and reclaim America. They impose exorbitant fees while delivering negligible value. Regrettably, the candidate often remains oblivious to the deception until the election concludes and they have been defeated. This very concern prompted the creation of this book—to enlighten candidates about the hallmarks of a high-quality campaign and to furnish them with the essential knowledge and understanding needed to triumph on election day. America First candidates ought to embody the finest candidates, executing the most exceptional campaigns across every ballot. To achieve this, candidates must be well-versed in the intricacies of exceptional performance. A meticulously devised campaign calendar—your master plan—serves as the portal to such elevated performance.

CHOOSE A
PROJECT MANAGEMENT SOFTWARE

Initiating your campaign demands understanding the entire endeavor as a singular project. At Dark Horse Political, we employ Smartsheet (www.smartsheet.com) to supervise all our federal and statewide candidate campaigns, as well as our PAC clients. This resource enables us to view the comprehensive election effort on a single dashboard, facilitating effective management by delving into the specifics of particular campaign aspects on a daily basis. We can recommend this solution to your campaign, as well. While Dark Horse Political currently harnesses advanced tools to oversee our clients, our methods were not always so refined. In the firm's early days, we relied on Microsoft Excel to organize client campaigns manually. While less efficient, we can also recommend this solution, particularly for smaller campaigns. Regardless of whether you opt for a more sophisticated solution like Smartsheet or a simpler alternative like Microsoft Excel, the process of structuring your campaign is crucial to your ultimate success.

To explore a more comprehensive range of project management tools, simply perform an internet search. Numerous solutions cater to a wide spectrum of campaign complexities. It is worth noting that the chosen solution should possess the capability to link budgetary expenses to specific tasks. For instance, when planning your social media campaign, it is essential to be aware of the associated expenditures. The same principle applies to direct mail, email, texting, and other marketing campaigns. This approach enables you to allocate resources effectively, assess outcomes, and confirm that your investments target identifiable voters through relevant activities.

LAYING THE BONES: THE MACRO-CALENDAR

The essential framework of the campaign calendar has been outlined throughout this book, as it is based on these very principles. Your campaign calendar consists of at least 10 distinct components: Phase 1: Pre-Campaign Analysis & Setup, Phase 2: Launch, Phase 3: Building Your Base, Phase 4: Establishing Your Base, Phase 5: Imposing Your Dominance, The General Election Plan, The Ground War, The Air War, Budgeting, and Fundraising. Each of these components has been extensively examined in previous chapters. It is now the moment to integrate them into a unified strategy.

The initial step in organizing these details involves allocating a timeframe for each item. For instance, in a Congressional race, Phase 1 generally takes two to four months, Phase 2 spans 30 to 45 days, Phase 3 lasts three to four months, Phase 4 requires two to three months, and Phase 5 typically spans two months. The General Election timeframe hinges on the period between the primary and general election dates, as determined by your state's election calendar.

To establish the starting point for your campaign, begin by adding your primary election date to your calendar and work backwards. For example, if your primary election takes place in the first week of August, initiate Phase 5 activities in the first or second week of June. In Phase 5, add the dates of ballots being mailed to vote-by-mail and absentee voters. Begin Phase 4 activities in March or April, Phase 3 activities in December or January, Phase 2 activities in October of the previous year, and Phase 1 activities between June and August. An important note, be sure to add the dates for filing your ballot qualification paperwork which typically occur in Phase 3. Forgetting to prepare for your official filing is a mistake that is always fatal. The timeframes suggested here serve as general guidelines, as factors such as the size of the race, location, and specific office pursued will influence the appropriate timing for each phase. Understandably, smaller races demand less time and financial resources due to fewer participating voters, whereas larger races necessitate a longer time horizon and increased budgetary provisions.

Upon establishing the foundational timeline for the campaign, enumerate the prescribed activities for each individual phase. For instance, in Phase 1, the following activities should be listed: SWOT Analysis, Race Analysis, Cost Analysis, Budget Formation, Team Identification, General Narrative Creation, Photoshoot, Logo Development, Digital Development, Promotional Material Creation, Digital Asset Creation, Initial Fundraising Calls, and Committee Setup.

The second step involves assigning a timeframe to each item and determining which items are dependent on the completion of others before they can commence. For example, SWOT Analysis is an independent item that does not rely on any other item's completion before starting the activity. In contrast, Budget Formation is contingent upon the completion of both Cost Analysis and Race Analysis. Consequently, this item will be executed sequentially, while SWOT Analysis, Race Analysis, and Cost Analysis can all begin simultaneously and run concurrently. Using this approach, assign a timeframe for each item and incorporate them into your Phase 1 calendar. Repeat this process for Phases 2 through 5. In the end, each specific activity required in each phase should be accurately listed within its corresponding phase. In particular, Phase 1 activities fall under Phase 1, Phase 2 activities under Phase 2, and so on.

These activities should establish the most essential elements of your primary election campaign calendar. The general election calendar will be determined later in the race (you don't want to get ahead of yourself).

Specifically, if the campaign believes it will win the primary election, the general election campaign calendar should be set at the onset of Phase 5. However, if the campaign has no credible opponents and is expected to easily prevail in the primary, the general election calendar can be set up at the beginning of the campaign.

Thirdly, create a fundraising calendar that includes the fundraising targets you determined in Phase 1, which will adequately fund the entire primary campaign. For example, if you determined that your entire Congressional campaign requires a fundraising haul of $5,500,000 with a primary fundraising target of $3,437,500 and a monthly average fundraising target of $343,750, your campaign calendar will reflect that monthly fundraising target. While this is a simplified example, the process of creating this fundraising calendar is the same for your specific targets.

Next, incorporate your marketing plan into your calendar, dividing the activities into two sections: ground war and air war. Each aspect of your marketing activity must be explicitly scheduled. This includes the event schedule, debate schedule (to be added once debates are formally agreed upon), email campaign schedule, text messaging schedule, social media posting schedule, direct mail schedule (including pre-production, production, and post-production timeframes), radio ad schedule, and television ad schedule. All of these (and any additional activities) should be clearly delineated on the campaign calendar.

While the specific timing of these activities may need to be flexible, adapting to the changing conditions on the ground, it is essential to place them on the calendar during their appropriate phases. This ensures they are not overlooked and can be adjusted as necessary. Once the marketing calendar is established, your macro-calendar will be complete, allowing for a well-organized and efficient campaign.

Lastly, allocate the appropriate budgetary costs to each item or phase. For example, many of your Phase 1 activities may be managed by your General Consultant or Campaign Manager for a set fee. Assign that amount to the specific activities covered by the fee. Other items, like website development and logo design, may have individual associated costs. Allocate the specific costs to each item. Repeat this process for each phase and activity. Budgetary information is particularly important for your marketing activity because marketing consists of 70% to 80% of your budget. This information will allow you to see where your money is being allocated each day and with each activity.

FLESHING OUT THE EFFORT:
THE MICRO-CALENDAR

Once the foundation of the campaign has been meticulously laid on your calendar, it becomes crucial to elaborate the specific intricacies of each identified item. To achieve this, the campaign ought to inquire how to accomplish each task. For instance, in Phase 1, your campaign conceived general narrative digital ads, intended to be displayed on websites and social media beginning in Phase 2. This serves as an integral part of your initial general awareness push preceding your announcement event. Although these items are present in your calendar, the methods of their creation and deployment are yet to be determined.

For example, your overarching items dictate that your social media ads campaign ought to commence on a designated date. How are these ads brought to life? Who is responsible for their creation? What are the costs involved? How long is this process? Who orchestrates the ad purchase? When is the ad purchase made? These are the details that enrich your calendar. If your macro calendar indicates that your team will be canvassing during a specific week, who rallies the volunteers? What resources are necessary (a walking app, palm cards, meals, etc.)? Who imparts the knowledge of using the app, and when and where does this training take place? What are the expenses incurred to provide food for the volunteers? Who delivers the palm cards to the volunteers, and when are they distributed? For every campaign activity, it is crucial to determine the specific details, as needed.

GIVING YOUR CAMPAIGN LIFE: UTILZING YOUR CAMPAIGN CALENDAR

The utility of your campaign calendar is contingent upon its active implementation. Serving not only to crystallize your master plan, the campaign calendar's fundamental purpose is to guide your daily endeavors, ensuring your team remains focused, within budget, and punctual. At any given moment, your calendar should provide insight into ongoing activities, requisite revenue, anticipated expenses, human resources assigned to oversee these activities, current campaign strategies (such as ground and air war efforts), active fundraising initiatives, voter engagement endeavors, and every nuance of daily campaign operations. This capacity bestows upon the candidate and the campaign team the precise knowledge of their daily responsibilities, fostering a well-coordinated and effective campaign.

In order to fully capitalize on the power of your campaign calendar, it is vital to embrace the following principles. First, develop the discipline of reviewing and updating your calendar on a daily basis, for this habit is the cornerstone of a thriving campaign. By constantly evaluating and adjusting your plans, you create a dynamic and responsive campaign, poised to overcome the uncertainties and challenges that may arise in the election process.

Indeed, your campaign calendar ought to serve as a reflection of your campaign's priorities, judiciously allocating resources and time to the tasks of utmost importance. Mastering the art of effective time management is key in avoiding squandered efforts and maintaining the momentum necessary for a winning campaign. By concentrating your resources and energy on the most vital tasks, you create an environment in which your team can flourish and steadily progress toward your goals. Success is built upon a foundation of well-executed plans, and a meticulously designed campaign calendar is no exception. By diligently planning and allocating time to each essential task, you empower your team to work with purpose and direction, ultimately fostering a sense of achievement and satisfaction. Moreover, this thoughtful approach to time management instills a sense of urgency and accountability, inspiring your team to consistently meet deadlines and maintain a high standard of performance.

As your campaign evolves and moves forward, the calendar should remain a dynamic tool, adapting to new priorities and shifting focus as necessary. In doing so, it ensures that your team remains nimble and responsive, able to tackle challenges and seize opportunities as they arise. In essence, a well-structured campaign calendar is an invaluable asset, guiding your team's efforts and paving the way for success. By allocating resources and time to the most crucial tasks and maintaining effective time management, you create a steadfast foundation upon which your campaign can thrive, ultimately securing a path to victory.

The campaign calendar also serves as a unifying force for your entire team, fostering a sense of shared responsibility. By regularly sharing calendar updates with your team members and encouraging open communication and collaboration, you promote trust and accountability, empowering your team to work in harmony and with greater efficiency.

Make it a priority to employ your calendar as a tool for assessing the effectiveness of distinct strategies and tactics, while also keeping a watchful eye on the broader progress of your campaign. By identifying areas in need of enhancement, celebrating the achievements of your team, and fine-tuning your plans when necessary, you create an environment that promotes continuous evaluation and growth. This process of constant refinement allows your campaign to evolve, become more resilient, and adjust to the ever-changing landscape of the political arena. In the pursuit of success, it is crucial to acknowledge that no plan is perfect, and that the path to victory often requires adaptation and flexibility. By embracing this mindset and regularly reviewing your campaign calendar, you empower your team to make informed decisions, optimize strategies, and ultimately, propel your campaign forward. In doing so, you foster a culture of learning and improvement, where challenges are seen as opportunities for growth and setbacks are transformed into valuable lessons.

Ultimately, a masterfully designed calendar skillfully intertwines long-term goals with short-term objectives, forging a coherent and unified vision for your campaign. It is of paramount importance to align your daily tasks with your overarching ambitions, ensuring that every action taken contributes meaningfully to the journey toward victory. By embracing these principles and applying them to your campaign calendar, you create a robust and dynamic campaign, primed to navigate the political landscape with confidence and secure the win.

This harmonious integration of long-term and short-term objectives helps to maintain focus and motivation within your team, providing a clear roadmap for success. As each milestone is achieved, team members can recognize the progress they are making and visualize the impact of their collective efforts, bolstering their resolve and determination to continue striving for the desired outcome. Furthermore, the seamless blending of goals and objectives within your campaign calendar fosters a sense of shared purpose and direction, uniting your team under a common banner. This unity not only enhances collaboration and communication but also promotes a sense of belonging and camaraderie, vital ingredients for a successful campaign.

FINAL THOUGHTS

The campaign calendar, when crafted correctly, serves as your overarching blueprint. It is vital to restrict access to the calendar's specifics to a select few individuals, with complete access granted only to the candidate, campaign manager, fundraising director, and general consultant. If your master plan falls into the hands of the opposition, they gain a strategic edge, outmaneuvering you at every turn. Safeguard this information by using password protection and avoid sending the campaign calendar as a file via email or storing it on a thumb drive. Losing control of the file may result in its leakage, compromising your campaign.

How you do anything is how you do everything. As we reach the conclusion of this chapter on the creation of the campaign calendar, let us revisit the essential concepts and their significance in ensuring your campaign's success. The journey begins with choosing the right project management software to effectively organize and manage the numerous aspects of your campaign. Whether opting for a comprehensive solution like Smartsheet or a simpler alternative like Microsoft Excel, the key lies in establishing a clear structure to guide your campaign's progression.

With the foundation laid, the next step is constructing the macro-calendar, which serves as the backbone of your campaign strategy. This involves integrating the 10 distinct components outlined in this book, including the various phases of your campaign, budgeting, fundraising, and the general election plan. By meticulously outlining each element, you create a coherent and unified blueprint that drives your campaign forward.

Once the macro-calendar is established, it's time to delve into the micro-calendar, which focuses on the specific intricacies of each task. This detailed approach ensures that every aspect of your campaign, from ad creation to voter engagement, is thoughtfully executed and monitored. The micro-calendar enables your campaign team to anticipate and address potential challenges while ensuring that your resources are allocated efficiently.

Finally, it's crucial to remember that the campaign calendar is not merely a planning tool, but a living, breathing document that should be actively utilized to guide your daily efforts. It is the very essence of your campaign, providing constant direction and insight into ongoing activities, financial requirements, and resource allocation. By consistently referring to your campaign calendar, both the candidate and the campaign team can maintain focus, stay within budget, and meet deadlines.

In the complex world of political campaigning, the campaign calendar is the lifeline that keeps your team united and informed. It is the strategic roadmap that illuminates the path to victory, detailing every milestone and challenge that lies ahead. By carefully crafting your campaign calendar, you instill a sense of purpose and direction in your team, empowering them to overcome obstacles and achieve the ultimate goal: winning the election. As you embark on this journey, never lose sight of the vital role your campaign calendar plays in shaping the outcome of your political endeavor. Use it to navigate the ever-changing landscape of political campaigns and stay true to your objectives, principles, and vision. The campaign calendar is a powerful instrument, but its effectiveness lies in your hands.

In the words of Sun Tzu, "Victorious warriors win first and then go to war, while defeated warriors go to war first and then seek to win." Your campaign calendar is the cornerstone of your victory; it's the strategy you devise before stepping onto the battlefield of politics. By diligently following the guidelines outlined in this chapter, you set the stage for a successful and well-orchestrated campaign. Remember, the journey of a thousand miles begins with a single step, and in this case, that step is the creation of a comprehensive campaign calendar.

As you venture forth, keep in mind that success in politics requires unwavering dedication, adaptability, and resourcefulness. Your campaign calendar is a testament to these qualities, and its ongoing utilization and refinement will be the deciding factor in the triumph of your political aspirations. Embrace the power of planning, and let your campaign calendar be the compass that steers you towards victory.

ABOUT THE AUTHOR

CHRISTOPHER GERGEN IS A HIGHLY skilled and experienced political strategist who has dedicated his career to conservative political organizations and candidates. He stands out from other political consultants by embracing unconventional political thinking. His unique ability to bring order to chaos through innovative tools and methods has proven to be a valuable asset to his clients.

Christopher's journey in politics began as a grassroots volunteer for Senator Bob Dole's Presidential campaign in 1995. Since then, he has been involved in numerous political campaigns ranging from local races to Presidential elections. After serving in the United States Navy in response to the 9/11 attacks, Christopher went on to build a successful financial planning practice with a Fortune 500 company. However, he saw an opportunity in the political arena and left his growing practice to establish Dark Horse Political in 2015. The following year, he was hired as the State Political Director for the Trump for President organization in Oregon. Since then, DHP has continued to provide advisory services to various campaigns at all levels of government.

He resides in Las Vegas, Nevada.

dhpolitical.com